# Dream No Little Dreams

Best wishes,

Clay

# Dream No Little Dreams

Clayton L. Mathile
and Echo M. Garrett

edited by Mary Beth Crain

DNLD Publishing

"On a Tree Fallen Across the Road" from
THE POETRY OF ROBERT FROST edited by Edward Connery Lathem.
Copyright 1923, 1969 by Henry Holt and Company. Copyright 1951 by Robert Frost
Reprinted by permission of Henry Holt and Company, LLC

First printing  2007
ISBN: 978-1-934282-03-8
LCCN: 2007920262

**ATTENTION CORPORATIONS, UNIVERSITIES, COLLEGES, AND PROFESSIONAL ORGANIZATIONS**: Quantity discounts are available on bulk purchases of this book for educational, gift purposes, or as premiums for increasing magazine subscriptions or renewals. Special books or book excerpts can also be created to fit specific needs. For information, please contact Aileron at 8860 Wildcat Road, Bethel Township, Ohio 45371 or director@aileron.net.

# CONTENTS

## CHAPTER 1

# A Win for Everyone: Selling the Iams Company

I share the wise Native American philosophy that we humans really don't own things. The earth, and everything on it, is on loan to us and we are here merely to guard its precious gifts. So, I never felt, for instance, that I owned The Iams Company. Rather, I felt that Iams belonged to everyone who had ever had a part in making it a success and that I was really only the caretaker of this unique and magnificent enterprise.

Reaching that frame of mind hasn't always been easy. I wasn't born a good listener or a great manager. I didn't always have my priorities straight. The Iams journey was also my personal journey of self-development as I learned how to be a better citizen, a better manager, a better president, a better CEO, a better chairman, and a better husband and father. I sure haven't been perfect, but I was and still am willing to learn how to improve. I have constantly asked, How can I grow? How can I help others? How can I help the company?

When you reach my age, somewhere between Dayton and heaven, you want to be able to look back on your life and know your biggest accomplishment wasn't making a pile of money but earning and keeping the love and respect of your family, your friends, and those who worked with and for you.

This all explains why, when I decided to sell Iams in 1999, my first consideration was not for myself. I was chiefly concerned about what effect the sale would have on my family, the employees, the community, and our most loyal customers, the dogs and cats of the world.

I've had to make many difficult decisions in my life. But probably the most difficult was whether or not to sell the company that had been my dream and vision for thirty years. For many CEOs, it's impossible to think of selling the company they've spent a lifetime building, because their egos are so invested in that company. It becomes more than a business; it's synonymous with their personal identity. It defines who they are, who they were, and where they're going.

Certainly, I had to struggle with these feelings. Iams was like a child I had adopted from Paul Iams, the pet nutrition pioneer, in 1982. At that time the company was worth $2 million, and I nurtured and loved it until it grew up to be a big, strapping billion-dollar international company that was on its way to being the world leader in dog and cat nutrition. As my wife, Mary, liked to joke, The Iams Company was really our sixth child, the one that might grow up but would never leave home.

Aside from the personal attachment I had to Iams were two much larger issues: 1) How would a sale impact the many employees who had served the company so loyally for so many years and the community of Dayton, Ohio, the hometown of Paul Iams and the home base of Iams since 1950? and 2) How could the quality and integrity of our product stay intact after a sale? The success of Iams, after all, was ultimately due to the fact that we never compromised on quality. We never reduced the quality of our ingredients to improve margins or make more money. The welfare of animals was as important to me as the welfare of people. My vision of Iams can be summed up in the following philosophy, which I'd be proud to have as my epitaph: "Dedicated to enhancing the well-being of dogs and cats."

Nothing could prepare me for the surge of emotions I experienced once I allowed the possibility of selling The Iams Company to penetrate my thoughts. So I decided to put down on paper what it would take for me to sell the company.

December 10, 1997

## What I Want

1) Assurance that Iams' presence remains in the Dayton community.

2) Assurance that all employees are rewarded for their loyalty on the basis of seniority for lower-level people and on (perceived) individual contribution at the higher levels. This (bonus) will be made without jeopardizing the buyer's opportunity to keep key people employed.

3) Assurance the buyer will protect the integrity of the company's science and technology. (The buyer must understand how good these products are before we do the deal.)

4) Valuation based on a strategic (not financial) perspective that will help the buyer achieve world leadership in nutrition and product quality. (We have the world's best pet foods and we can prove it!) The combined entity could challenge the Mars Company for world leadership within five to seven years.

---

My philosophy in business has always been, "Never make a decision before you have to. Gather all the facts and information you need first. Taking your time doesn't mean procrastination. It means having knowledge and insight about when a decision should be made." As a result, I've always had the ability to make big decisions, even if it took me a heck of a long time to come around to them.

It took me two years to sell Iams. During those two years, I vacillated more than I have over any decision in my life, and it was pure agony. Under normal circumstances, I counted my ability to tolerate indecision as one of my strengths. I'm comfortable remaining in the state of information-gathering for months and even years, because then when I finally make a decision, I'm able to rest easy knowing I did the best I could with the most information available.

Why was I considering selling in the first place? Perhaps that is best answered in a letter I wrote to my family on April 15, 1998.

---

## Reasons for Changing Ownership of The Iams Company

For the past year I have been contemplating doing something with The Iams Company. This has been one of the most difficult decisions of my life because I have put so much time, energy, thought, and creativity into the company. It is very much a part of me and me of it. Disengaging from the company emotionally will require a lot of counseling and prayer. I am writing this for those people who are most important to me and for future generations, so they will understand my decision.

I was born in 1941 on a family farm in northwestern Ohio. My father was a farmer, and my mother was a schoolteacher. I am the oldest of three and have one brother and one sister. My mother passed away in 1983 and my father in 1986. She was 66 and he was 74. I married my childhood sweetheart in 1962, and we had five children: three daughters and two sons. Currently we have nine grandchildren. We have no family members in the business. I have worked hard all my life and now, at age fifty-seven, I am ready to do something different. I have plenty of money and recently started a family office to manage our family's current and future assets. We have formed a family council, which ultimately will be responsible for governance of the family office.

This is my twenty-eighth year with The Iams Company. When I joined it in 1970, we had five full-time employees and [dog food] sales of $500,000. Our products were better than any in the industry, but only a few people knew of us. Our customers were comprised of two distributors and mostly local kennels. Our nutrition was outstanding, but the form and packaging of the

4

product were not consumer-friendly, and our prices were double that of nationally known brands. Those who knew about and used our products believed, as I did, that this was the only way to feed dogs and cats. My vision was for every dog and cat to have a shiny coat. If their coats were shiny, then you could rest assured they were healthy inside. Through our efforts we've helped make a lot of dogs, cats, and owners happy. In addition, we have changed an entire industry. Our sales will exceed $800 million in 1998.

### Industry

Because we have been so successful in selling premium dog and cat foods, the industry has had to change the way it formulates, markets, and distributes products. Many of the leading companies, Mars, Ralston, Nestlé, and Heinz, have or will have premium products that will compete directly with us in all retail channels. Their aim is to have products that are equal to Iams or better. But none has been able to come close to our quality.

There are three major premium companies: Hill's, Iams, and Nutro. Hill's, a division of Colgate, announced it was for sale last year and was negotiating with Nestlé until the negotiations broke down over price. The owner of Nutro is in his early 60s and has no apparent successor in the business. An acquisition of one of our competitors by Ralston, Nestlé, or Heinz would make things difficult for us.

The choices are either to be a consolidator or a consolidatee. When we look at the sizes of the leaders in the industry, it is improbable that we could become the former. We plan to hire an investment banker to help us figure this out.

Below are listed the leaders in our industry, ranked by estimated sales today:

| | |
|---|---|
| 1) Mars | $5.5 billion |
| 2) Nestlé | $3.5 billion *(includes acquisition of Dalgety)* |
| 3) Heinz | $2.3 billion |
| 4) Ralston | $2.3 billion |
| 5) Hill's | $0.9 billion |
| 6) Iams | $0.8 billion |
| 7) Doane | $0.6 billion |
| 8) Royal Canine | $0.5 billion |
| 9) Nutro | $0.3 billion |
| 10) Sunshine | $0.2 billion |

My opinion is that within five years this top ten list will be whittled down to only four to six players, comprising nearly 80 percent of the market worldwide.

### Retail Channel

We were able to grow in our industry because we made a better product, and we only sold through specialty retailers. In the late 1980s, the pet industry began consolidation of specialty retailers with the appearance of PETsMART and PETCO. They, along with other regional players, began opening very nice stores in good locations, and this factor propelled the growth of premium pet foods. In the mid-1990s, both PETsMART and PETCO went public and began acquiring many of the leading regional players. Currently, neither of these companies is making money, and PETsMART is reorganizing its management team for the second time in five years and is in jeopardy of bankruptcy. I feel the specialty pet retail channel is blurring, and we must find another channel in which to sell our products. This change requires great risk and causes me a great deal of concern.

### Debt

For a family-owned business to grow, it must take on debt. In 1997, we negotiated a $200 million credit facility. It was structured with $50 million being a private placement and $150 million as a revolver. Our capital outlay for 1998 will be in the neighborhood of $140 million. Nearly all the capital will be for the construction of two new dry (food) plants: one in Coevorden, the Netherlands, and the other in Leipsic, Ohio. In addition, our systems project, including the Y2K problem, will consume another $20 million. This level of debt is new to me and at my age (fifty-seven) concerns me, since it equals more than all the assets we have accumulated in our entire lives!

### Culture

We have created a unique culture at Iams. It was built around my philosophies of business and of life. I am the main promoter of that culture. The larger we get and the more I am away from the people, the more I see this culture changing, from a friendly, family atmosphere to that of a big, impersonal company. It is very hard to manage a company in this way. Very few professional managers recognize the need or have the skills to manage The Iams Way! That is unfortunate, because this way is the path to higher quality and higher productivity and could be applied to any business. In another life, I will probably teach other entrepreneurs how to create similar cultures in their businesses.

### Second Generation

We have five children ranging in age from twenty-five to thirty-five. None of them has an interest in being involved in the management of Iams and none has an interest in keeping the company private. A few years back, we hired consultants to assist us in perpetuation of the family through the development of a family council and family office. In 1997 we acquired space for the family office and hired our first president. The second generation is very excited about the family activities and has taken a keen interest in the family office. I feel the family, the family office, and the family foundation will become our legacies. The Iams Company was the vehicle to produce the wealth, which will allow us to do that.

## *Conditions of Sale*

If I am to do something with the company, the following conditions must be met:

1) I will need absolute assurance that the acquirer will maintain a significant presence in the Dayton community. I am committed to the economic development of the Miami Valley (a part of Dayton), and I do not want to be remembered as someone who, through greed, had a negative impact on the community where my family and I will continue to live.

2) The people who helped me build this company must have job security and/or be well compensated for their loyalty. This requirement will be met in such a way that it will not jeopardize the future of the enterprise or the buyer's ability to operate the combined businesses effectively.

3) I will need assurance that the buyer will continue to use our science, scientists, and scientific philosophies to develop products that enhance the well-being of dogs and cats.

4) We are aware that valuation of the business may be sub-optimized to satisfy the above conditions.

### *What I Want*

More than twenty years ago, I articulated four dreams for myself. (A wise man once said, "A vision is a dream with a plan.") These dreams could also be called prayers!

My dreams were as follows:

1)  The Iams Company would survive and prosper forever.

2)  The Iams Company would be recognized as the world leader in dog and cat nutrition.

3)  I would use my talent, knowledge, and wealth to help people less fortunate reach their full potential.

4)  I would do my part to perpetuate the "Great American Dream" by supporting our free enterprise system and entrepreneurism. (Give back!) I believe I have achieved the first two dreams, and I need to move on to the next ones before I lose my interest, enthusiasm, and strength to pursue them.

Love,
Dad

---

The first critical step in selling The Iams Company was to find an investment banker to review our options:

- Making an initial public offering that would allow continuing as an independent company.

- Merging with an equal company.

- Agreeing to an acquisition.

- Bringing in a significant investor who might take the family out of the equation but would keep the management and continue to build the company as an independent entity.

Who would initiate the search? In his previous positions, Iams COO Tom MacLeod had acquired a few small entrepreneurial companies but had never been involved in a sale. However, our CFO, George Morris, who had been Borden's COO, had been involved with twenty-two transactions in his career, including fifteen sales and seven acquisitions, so he led the charge.

We narrowed the investment banking firm search down to five choices. Roberto Mendoza, vice chairman of J.P. Morgan at the firm's New York headquarters, charmed us from the start. "I know this might sound hokey," he said, when Tom MacLeod, George Morris, and I met him, "but I'm an Iams user, and I want to introduce you to some of my friends."

With that, Roberto ushered us into his office, where his dogs were waiting. His favorite was a Pekinese mix nicknamed "Cat Dog" because he did indeed resemble a cat. An avowed animal lover, Roberto kept a virtual menagerie in his city apartment. At his house on Long Island, he even had llamas and monkeys.

Both Tom and I were impressed with the high degree of personal interest Roberto took in our business and with his team, a group of bright, energetic young people who nearly knew as much about our company as we did. Moreover, J.P. Morgan demonstrated a strong understanding of the players in the Midwest and had the upper hand in the international arena. The firm's global reach was important to us, since we had identified a couple of big international companies not based in the United States as potential buyers.

Roberto and Cat Dog won our business. We hired J.P. Morgan to do a valuation of the company, which occupied the first six months of the process.

We conducted the same kind of beauty contest for a legal firm to represent us and chose the eminent Wall Street firm of Davis, Polk, Sullivan & Cromwell. My longtime trusted legal advisor, Dick Chernesky of Chernesky, Heyman & Kress, guided us on that pick. We made sure good synergy existed between our investment banking and law firms, so they would work well together and not try to do each other's job.

Next on J.P. Morgan's agenda was conducting an analysis of our options to monetize the company. Only after those tasks were completed did I want to entertain offers seriously. However, I sensed that a window of opportunity was opening for us to make a move and sell the company.

And I knew the window wouldn't stay open long.

If Nestlé were to acquire Hill's, for example, that would eliminate one of the more attractive buyers from the market. Nestlé inherited the pet food business via its acquisition of Carnation. A lot of the old-timers at Nestlé, including the outgoing chairman, were not enthused about pet food, but Nestlé's new chairman was eager to beef up its pet food business.

My roster of potential buyers was narrowing. Although selling the company was still just one option, it appealed to me because it would simplify my life and afford me the time and means to get on with accomplishing my next two big dreams.

The company that initially showed the most interest in buying Iams wanted a thirty-day exclusive opportunity to bid. I expected it to pay a premium for us to grant the privilege to preempt anyone. J.P. Morgan, who stepped in to run interference for us, asked the conglomerate to make an offer before we gave it that exclusive right.

*As we sifted through the options, I became a regular agenda item at the family council meetings. The family asked good questions. They wanted to know my thoughts on Clay's interest in selling the company, the probability of success in expanding our distribution channels and building factories, and many other issues. Ultimately, though, the kids said, "What Dad wants is what we want, because it's his company." They were respectful of that.*

Tom MacLeod

"The number has to have a '2' in front of it," I told Roberto (as in $2 billion), "or I'm not interested."

On August 2, 1999, after two years of interviewing potential buyers, I finally sold The Iams Company to Procter & Gamble for an astonishing $2.3 billion, the largest acquisition P&G had made at the time.

But the deal wasn't about the money, it was about the fact that P&G was the kind of company I knew would take good care of Iams and all the people associated with Iams. From the very beginning, the P&G management team expressed willingness to meet every one of the criteria I had set forth. They had enormous respect for me and for our company. They planned to take the Iams brand to the mass market, the exact strategy we had intended to deploy if we had decided to keep the company. And P&G is an Ohio-based company, which meant the key players understood the community and its values and needs. Finally, P&G was a veritable consumer products giant, with a sterling reputation and more than three hundred brands under its banner. It had been in business since 1837, which meant it was doing something right.

And, most importantly, P&G passed the ultimate hurdle, the Mary Test. When my brilliant, insightful wife, Mary, approves of a person or a decision, it automatically gets the green light in my book.

We had a meeting with Durk Jager, P&G's chairman and CEO. After Durk left, Mary stood up and said, "If we are ever going to sell, P&G is the company that should own The Iams Company. I'm convinced it would be right for Clay, right for the family, right for P&G, and good for the community. Everybody would win."

On the momentous day of the sale, Durk toasted the deal with a bottle of sparkling apple cider. "The first day we saw this company, we knew we had to own it," he said. "It is such a fine company. We were shocked at how poised the company is to grow. We turned this company upside-down, and we have never seen a company in an acquisition run as well as this one."

Then he added, "We must keep this utterly confidential until August 11. Since we are publicly held, we have to get things in place before we make an announcement." Coincidentally, the announcement of the deal was scheduled on Paul Iams' birthday.

After getting P&G's approval to tell Paul Iams of the sale ahead of the formal announcement, Mary and I flew out to see him in Sun City, Arizona. I didn't want him to hear about the sale from someone else. And I wanted to see his reaction. He was shocked. Paul has always been anti-corporate, and he had worked for P&G. Plus, Paul was never impressed with numbers. The money didn't mean anything to him. He asked the same questions I had: What would happen to the people, the quality of the products, and the research department? I assured him I'd covered all the bases.

At 4:30 P.M. on August 10, we sent out a worldwide email instructing everyone in the company to dial in for an important conference call at 8 A.M. the next morning. Distributors were asked to join the call at 8:30 A.M.

The night before the announcement I scarcely slept. Colle+McVoy, the Minneapolis-based firm that handled our public relations and had conducted our media training, helped me with my speech. CEO and President Tom MacLeod and I, along with George Morris, John Polson, Diane Hirakawa, Marty Walker, Rob Easterling, John Meyer, Mike Jackson, as well as our two assistants, Jane Trout and Jackie Sammons, crowded into the company's fourth-floor conference room.

Before I picked up the phone to start the conference call at 8 A.M., prior to the stock market's opening bell (required since P&G is a public company), I drew in a deep breath and said a prayer. My heart was pounding, and I scarcely remember a word I said.

I explained that our family had decided to do this deal with P&G and the terms and conditions of the sale. I reassured the troops of P&G's commitment to the brands, the quality, and the Dayton community.

"I am confident P&G will be a good corporate citizen and will continue corporate contributions at our current rate of about $1 million a year," I said.

"Headquarters will remain in Dayton, and the worldwide pet nutrition research center will continue to operate locally. P&G is excellent to employees. They will continue to promote from within, and they offer great benefits and a terrific retirement plan." Then Tom took over and talked about how exciting the acquisition would be.

P&G dropped the press release at 8:30 A.M. before Wall Street opened. Then, at 9:30 A.M., Durk Jager conducted a teleconference with key analysts. The business community appeared stunned, first, that P&G would buy a pet food company, and, second, by the fact that we were approaching $1 billion in sales. Most industry observers pegged us at around $400 million in sales. After our teleconference calls with the employees and distributors, Tom, George, and I spent the latter part of the morning on the phone individually with our distributors and certain suppliers, so we could answer their questions and address their concerns.

In the early afternoon, Bruce Byrnes of P&G, Tom, and I conducted a local press conference at the Dayton Marriott. There I said, "I see this sale as a win-win: A win for P&G, a win for our employees, a win for Dayton, and a win for me.

"It's a win for P&G because it has a great platform from which to enter the $25 billion worldwide pet food market. The company gets excellent scientific and processing technology and outstanding, dedicated employees, the best in the pet food industry. P&G gets two outstanding brands, Iams and Eukanuba, which afford many options for growth. P&G has the resources to leverage our technology, our brands, and our people to continue to grow the business.

"It's a win for our employees because P&G has an excellent reputation as one of America's best employers. P&G is committed to growing its people through training and development, and it promotes from within. This philosophy will fit right in at Iams, because that's what we've done here for the last twenty years. P&G has an excellent compensation and benefits package, and its retirement plan is one of the best I have ever seen.

"It's a win for the Dayton community because the pet food division's worldwide headquarters stays here. The R&D center stays in the local area. P&G will add significant resources to this business and will continue growth, which will provide lots of employment opportunities in this region for a long time to come."

Then I dropped the second bombshell of the day. I announced the endowment of a $100 million community fund for the Dayton region within the Mathile Family Foundation, which we endowed with an additional $200 million. An audible gasp went up from the crowd. "The proceeds of this endowment will be used to help fund major community projects such as Second & Main, Riverscape, and Carillon Park, just to name a few, and we intend to continue our support of the local humane societies as well."

I concluded, "It's a win for me because, although I plan to help P&G in any way I can to achieve a smooth transition of the business to the new management, I'm excited about the fact that this sale will afford me more time to work at the Center for Entrepreneurial Education, as well as our family foundation activities. And maybe I'll be able to finally work on my golf game. It sure needs it!"

We were not ready to announce that we'd earmarked $100 million to be distributed among the employees. Some of the proceeds would be divided evenly among our five children, and we paid about $500 million in taxes on the transaction.

After the press conference, I went back to my office, which was strangely quiet as the day wore on. Jane Trout and I were prepared for the phone to ring off the hook, but it didn't. I was surprised but grateful because I was emotionally exhausted by the end of the day. The Iams employees were astounded by the news. Hardly anyone got much done that day. Other than the top managers, no one had had an inkling we were planning to sell the company. To this day, I'm amazed we were able to keep the process under wraps. I left early to go home to be with Mary and most of our kids, who had gathered to watch the evening news coverage of the sale.

As I watched the news with the family, I thought about the kind of company Iams had been. I was proud to be able to say that it was like a family, that we worked with our employees to create an environment where they could operate at their happiest and most productive, and that part of that family included everybody's pets. For instance, Tom MacLeod had routinely brought Kramer, his beloved basset hound, to our quarterly meetings. A former shelter dog, Kramer literally ascended to heights undreamed of in the rescue world when he accompanied Tom on our corporate jet. They were quite a team: Tom, with his dry sense of humor, and Kramer, with his droopy eyes and laid-back air. And so I found it most appropriate when a photo of Kramer made the front page of the following day's *Cincinnati Enquirer*, accompanying the story on the sale. Not bad, I thought, for a little dog nobody wanted or for a small, regional dog food company that scarcely anyone had heard of when I signed on. We'd both come a long way.

The next day, I vacated my office and set up shop down the street at CYMI, the family office, and the following week I went to Cincinnati to make a presentation to P&G's board of directors.

Because Iams was, above all, a family-style company, I wanted to reward all its members. I couldn't possibly have considered not sharing our good fortune with my employees. So Tom and I spent a lot of time establishing the ground rules and the formulas for exactly how to distribute bonuses. Then, since we were talking about a lot of money, we went over it and over it again, because it had to be right.

Tom put everything on a big chart, so we could look at it across the company. We devised a fair and equitable formula based on each person's level in the company, base salary, and bonus level, plus length of service. To a lesser degree, discretionary contribution to the company was considered. Every single employee got a bonus. Hourly people got one week's pay per year of service, and even an employee who had worked just one day at The Iams Company at the time of the sale got a bonus check. The reactions of absolute joy and gratitude were a reminder to me that when we give, it's we who receive the most. Some people broke down and cried. They never expected to have, all at one time, that kind of money.

I also rewarded some people who had retired and some who weren't even employees of the company. Nobody got left out. Giving the employees a share of the sale proceeds was completely voluntary, but there were so many people who had so much to do with my success. I couldn't just hoard all of that money and walk away. Still, because I had never promised anyone anything, it was so much fun, because it came as such a shock to people.

The next celebration came on September 1, 1999, when our big check came from P&G as it officially took possession of the company.

As I held that check in my hand, I thought of the passage from Ecclesiastes:

*Then I realized that it is good and proper for a man to...find satisfaction in his toilsome labor under the sun during the few days of life God has given him, for this is his lot. Moreover, when God gives any man wealth and possessions, and enables him to enjoy them, to accept his lot and be happy in his work, this is a gift of God.*

---

I was saying goodbye to the company I'd spent the last twenty-nine years building into an enterprise of pride, passion, and promise. It had been a labor of love. Even in the early days when I was struggling and didn't seem to be getting ahead, I loved every minute of it. I was that lucky man in Ecclesiastes: At age fifty-eight, I had more money than I could ever need, and only God knew how many years I had left to do the most I could with it. I had been happy in my work. I felt overwhelmed with gratitude.

And now, I was standing not at the end of the road of my life, but at one more turning point. That road had been one of risk and faith, one most men never choose or never get the opportunity to travel. I recalled Robert Frost's most famous poem, "The Road Not Taken."

I've never been one to look back in regret over things I haven't done or should have done. I learn from my mistakes, but I don't dwell on them. Yet, as I stood on the threshold of a new future, a new road not taken, it seemed a good time to reflect upon the road I had taken, the one that began on a family farm in northwest Ohio in the winter of 1941.

## The Road Not Taken

*Two roads diverged in a yellow wood,*
*And sorry I could not travel both*
*And be one traveler, long I stood*
*And looked down one as far as I could*
*To where it bent in the undergrowth;*

*Then took the other, as just as fair,*
*And having perhaps the better claim,*
*Because it was grassy and wanted wear;*
*Though as for that the passing there*
*Had worn them really about the same,*

*And both that morning equally lay*
*In leaves no step had trodden black.*
*Oh, I kept the first for another day!*
*Yet knowing how way leads on to way,*
*I doubted if I should ever come back.*

*I shall be telling this with a sigh*
*Somewhere ages and ages hence:*
*Two roads diverged in a wood, and I—*
*I took the one less traveled by,*
*And that has made all the difference.*

—Robert Frost

19

## CHAPTER 2

# The Boy Who Begged to Go to School

I f you ask a four-year-old boy what he wants more than anything, the last thing you'd expect him to say is, "To start school." But when I was four, that was my big dream. My mother and my father's sister, Aunt Evron, were both elementary school teachers and had taught me to read by age three, so from the moment I could open a book and figure out what was in it, I began driving my mother crazy, pestering her daily about when I'd be old enough to go to school.

On the Tuesday after Labor Day in 1945, when my best friend Jim, who lived nearby and was two years my senior, went off to his first day of elementary school, I decided I was going, too.

Of course, the authorities wouldn't let you start school until age six, but silly rules and regulations didn't impress me then any more than they do now. At four years old, it's tough to wait a week for something, let alone two whole years. I was ready for school, and that was that! So the night before the big day, I carefully plotted my strategy, and the following morning, I marched out bright and early and stretched out in the middle of the asphalt road in front of our Portage, Ohio, farmhouse, forcing the school bus that trundled past to grind to a halt.

It was very Mahatma Gandhi-esque, a shining example of nonviolent protest. My mother was horrified and swiftly removed me from the premises, but the bus driver, our neighbor Frank Kominek, thought the whole thing was hilarious and laughed heartily. Back inside the house, I received a spanking I've never forgotten. Of course, those were the days when spanking was not only legal but the prevailing disciplinary philosophy. In my case, I don't know how much good it did; although I undoubtedly thought twice about taking such rash action again, I never gave up on my dream.

And I never let up on my mother. I continued to pester her about going to school until the following year when, even though I was born on January 11, past the cutoff date of December 31 for acceptance into first grade, Mother convinced (begged is more like it) the school superintendent to let me into first grade at age five. What a sigh of relief she must have breathed as I excitedly, and legitimately, boarded that school bus at last. I was a handful, and mothers, even those as active and ambitious as mine was, only have so much energy.

Born Helen Good, the youngest daughter of John and Sally Good, she was a brilliant, intellectual women's libber before there was women's liberation. One of just a few college-educated women from her tiny town of Vaughnsville, Ohio, she used to joke that she was "the only Good girl in town." An incredibly bright and capable woman, my mother graduated with a two-year associate's degree and teaching certificate in 1936, went back to her hometown, and taught fifth grade for the next three years. She was a creative forward-thinker, full of dreams of life beyond the farm and aspirations to be financially independent.

My father, Wilbert Ray Mathile (everyone called him "Bill"), was a hard-scrabble farmer, always struggling to make ends meet. Mother met Dad when she was studying to be a teacher at Bowling Green State University and he farmed nearby. They certainly seemed like opposites in both temperament and outlook. Whereas Mother put the highest premium on education (the higher, the better), Dad never even graduated high school. Instead, he stayed home to help his father on the family farm. When his father died in 1935, my father was 23. It was the height of the Great Depression, and Dad inherited more debt than value.

Whereas Mother was ambitious and goal-oriented, Dad was anything but a visionary. A miser who had an aversion to debt after seeing his own family suffer in the Depression, Dad only owned forty acres. He farmed another 160 for gentlemen farmers in Wood County, an area in Ohio where the farmland isn't quite as rich as in neighboring counties. The small farming communities dotting that flat countryside have scarcely changed since then.

Why did Mom marry Dad? He certainly was a reliable prospect; a typical no-nonsense Midwesterner, he thrived on hard work. And maybe it had something to do with the fact that he was strong as steel, stood six feet tall and weighed 185 pounds, and had dark hair, blue eyes, and movie-star good looks. He took after his mother in that department; she was a stunning woman who resembled the actress Anne Bancroft.

Tragically, Dad's mother died in a cook-stove fire when he was just twenty-six. The first thing each morning, she would stoke the fire with coal oil. On that terrible morning, burning embers still smoldered in the box. The stove blew up, and flames roared back up to the oil can in her hand. She ran outside with my father chasing her. He smothered the flames by wrapping her with a blanket, but she died in the hospital a few days later. That horrible event deeply traumatized Dad. Mother told me that when she visited Dad at his house during their three-year courtship, my grandmother's scorched footprints remained visible, seared into the wool carpet, a grisly reminder of that horrific day when she fled through the living room and out the front door.

My parents were married in 1939. Dad, who never wore a watch and was chronically late, showed up three hours late for the ceremony. No one seems to remember why.

They quickly settled into traditional roles, with Mom's domain being the house and yard, which she kept immaculate. An accomplished seamstress and good country cook, she was constantly sweeping, canning vegetables, darning socks, and keeping track of every penny our household spent. The few times she managed to convince Dad to take a vacation, she carefully noted all expenditures on the trip in a small spiral notebook. And she insisted on separate checkbooks, in accordance with her fierce independent streak.

Dad paid one farmhand to help him, which he could barely afford. He grew feed grains, including wheat, soybeans, hay, and oats, and raised dairy and beef cattle. Like most farm families back then, we had chickens, too. We lived off the land, eating fresh vegetables from the garden in the summer and canned vegetables in the winter, eggs from the henhouse, and meat from the livestock Dad raised. Our modest farmhouse, which dated to the late 1800s, was next to a creek where I learned to swim. Like others in our region, our house was a practical, unadorned saltbox, typical of those built by Germans who settled Ohio's farmlands. We didn't have a decent barn until 1951. Although our address was Portage, we were closer to a spot in the road called Mermill, which amounted to a collection of junk cars, rusted farm equipment, and ramshackle houses.

I was born on January 11, 1941, and given the name Clayton Lee Mathile in honor of my grandfathers. (We've traced the name "Mathile," pronounced "Ma-till," to Swiss watchmakers in the Alsace region of France.) Everyone called me "Clayt," though on occasion Mom used "Clayton Lee" when I was in trouble. My brother Dallas was born three years later on March 25, 1944, and my sister Sally arrived on December 3, 1947.

My dad had the nature of a pessimistic farmer. Prices for our crops were always too low. There was never enough rain, or there was too much rain. Only one thing was certain: We never had enough money. Seventy-five percent of the conversation at every meal revolved around that topic.

Our narrow kitchen couldn't accommodate a table and chairs comfortably, so at mealtime Mother pulled a small white wooden table and fold-up benches out from the kitchen wall. Some of my earliest memories are of sitting at that narrow table, listening to my dad discuss farm business, like whether to sell our bull or whether to buy a new tractor. Even before I entered elementary school, I'd mentally weigh the pros and cons of whatever decision he was trying to make. I'd think to myself, "If I owned this farm, what would I do?" I never thought like an employee. I always took the position of an owner.

As a teenager, I sometimes tested my father. Once, I asked him if we could run the numbers to figure out exactly how much money we made from our herd of milk cows. He turned red with anger and accused me of being lazy. I explained that I thought we probably made so little from the milk that keeping the cows didn't make any sense, but he ended the discussion by stomping out of the barn.

Unlike my father, my mother encouraged me to dream. She loved quotations and used them liberally in her speech to encourage me to make the right choices. One of her favorite sayings was, "If you don't listen, you'll have to feel," meaning that those who don't learn from history will have to learn by making their own mistakes. Her advice was both inspirational and uncompromisingly practical:

- "Do the best you can with what you have. Don't go crying about what you don't have."

- "Eliminate 'can't' and 'too hard' from your vocabulary."

- "Education is the great equalizer. That's how poor kids get to be rich kids."

I'm a lot like my mom; I have very high standards. In the early days of running Iams, I didn't tell my employees what those standards were; I guess I figured they could read my mind. But as time went on and I learned how to be a good CEO and manager, I saw how important it was to set those standards at the outset with employees, then work with them to achieve our goals. That's what Mother did. She never kept me guessing as to her expectations; she spelled them out, then gave me support and encouragement to help me to meet them.

The two strongest female influences in my childhood were my mother and Dad's sister Evron, nicknamed "Bud." Aunt Bud was a frail childhood diabetic, six years younger than my dad, who lived with us because she needed someone close at hand in case she slipped into insulin shock. Smart as a whip and the valedictorian of her high school class, Aunt Bud stands out in my mind as the one person I knew as I was growing up who made me feel completely safe and unconditionally loved. She cherished me like a son and read to me constantly. She cheerfully took me on adventures and, like Mother, encouraged me to dream. Thanks to the two of them, I never thought the world stopped at the edge of Portage.

I missed Aunt Bud terribly when she got married and moved out that year. She died ten years later when I was fourteen and she had just celebrated her thirty-sixth birthday, leaving her own young son behind.

Then there was my maternal grandfather, John Ernest Lee Good. Now there was a character! A tough guy who worked hard like my dad and had high expectations like my mom, Grandpa Good was a hog farmer, a carpenter, and a maintenance man for grain elevators. He came to live with us for a few months in order to construct an indoor bathroom for our house. During the war, copper piping had been impossible to get, so we didn't have indoor plumbing.

Grandpa Good, who came from stern German stock, subscribed to the old-school theory that children should be seen but not heard. Everything about me grated on his nerves. A blur of frenetic energy, constantly moving and asking questions, I would absentmindedly pull the tops off my socks, much to my frugal mother's chagrin. Grandpa Good seemed to have forgotten what it was like to be a little boy, because after he finished the plumbing job, he told my mother, "That's the rottenest kid I've ever seen. He's a spoiled brat. You've got to do something with him."

Even though he was only five feet six inches tall, Grandpa Good was a formidable presence. At two hundred pounds, he knew how to throw his weight around. Not exactly the sweet old granddad type and very dogmatic, he loved to talk "at" you, as though he were a professor and you were in his class. Grandpa Good was a real curmudgeon, anti-everything. The soul of intolerance, he was a rabid conservative who hated Franklin Roosevelt and Harry Truman.

As a Protestant in a Catholic county, he naturally hated Catholics. He also hated anyone who wasn't being productive. He had an obsessive devotion to the Teutonic work ethic; Social Security came into effect when he lacked only three years to be eligible to draw the full amount, but he refused it, saying it was only a fancy name for a form of welfare.

Despite his gruff, intimidating personality, I genuinely admired Grandpa Good. He had a tool shop and had developed a reputation as an exceptionally skilled millwright. Farmers from miles around brought their saws to him for sharpening, because of his fanaticism about quality work. To be good at that job, he had to be exact. Sharpen a saw incorrectly, and the sharpening only lasts a little while. On the other hand, sharpen the saw too much, and it will be weak.

As a kid, I liked to explore the tools in his tidy workshop. A perfectionist, he kept each tool in such a precise spot that he could tell at a glance if someone had been in his tool shop. Even if you put a tool back in its appointed place, he somehow still knew it had been moved. Relatives often told me that I looked somewhat like him and that I inherited his work ethic. I was very impressed by his commitment to quality.

At age seventy-six, Grandpa Good fell off a twenty-foot-high scaffold, broke his back, and required a full body cast. This was in the middle of summer, so you can imagine what the discomfort and inactivity did to Grandpa's already cantankerous personality. He became absolutely impossible and drove my mother nuts! The doctors told him he'd never walk again, but they didn't know Grandpa Good. Within a year, through sheer willpower, he walked. He died a few years later in 1958 at the ripe old age of eighty-one, irascible to the end.

School never was a struggle for me, but the farm had its challenges. My father expected me to work with the intensity of a man, so by the age of six, every morning between 5 A.M. and 6 A.M., I helped milk and feed our twenty cows. I learned early not to shirk hard work and devoted much of the time I wasn't in school to my farm chores. At the same time, I also knew that I didn't want to follow in my father's footsteps. I hated everything about farming, and my obvious distaste for it deepened the chasm between my father and me.

When I was six, we took a road trip out of northern Ohio for the first time. I trace my fascination with entrepreneurship to that two-day, seven-hundred-mile drive to visit my Great-Uncle Bert in Arkansas. Uncle Bert left Ohio with his wife Elsie in a covered wagon in 1909, three years before Arkansas achieved statehood, to become a homesteader. He squatted on 80 acres north of Walnut Ridge long enough to claim it, then cleared the tract of pine trees, sold the wood, and planted cotton and soybeans.

Following this process, he eventually cobbled together two thousand acres of land, then built a sawmill and cotton gin. Aunt Elsie, a slight woman who kept her long hair pinned up in a neat bun, operated their general store in town. By the time we visited them in 1947, my prosperous aunt and uncle resided in a big, rambling ranch house in town.

Mechanical cotton pickers had just been invented, and Uncle Bert, quick to embrace innovations, purchased one of the first in the area to use in his fields. That was the big time to me. We took a tour of Uncle Bert's cotton gin. Sharecroppers would pull up outside the gin with their cotton in wagons, and a giant vacuum machine would suck the crop out of their trailers. Transfixed, I watched the gin comb the cotton to extract the seeds and stretch the fibers to form the end product: a one thousand-pound cotton bale. For the first time, I made the connection that a business owner exercised far greater control over his or her own destiny.

As a member of the local bank board, Uncle Bert enjoyed his status as a real player in the area. Besides his office downtown, he set up an office on the back sun porch of his house. He'd sit behind his desk with a small safe in one corner and comfortable chairs on the other side. On Saturday mornings, a steady stream of people, white and black, would come to the back door and bring him money. Sometimes they'd apologize for not having more to pay him, but he'd reply, "Just pay me the interest and don't worry about it." He'd carefully note what they'd paid in a black ledger book he kept in his desk.

Some of the amounts totaled as little as $2. I asked him about all the activity, and he explained that he made personal loans. "These folks are poor, and they couldn't get loans at the bank, because they didn't have collateral," he said. "But I know them, and they are good people." Despite his success, Uncle Bert always made time for the working man and treated everyone who came to him with dignity and respect.

I gravitated to successful men in our community. Harry Moran, who owned one of the farms we worked, made a big impression on me. A wildcatter, Harry found oil on his land and sold the rights to Ohio Oil, now Marathon Oil Company. He always wore a broad-brimmed hat like Harry Truman, a long-sleeved white shirt, and a tie with a ruby stickpin. He'd drive up in his Buick Roadmaster to check his oil wells on the farms he'd purchased with proceeds from the oil rights. Lighting up an R.G. Dunn stogie, he'd lean on his car and visit with me a few minutes. I was all ears as he told me how he made his money and why he invested in land.

Harry gave me my first paying job. I checked the oil wells every day for leaks. Every two or three weeks the oil wells would top off, and I called for the oil truck. I got $20 a month for that job, but it was worth much more in terms of a lesson it taught me about honesty.

In those days saltwater was mixed with the oil so that when you pumped out the oil and put it in big wooden tanks, the water would go to the bottom. Before the truck came to pick up the oil, you had to drain off the water. One particular day, the valve was so corroded that I couldn't shut it off, and the oil spilled everywhere. I had to run more than a mile to get my dad so he could turn it off. The following week, Harry came over to our house and wanted to know what happened. I could have lied and said I didn't know, but I told him the truth. And he thanked me.

"I'm glad you were honest," he smiled, "because I would have traced the slick back to you anyway!"

At one point Harry offered to sell my father an eighty-acre farm across the road from us. On one of his frequent forays to visit our family, Uncle Bert stepped in, offering to bankroll my dad the $200-an-acre asking price. Dad turned him down flat, refusing to take on any debt. So Uncle Bert bought the farm instead and Dad farmed it. Dad deposited half the farm's profits into an account for Uncle Bert, and, in return for farming the land, kept the other half.

In six years, Uncle Bert's profits from the farm grew to an amount that would have paid off the entire note. My dad just wouldn't take the gamble. The shadow of the Great Depression and what he'd seen all around him during those painful years caused him to fear stepping out on faith in his own abilities. But I inherited my mother's optimism. I thought, "Why work for the man when you can have the man work for you?" I wanted to be like Uncle Bert and own the land.

Dad liked to tell me the story of a man he viewed as a hero during the Depression. He was Carl Schwinn, the banker at Cygnet Bank in one of the many small towns that sprang up after wildcatters struck oil in Ohio in the late 1800s. During the Depression, the banker deposited all his personal wealth in his bank to ensure that it stayed solvent. He even stayed open on bank holidays throughout the Depression years to reassure local farmers who put their money in his bank.

In those days, the banker was a farmer's trusted business advisor. When times improved, locals revered Carl Schwinn for his integrity. Everybody wanted to do business with him. That taught me a powerful lesson: People want to do business with an honest person. Integrity is everything. Without it, you have nothing!

School continued to be easy for me academically. I loved math and science. I don't remember bringing home a book, though, because I focused enough to get my homework done during study halls.

My father and I had little in common, but we shared a mutual passion for basketball. My dad mounted a rim on the corncrib inside our barn, which had a smooth concrete floor, perfect for dribbling. On Sundays I'd back the tractors out of the barn to make room for the half-dozen kids from the area who showed up to play several games. Every spare moment I could grab, as much as three hours a day, I'd practice shooting hoops.

Short for my age and the smallest guy in my class, I decided I'd work harder than everybody else. In the severe Ohio winters, I'd stay out in the barn shooting and practicing my ball handling for hours, despite the bone-chilling cold. Sometimes my hands swelled and turned practically purple from the frigid temperatures, but I doggedly kept working on my game.

In my sophomore year, my raging hormones and simmering anger boiled over one afternoon during a basketball scrimmage. Younger twins on my team kept fouling me and mouthing off. I warned them that if they kept it up, I'd deck them. Coach stepped in, chastising me for threatening my teammates, and sent me to the locker room to cool off. It was history eerily repeating itself; I remembered how my dad had been thrown off the high school basketball team for losing his temper and how that incident had cast a shadow over his life, as it led to his quitting school.

But that didn't diminish my anger. I threw chairs and basketball shoes and kicked lockers. Instead of letting me work off my head of steam, Coach came in, grabbed me, and started grappling with me. I snapped and punched him hard in the face. He knocked me to the ground and stalked out. Later he told me he'd put my fate to a team vote, and my teammates had decided that I'd ride the bench for the rest of the season. I was forced to re-earn my position on the varsity team.

Our team's record was 0-16 that year. I sat on the bench and watched as we got thrashed time after time. Finally, when the tournaments rolled around, Coach put me in against our archrival Westwood. I scored several baskets and rebounded with a vengeance, and we upset the opposing team. Although I craved winning, and that victory undeniably tasted sweet, my time riding the pine taught me a far more powerful lesson. I began to grasp that lack of control over my anger could jeopardize my team and have dire consequences.

A cheerleader caught my eye the following year when we played Westwood again. Mary Ann Maas lived in the nearby town of Custar, a farming town with slightly more fertile soil than Portage and a population of two hundred, almost all of them Catholic. Mary, the most popular girl there, was a petite redhead with sparkling blue eyes. I asked around and discovered she already had a boyfriend. My friends all ribbed me and assured me I didn't stand a chance with Mary. I already had a strike against me as a star on the rival high school's basketball team.

Sixteen years old and a hotshot athlete, I certainly didn't lack confidence. When I spotted Mary again, I convinced a mutual friend to arrange a date for us. Mary, who was between her sophomore and junior years in high school, finally consented.

That August we spent a day together at the Wood County Fair in Bowling Green, a popular hangout with the teens in our crowd. I talked about my plans for the future, telling Mary I wanted to own a business someday. She encouraged me to talk about my dreams, and I asked for another date. The following Saturday we went to the drive-in; at the end of the evening, I brashly announced that I planned to marry her someday. Mary laughed, shaking her head and arching her brow, but soon afterward, we were steady.

If Mary was impressed by my boldness and confidence, I was impressed by her concern for others. If she noticed another kid alone on the school bus, Mary would sit with him or her. Her great compassion and desire to help others was perhaps the thing I most loved—and still love—about her.

That same summer, a farmer came to me and told me he'd pay me $10 a day to keep his soybeans weeded during the growing season. I asked my dad if I could do it, as long as I kept up with my chores at home. By summer's end I could make about $800, money I could sorely use for college. Dad caught me by surprise when he offered me a business deal instead. "I'll give you eight acres of land that will be yours to work, and when we harvest in the fall, I'll give you the profits from your crop."

After calculating the potential in my head, I figured I could make about the same as the other farmer was offering me, so I eagerly agreed. All that summer, I carefully cultivated that field and weeded the soybeans that I planted. I worked hard on my little plot, doing everything in my power to improve the yield. That summer we got good rains, and I figured my yield would be about twenty-five bushels to an acre at $4 a bushel for a grand total of $800. For the first time, I felt the pride of ownership and looked forward to getting a reward for my hard work.

In late September while I attended school, Dad harvested my field and dumped my soybeans in with his in the old wagon he took to market. When I got home from school and asked him about my crop, he admitted that he had forgotten all about our deal. I didn't ask him about the money, and he never brought it up. To him, those soybeans simply needed to be harvested and taken to market, and that was that. It was my first financial failure. But like all failures, it was a valuable lesson in disguise, clearly showing me a profound difference between my father and me that would shape my future. My dad dreamed little dreams, if he dreamed at all, but I longed to have something I could claim and was more determined than ever to make that dream come true.

By my senior year on the Portage basketball team, I had finally hit a growth spurt and topped six feet. That year I averaged 22 points a game. In the final game of the county tournament, our team trailed by one point and got the ball with the last seconds ticking away. My teammate froze with the ball, paralyzed at the thought that in his hands rested the deciding points of the game. I swooped by and snatched the ball from his grasp and tossed it up. It rolled around the rim and then plopped into the basket, giving us the victory.

Dad's buttons popped, but mom was more interested in my grades. When they slipped a little in my sophomore year, she warned, "Clayt, if you aren't valedictorian, I'm not coming to your graduation."

She pushed herself, too, and set a good example. She'd gone back to college to get her four-year degree, and many evenings when I went to bed, she would be sitting in the kitchen doing her own homework and writing her own lesson plans for teaching the next day.

I made valedictorian. Of course, my graduating class had only fourteen people, five boys and nine girls, but Mother was so proud of me that you'd have thought I'd beat out five hundred kids for the honor.

In my community, where virtually everyone was either a farmer or a factory worker, the big achievement was to earn a college degree so you could qualify for an office job. I was only the fifth graduate from Portage to ultimately get a college degree. Without my father's knowledge, my mother had squirreled away enough money from her measly teacher's salary to help me with my first year of college. Then she went to the bank and took out a loan to fund what her savings wouldn't cover.

I wasn't given a vote. She insisted I attend at least one year of college. She thought that if she could get her children off the farm, ultimately we would finish school. My mother taught me to believe in the Great American Dream, even though we weren't sharing in it.

Two years after I left the farm, my dad sold off our milk cows, declaring them unprofitable.

## CHAPTER 3

# Hoop Dreams, Soup Realities, and a Man Named Paul Iams

A basketball coach in our county, a graduate of a small, conservative Methodist school called Ohio Northern University, caught wind that I wanted to play college ball. He introduced me to the Ohio Northern coach, who had already doled out the scholarships for that year but agreed to give me a look.

I made the squad. Thanks to the one thousand dollars I had saved up, winnings from showing my steer calves at county fairs, and Mom's efforts (she paid for books and tuition), I could afford the first year of school without scholarship help. As for my sophomore year, the coach promised to give me one of those precious scholarships if I played well and kept my grades up.

So off I went to Ada, Ohio. Surrounded by corn, wheat, and soybean fields, the small, windswept college town consisted of one main street and a pretty campus founded in 1871. In the café near the railroad tracks, your cup and saucer practically rattled off the table when a train roared past. I enjoyed watching the trains rush by and wished I were on them, bound for adventure.

I was a typical clueless freshman with no idea what I wanted to do with my life. Undecided on a major, I settled on mechanical engineering, because I'd heard that engineers earned big bucks and snagged jobs easily. There was just one problem: I hated mechanical drawing.

Fortunately, my professor, a big basketball fan, took a special interest in me as the engineering school's lone varsity basketball player. One day, he mentioned that my declared major meant "two or three more years at the drawing board after you graduate."

"I'll go crazy," I blurted out. "Save me from that."

He answered, "You either have to learn to draw or do something else. What do you want to be?"

"I want to own my own business," I replied. I transferred to the business school the next day.

The highlight of my freshman year came at the athletic banquet. I'd lettered in basketball and as the second baseman for the college baseball team. The basketball coach stood up and declared that I had the potential to be one of the best guards ever to come out of the school and that I'd be on scholarship the next season.

But that summer he gave away my scholarship to an incoming freshman. Shades of Dad and the soybeans. Again I had been betrayed by an authority figure. Although I was deeply hurt, the disappointment had a silver lining: I became more determined than ever to chart my own course, trusting none of the traditional, safe routes. And as much as I despised Coach for breaking his promise, I was forced to admit that perhaps he'd inadvertently done me a favor; when it came right down to it, I knew I would never make my living playing basketball.

Without the promised scholarship to lighten the financial burden of school, I rolled up my sleeves and took a job at one of the gas stations on Main Street. Ray Long, the station owner, was stricken with Parkinson's disease. He positioned himself against a doorway where he could keep an eye on the pumps and the cash register simultaneously.

I noticed that several of the college kids from wealthy families drove foreign cars such as Porsches and MGs, so I suggested that Mr. Long gear up to carry foreign auto parts. I made the rounds at the fraternity houses, offering free car washes and oil changes whenever someone brought a car in to be fixed. His business increased tremendously, because our station stood out as the only one for miles around that stocked foreign parts.

During summer breaks, I gave Dad a hand on the farm and worked at nearby factories. I took a job as the night watchman and janitor at Day Brooks, which made truck bodies. That experience led me to conclude the savvy manager who isn't sure what's going on in a department should talk with the janitor. You can learn a startling amount about how a company operates from roaming the offices after hours and handling its trash.

Another summer, I joined the decontamination crew and ore-crushing department for a plant that smelted beryllium, an ore so dangerous that plant workers submitted to weekly pulmonary tests. Every day, I lifted heavy burlap bags filled with the beryllium ore, an extremely strong metal used to make the cones for spacecrafts.

It seemed I was always working and always learning. Every one of those early jobs taught me invaluable lessons about persistence, patience, and trying, whenever possible, to stimulate and improve sales by taking a more creative approach to the product. Whether it was adding foreign auto parts to Mr. Long's service station, using a lowly custodial position to get a feel for Day Brooks, or increasing my physical strength and endurance as a crew laborer at the beryllium smelting plant, each job was a building block that helped me develop the qualities I'd need when I finally ran my own company.

Mary graduated high school a year after I did and joined me the following fall at Ohio Northern, where she studied business and I pretended to study business. I don't know if it's something to be proud or ashamed of, but I managed to get my college degree while rarely cracking a book. My mom told me that as long as I made Bs and Cs that was good enough, so that's exactly what I did. The one time I screwed up was when I made a D in "Money and Banking," a rather charming irony in view of my later entrepreneurial success. Another time, when I showed up to take the midterm exam for a five-hour accounting course that met at 8 A.M., I had to convince Mrs. Ritz, the instructor, that I'd actually enrolled in her class, because I'd attended so infrequently.

"Mr. Matheel," she declared, loudly mispronouncing my name, "why are you here? You aren't in this class!"

"Why on earth would I be here this early in the morning if I'm not on the roll?" I shot back. She checked her book and grudgingly let me take the midterm. I got a B on it.

For the most part, the business courses at Ohio Northern did little to inspire me in my quest to be an entrepreneur. The curriculum was geared toward students who wanted to go on to work in large corporations. I'd listen to some professor and think, "That guy couldn't run a popcorn stand."

One professor, however, made an important impression on me. Dr. Palmer, formerly a banker with Mellon Bank in Pittsburgh, taught corporate finance. "The most important element in business is timing," he often intoned. "Being in the right place at the right time with the right stuff; if you can figure out how to do that, you'll be a success."

Many of my classmates were contemptuous of the seventy-year-old, $1-a-year man. (He'd already made plenty of money, so he took only $1 for his annual teaching salary.) But I frequently visited with him in his office, peppering him with questions about what industries and career opportunities I should consider. I spoiled my B and C record by earning an A in his class.

After my pressure-cooker life on the farm, college was like a four-year vacation. I divided my social time between Mary, the love of my life, and my buddies. Mary never drank, so I routinely escorted her back to her dorm and then went out partying with the guys.

We guzzled beer at The Forest Inn, a watering hole a few miles outside of the dry town, or at Kribley's, known as The Krib, a dive in downtown Ada authorized to sell "3.2" beer (it only had 3.2 percent alcohol). At frat parties, we smuggled in beer.

If people had said to me back then, "Clay, you're developing a drinking problem," I would have thought they were crazy. I was your ultra-normal collegiate guy, period. What I didn't realize was that I was indeed developing an alcohol problem that gradually escalated through the years until, in the 1980s, I was forced to confront the painful fact that what had begun as an innocent social activity had become a palliative for anger and frustration and an emotional escape. Because drinking never impaired my ability to function, I assumed it was "under control." In reality, it would one day threaten to destroy my marriage and everything I held most dear.

The next fall, Mary, ever practical, announced she didn't find college life a good fit for her. She left school, moved back to Custar, and took a secretarial job at Campbell Soup Company in Napoleon, forty miles away.

I never formally got down on my knees and proposed. Our understanding was that we'd marry as soon as I graduated and landed a steady job.

Although I had scarcely a dime to my name, Mary unwaveringly bought into my vision of owning a business. Her staunch support inspired me to be more determined than ever to transform that dream into reality.

In the cold, hard reality of the moment, however, I couldn't even afford to buy her a proper engagement ring. As a result, Mary ended up fronting most of the money for her own ring. She put down $200, and I chipped in $100 on a ring we bought at a jewelry store where one of my fraternity brothers worked and got us a good deal. Technically, I have yet to repay Mary for that loan.

I graduated one quarter early in February 1962. A month later, I landed my first job as an accountant in the plant accounting office of the Chevrolet Division of General Motors in Toledo, Ohio, where the plant made passenger car transmissions. The benefits were particularly enticing; in those days, the accepted career path meant spending thirty-five years with a big company so that you could claim the pot of gold, in the form of a nice pension and retirement, at the end of the rainbow.

On July 7, 1962, Mary and I were married in a simple wedding mass at St. Louis Catholic Church in her hometown of Custar. It was a typical Custar wedding. During midday, most of the attendees scurried back to their fields to finish cultivating the corn or harvesting wheat, so our cake and punch reception was delayed until 4 P.M., customary for the farming communities in that area. A few of my relatives refused to attend because

Mary was Catholic and I had converted, but nothing could put a damper on the day.

We were the quintessential struggling newlyweds. I could barely cover all our expenses with my $450-a-month salary, and we quickly racked up every kind of debt you can imagine. Our new Sears credit card helped with rent, furniture, and appliances, and we were saddled with payments on a shiny new red Buick Skylark with a white convertible top. I wisely or unwisely, as the case may be, bought that car right before we got married. Mary's practical nature would have kept me from making such a wildly extravagant purchase.

We'd planned on Mary working, but on the day of her final interview for a secretarial job assisting the owner of a tool-and-die shop, she discovered she was pregnant.

We decided to move, because our efficiency apartment was so tiny that we couldn't figure out where we could squeeze in a crib.

Only a few weeks after starting at GM, I knew I'd never be happy in the corporate life. Bureaucrats filled the ranks, and I stood out like a sore thumb, chafing at the tedium of shuffling papers all day in a mundane job. Yet even though I felt choked by the company's militaristic policies and procedures, I couldn't quit. We needed the insurance coverage for Mary's pregnancy.

Catherine, a blue-eyed redhead like her mother, came into the world on April 28, 1963, a scant ten months after our three-day honeymoon in Pigeon Forge—now best known as Dolly Parton's hometown—in the Smokey Mountains of Tennessee.

I developed a bad case of workplace cabin fever that propelled me to interview for a position as a supervisor of accounts payable at the Campbell Soup Company plant in Napoleon, Ohio, where Mary had worked. The personnel director asked me to take a test to determine creativity, and I scored one of the highest grades ever recorded at the plant. He subsequently recruited me for a management trainee position that paid $120 a week with $100 per month extra for overtime directly from headquarters' payroll. The promise of a 10 percent raise every six months and a move to a new job within the company every few years appealed to my restless nature. After a little more than a year at GM, I ditched my job and joined the Campbell Soup Company.

My first order of business was not exactly thrilling. I was told to bring order to the chaos of dozens of invoices that had gotten bogged down in an unwieldy system. Suppliers peppered our department with calls, demanding to be paid. Within months, I needed glasses after spending hours poring over invoices and trying to sort out the mess.

Over the next seven years I moved through a succession of positions in cost accounting, inventory control, and purchasing. By age twenty-five, I was an assistant purchasing agent, a coveted position previously reserved primarily for men in their forties and fifties, signaling that I'd made it onto the fast track for a vice president's spot within Campbell Soup.

I steadily worked out from under the debt we'd incurred; I wanted independence. We didn't buy a new car or a house. We rented a modest apartment and then a small house near the Elks Club, an elementary school, and our church, about two blocks from the main street in Napoleon to accommodate our growing family.

Timothy was born in 1965, followed by Michael, three years later. Even though we were strapped financially, we welcomed each new arrival with great happiness. Mary never asked for material things, so she relieved the pressure on me to adhere to the corporate culture out of fear of losing my job. Thanks to my undemanding wife, I gained a lot of insight into what one can do in a system where the corporation doesn't have power over you. You can behave in interesting ways and accomplish a lot.

From the outset, I set a personal goal to be either a saver or maker of at least $100,000 every year for the company. I wanted to stand up in front of my boss when performance reviews rolled around and say, "I made or saved you more money than you paid me, and I can document that."

Each of the six Campbell Soup plants employed two cost accountants, one for the can manufacturing side of the business and one for soup manufacturing. After our can manufacturing cost accountant left, I split my time between the can manufacturing and soup manufacturing sides of the business. I was in the can manufacturing side four days out of the month for twenty-hour days, crunching numbers like crazy. But I noticed that the material costs for making the cans never varied more than 1 to 2 percent. The only variable was tin plate. By giving my boss an estimated number and burying the reserve in the tin plate inventory, I created a standard cost system and relieved the cost during the next month to balance the books.

One afternoon, as I prepared to leave at my customary time of 4:30 P.M. on the dot, my boss confronted me. He was confused because my predecessor had previously worked crazy hours during that time of month, and I was leaving right on time. "What on earth are you doing over here, Mathile?" he demanded, eyeing me suspiciously.

Delighted that one of the higher-ups had noticed, I explained my new system. "You could be fired for that," he growled, but then added grudgingly. "But what you've done is actually ingenious." He helped me make an adjustment and get the rules changed. Subsequently, the company only needed one cost accountant at each of the plants, because the can side could be reconciled after the monthly closing, which was much faster now. Soon I was promoted to purchasing.

The average person buying a can of Campbell's Double Noodle soup doesn't do much reflecting upon all the elements that went into making that can of soup. For all they know or care, it simply materialized on the supermarket shelf. It's truly mind-boggling when you not only realize the many intricate mechanisms involved in manufacturing a product, but are also in charge of inspecting, maintaining, and improving them.

For instance, Campbell's machine specifications and U.S. Department of Agriculture regulations called for stainless-steel rollers on filler machines, along with stainless-steel cams to move the cans along as they were filled. It's something like a roller coaster track. But under tremendous pressure, stainless steel on stainless steel is the worst possible combination. The cams and stainless steel rollers had to be replaced each year.

One day I noticed that Ernie Tobias, a maintenance supervisor with twenty-five years of experience under his tool belt, had been putting in requests for nylon rollers. I went to the plant floor to question him.

"Ernie," I asked, "why are you using nylon rollers?"

"Because they're much more durable and cost-effective, Mr. Mathile," Ernie explained. "The stainless-steel rollers last about a year, and then they've got to be replaced. The nylon rollers last a lot longer and really cut down the wear and tear on the cam shafts, meaning they could last up to a decade."

I was impressed. The annual cost of replacing cams and steel rollers was $60,000 per filling machine. If they only had to be replaced every ten years...you do the math. I did and realized Ernie had hit upon a brilliant improvement in our process.

There was one main hitch. Because the machine specs and USDA regulations called for stainless steel, putting nylon rollers went against procedure. Worse, Ernie didn't feel he had the ability to navigate the bureaucracy to get the change approved. Even though I had that ability, I was paddling upstream if I put my stamp of approval on something that ran counter to policy.

But I believed in Ernie and decided to gamble that the money he was saving the company would justify the infraction. I never worried about my job. My bigger concern revolved around doing the right thing for the company.

I called the local USDA inspector, invited him to come to the plant, and convinced him to approve the change in specs. Then I recorded the change and resulting savings in my monthly report. The vice president of purchasing picked up on it. Other plants subsequently integrated the use of nylon rollers, which ultimately meant $600,000 to $1 million in savings each year for Campbell.

And to think that the idea came from a guy who worked with the machinery day after day but had no voice in the company. My belief that the best ideas often come from the front lines, from people management routinely overlooks, was validated.

Being in the corporate environment for almost a decade taught me what not to do. One example of self-defeating corporate behavior that's always driven me up the wall is valuing rules and regulations at the expense of employee talent and creativity. It's illogical. Why hire intelligent people if you ask them to check their brains at the door and don't allow them to make decisions? Rather than empowering people to do the best job they can, you are sending your employees a strong message that you don't trust or value them.

I've always believed in getting to know employees at every level of the company and getting firsthand experience with every job, from bottom to top. I've never felt that I was too good for a job. At Iams, I did everything from driving a delivery truck on up. If more executives adopted this attitude, corporations would change for the better. It promotes mutual respect and trust between management and employees, and no company can operate successfully without trust.

I owe Uncle Bert a vote of thanks for my ability to relate to people at many different levels in an organization. Because I observed him treating everyone with dignity and respect and decided to follow his example, I moved easily between the upper echelons and the everyday workers. This was one of the chief reasons for my business success.

*I believe you can learn something from anyone and the wisdom of the decision has nothing to do with the power of the position.*

I continued looking for ways to save company money. For years, Campbell purchased finished hardwood pallets for can storage. The specs required the pallets to be kiln-dried because the tin cans would start to rust if the wood in the pallets was green. These pricey pallets were delivered in bulk once a year because that gave the best price, but then they sat outside year-round since the warehouse couldn't hold them. I saw all these kiln-dried pallets sitting outside in the rain because someone in the corporation decreed that bulk-buying was always the way to go without looking at individual pieces of the puzzle. No one dared challenge thinking that came from headquarters.

I asked the warehouse manager if he could allow me room to have truckloads of green-wood pallets delivered on an as-needed basis and then air-dry inside the warehouse. He readily agreed, because the old procedure meant that the pallets required a good deal of unnecessary handling for the warehouse department. We wound up with much drier pallets at $9 each versus $12 each for the kiln-dried hardwood pallets. Just like when I'd listen at the supper table to my dad talk about farm decisions, I always thought, "What would I do if this were my business?" In 95 percent of the cases, my decisions either saved or made the company money.

At Campbell Soup, I observed firsthand what happens when a company has conflicting objectives. On one hand, managers subscribed to renowned quality expert W. Edwards Deming's exhortations to be fanatics about quality and to require that suppliers guarantee quality systems and quality raw products. At that time Dr. Deming's radical "quality theory," which he began teaching to top management in Japan in 1950, had galvanized Japanese businesses and had subsequently been embraced by many U.S. manufacturers.

From the store to the warehouse, Campbell Soup sought a total quality ethic from everyone involved. Simultaneously, the company subscribed to high production efficiency so onerous that it threatened the quality system. You had to circumvent the system to make your numbers. As a result, the quality manager spent most of the time watching the production manager, who, in turn, devoted most of his time to figuring out how to cheat the system.

In the early 1960s, the whole concept of value analysis—looking not just at what you paid for a product but what value you got from it—revolutionized industry and captured my imagination. I reasoned that if we stopped looking purely for the cheapest price on raw materials and treated suppliers like trusted partners who added value, we'd improve quality and be able to work together to hold down costs and produce a better final product. I looked at food as a nutrient, for example, rather than a commodity. But status quo at Campbell meant working with myriad suppliers and pitting them against each other to keep prices low.

At one point during my purchasing agent stint at Campbell, I got the assignment to source the raw materials, beef bones and beef, that produced beef stock for our soups. I studied the meat-rendering industry carefully, thinking about our processes.

The beef bones and meat I bought produced two by-products: beef broth and fat. My predecessor bought the bones for 3.5 cents a pound. Campbell used the beef broth in soups and other products within the company for human consumption, but the previous purchasing agent then sold the fat to the inedible market for 2.5 cents a pound. I hit upon a simple fix that enabled us to sell the beef fat to the edible market (for human consumption, a more valuable option) by switching the pipe in the shipping department from galvanized iron to sanitized stainless steel.

That little change in the way we transported the fat meant we could charge 5 cents a pound for it. With three to five truckloads a month transporting forty thousand pounds of fat fit for human consumption, what had previously been a cost to Campbell now produced a tidy profit.

During my time as a purchasing agent, I met some impressive entrepreneurs: the businessmen who owned meat-boning operations in New York, Boston, Detroit, and Chicago. Part of my responsibility was to cultivate suppliers in those territories. These guys sold a high volume of boneless beef on razor-thin margins but managed to make a nice living at it. They were tough negotiators, and I admired their tenacity.

Three years into my stint with Campbell, I started looking for the quickest route to getting ahead. Tired of lateral transfers, I asked my boss about a prestigious program where Campbell Soup sponsored a Sloan fellow for an MBA at the Massachusetts Institute of Technology (MIT), a two-year sabbatical. The company paid to move the employee's family to Cambridge, Massachusetts, and paid both salary and school expenses. Sloan fellows typically landed plum jobs as vice presidents at Campbell Soup after completing the program. But year after year, the fellowship went to another candidate.

I took classes at Bowling Green, thinking that beefing up my undistinguished academic record might help. My boss kept telling me to be patient and wait my turn, reminding me that I wasn't even thirty yet. By 1968, I asked that he put his promises in writing, but he refused, chiding me for my impatience, saying, "You'll get your shot."

By 1970, I had developed a severe case of the corporate equivalent of the seven-year itch. While working on a better way to handle the fat by-product from the beef bones, I called Frank Pachin, a broker with A.L. Pachin & Sons in Dayton. Well-versed in the pet food industry, Frank purchased inedible fat from me, then brokered much of it to Procter & Gamble for use in making soap. Frank helped me figure out how to make the fat we were producing work for the edible market. He was also a supplier to Iams Food Company.

Frank called me one day and said, "I've sensed for some time that you aren't entirely happy at Campbell Soup. There's a fellow I want you to meet. I know you are developing a supplier for Campbell's new dog food brand, Lassie's Recipe. This fellow, Paul Iams, knows more about the dog food industry than anyone I know, and you might have an opportunity with his company."

Intrigued, I took down the information and called Paul Iams later that afternoon. "When Frank tells me somebody is good, I know it's worth talking to you," he said. "Why don't you come down?"

I said okay, thanked him, and hung up. Little did I suspect this informal offer would mark the key turning point in my life.

## CHAPTER 4

# Any Title but President

I drove down to the Iams plant in Dayton on a gray Saturday morning in late February 1970. In business for nearly a quarter-century, Iams Food Company, as it was called then, still fit into the small, nondescript, drafty building it had occupied since 1950 on Delphos Avenue. It stood next to a railroad track in a rough neighborhood on Dayton's west side. The smells of meat meal and fat permeated the air. Dirt, grit, and black beet pulp dust covered every surface. The place certainly wouldn't win any sanitation awards.

Fifty-four-year-old Paul Iams was a tall man who smoked cigarettes and an occasional pipe. With his strong jaw, he bore a remarkable resemblance to Senator Barry Goldwater. After meeting me with a firm handshake, Paul ushered me into his office, a small cluttered space with a plain desk and a worn couch from the Army surplus store that belched dust when I sat down. He flicked ashes everywhere as he told me about his company's history.

When Paul launched the Iams Food Company in October 1946 at the Tipp City Feed Mill fifteen miles north of Dayton, he had no inkling it would one day be recognized as a world-class pet food manufacturer noted for its devotion to dog and cat nutrition. Like many entrepreneurs, the thirty-one-year-old war veteran spent the early years fighting to keep his fledgling business afloat.

Paul had spied a vacant building on the feed mill's grounds and struck a deal with the owner to use the facility for his new dog food business. He became close friends with the sales manager of the mill's largest customer,

Kentucky Chemical, who suggested the infant company's line of feed would be more complete with a dry dog food. The sales manager procured a dog food formula for Paul that a Tennessee company had been using successfully.

Paul and his father, a grain broker and consultant, set up a thousand-pound mixer and rudimentary bagging machine. With a contract in hand from Kentucky Chemical, which agreed to provide distribution and a sales force, Paul produced ten tons of dry dog food he named Provico, then waited anxiously for orders to pour in.

When weeks passed with precious few orders, Paul realized he'd made two mistakes: one, he was relying solely on someone else's sales force, and two, his dog food, although good, wasn't distinguishable from other brands, which made dog owners reluctant to switch to his new food.

Looking for something that would give his formula an edge, the young entrepreneur set about educating himself on dog nutrition. He talked to dozens of breeders and other experts and worked with Kentucky Chemical's nutritionists to find answers. When protein emerged as the key, Paul contracted with Eli Lilly, the pharmaceutical company, to purchase pig pancreases that had been discarded after the company had extracted insulin from them. This unique high-protein ingredient boosted Provico sales, but Paul wasn't satisfied. He noticed his customers were adding fat to the dry food, which already contained 9 percent fat. At the time, animal experts were declaring dogs could tolerate no more than 10 percent fat.

Paul knew the experts must be wrong and set out to prove it by producing Hi Fat Pro Lite dog food that contained 15 percent fat. Customers reported the new product gave their dogs the best coats they'd ever seen.

Despite this achievement, by 1953 Paul's confidence in the future of his dry dog food business, which he'd moved to Dayton, was waning fast. He had a wife and young son to support and, after seven years in business, too few loyal customers for his products, including Iams 999, so named because Paul believed it was almost perfect. He began looking for a buyer for his company.

But no suitable buyers surfaced. Paul had no choice but to redouble his efforts to find new customers. Seeking larger orders, he began driving regularly to Cleveland, which happened to be the backyard of one of his competitors: Bil-Jac, which manufactured its own dog food brand and distributed several others.

One morning, Paul rose at 3 A.M. to meet one of Bil-Jac's owners, Bill Kelly, two hours away in Medina, Ohio, where Bill was delivering his dog food by truck. Paul left a 25-pound bag of Iams 999 with Bill to sample. Despite Bill's initial criticism of Iams 999 (he judged the food to be too greasy), he was soon surprised to be selling as much as five thousand pounds of Iams 999 every week. Paul and Bill Kelly became good friends, often handling sales calls together.

One day, between calling on kennels, Bill suggested they visit a mink ranch owner he knew in western Pennsylvania. Paul, always eager for new experiences, agreed. At the ranch, the owner sadly pointed out twenty young mink that had failed to thrive, adding that he planned to do away with them.

Back on the road, Bill and Paul had traveled only a mile from the ranch when Paul had an idea. They drove back and offered to supply the rancher with free Iams 999 to see if it would help the poor-doing mink. The rancher was skeptical, since previous experiments with feeding dry dog food to mink had failed miserably. Still, he had nothing to lose, so agreed to the trial.

The mink began eating the nutrient-dense dog food in August 1953. By the December pelting season, they were thriving, with luxurious coats. The rancher credited Iams 999's high protein and fat content with the transformation. Paul did further research to prove his unique formula was behind the improvement. He invested a whopping $71 on a set of books that explained protein and amino acids.

By 1957, Paul Iams and Bill Kelly had taken their mink supplement, formulated after their success with those twenty mink, nationwide. The mink supplement business brought steady income for the partners while the Iams dog food business lagged behind. In fact, more than a decade into making and selling dog food, that piece of Paul's business barely broke even. The mink supplement's success, however, allowed him to buy a small farm and build a new home for his family.

Common sense might have led Paul to ditch his dream of creating the complete dog food diet in order to concentrate on the mink industry. But Paul sensed the answer to producing the perfect dog food had been right under their noses all along. Whenever he called on mink ranches, he noticed the big guard dogs there seemed to be in exceptionally good health, even when they neared fifteen years of age.

Bright-eyed and bushy-tailed, the dogs romped like puppies. Their stools were firm, and they didn't have the kidney problems often seen in older large-breed dogs. When Paul asked what the dogs were eating, the answer left him thunderstruck: The dogs ate the same food as the mink. Although canine experts were touting the 10 percent fat/25 percent protein diet for dogs, Paul's mink diet was working beautifully, despite its remarkable 20 to 25 percent fat and 35 to 45 percent protein content. Ever the experimenter, Paul's quest for the perfect dog food was reinvigorated.

But first he had a problem to solve. An avalanche of calls from both mink supplement and dog food customers complained that something had drastically changed with the Iams products they were feeding their animals, who were no longer thriving. Paul deduced that one of his raw-material suppliers must have made a switch without alerting him. He was right. Eli Lilly, which supplied the all-important pig pancreas component, had begun running pancreases through a solvent during the insulin extraction process. The solvent destroyed the protein's nutritive value, rendering it useless for both mink and dog food.

Paul moved fast to contain the damage. He secured a source of meat scraps that yielded enough protein and could supply him the ten tons per week he needed to compensate for the loss of pancreas protein. But this new source presented still another problem: It contained as much bone meal as meat meal, and Paul's research had told him the high mineral content contributed by all that bone meal would cause problems in a carnivore's diet.

Jay Hoke, Paul's first employee, sighed. "Paul," he said sadly, "I guess this is the end of the line."

Paul leaned against the wall, puffing his pipe and thinking. Then he asked, "Jay, does your wife have a hair dryer?"

"Yes."

"Go home and get it."

A strange request, but Jay complied. He knew his boss. If Paul had an idea, however bizarre, it was based on logic. The rest of the afternoon and into the night, the duo worked feverishly on a process to remove bone meal from the meat scraps. The resulting process remains a trade secret that is still used today.

So the fate of Iams Food Company hinged on creative use of a portable hair dryer circa 1950. Thanks to that ingenious process, the company continued to produce high-quality protein products while eliminating the high mineral levels and ash that made competitive products less effective.

In 1961, Paul introduced the first of what would become a new breed of breakthrough products: Iams Plus. He considered naming it "U-kanuba," a nonsense word that appealed to him, but those he tried it out on dismissed it as a goofy name for a dog food. Iams Plus came in meal form and had even more protein than Paul's previous formulations. He had finally succeeded in making a "complete" dog food, needing no added supplements to achieve good results.

Once again, Paul faced many obstacles. His tiny company lacked funds for advertising. Consumers were skeptics when it came to a complete dog food, thanks to the failure of previous pet food companies to deliver on that same promise over the years. And virtually all popular pet foods of the day were sold as kibble. Even the size of the Iams Plus bag, 20 pounds, compared to the hefty 50-pound bags of its competitors, testified to the company's David-and-Goliath battle with the big players in the field.

None of this bothered Paul. He was convinced he simply needed to create a superior product and customers would find him. His strategy was strictly word of mouth; converting one breeder and one kennel owner at a time to Iams Plus.

Confident of the future success of Iams Plus, Paul turned over day-to-day operations at the plant to Jay. Aided by moonlighting firemen, Jay kept up with the steadily growing demand for the dog food, and Paul turned his attention back to what he loved: his research farm at West Alexandria, Ohio, where he continued to fine-tune his nutritional theories for mink.

In January 1969, Paul met Loyal Wells of Ross Wells, Inc., at a mink convention in Milwaukee. The two men discussed what they did, and Paul became excited when he realized that Ross Wells, a division of Beatrice Foods, was a former rendering company. Loyal owned processing equipment that could produce the undamaged protein Paul needed to make his complete mink food. A complete diet would save mink ranchers many hours a day currently spent mixing ingredients and held much more potential to drive his company's success than a mink supplement. Instead of using chicken parts not intended for human food, including the head, feathers, feet, and internal organs, Paul planned to use only chicken entrails in his new mink food, making it incredibly high in protein with very little of the ash found in processed bones.

With a handshake, Paul and Loyal agreed the Berlin, Maryland, plant would co-pack a complete mink diet using Paul's formula and to his specifications. As a side project, Ross Wells also agreed to co-pack a new dog food Paul had been tinkering with. Unlike any other dry dog food on the market but like his dry mink food, this new dog food would be made using only chicken entrails, making its high-protein makeup unbeatable and difficult to copy. This time, Paul wouldn't be dissuaded. He called the new dog food "Eukanuba."

The finishing touches on Paul's long-awaited mink diet were made over the next year, just in time for the mink industry's collapse in 1970. As I listened to Paul's amazing story, I looked around the shabby little office and marveled at this no-nonsense business genius who was too busy creating the perfect dog food to care about the trappings of success. Like

Harry Moran, who owned land my father had farmed, Paul struck me as a straight shooter, a true entrepreneur passionate about his product, which he insisted far surpassed the nutritional value of any other pet foods on the market.

A self-taught scientist, Paul focused on continually improving the quality of his dog food, but he was less savvy about improving its distribution. Although Iams dog food was viewed as the gold standard by many kennel operators, it had yet to win star status in the mainstream. Iams Plus was sold primarily to feed stores and breeders. Paul was relying on word of mouth to move his products, which had limited distribution in Chicago and Detroit, plus parts of Ohio, Indiana, and California.

"I am looking for someone to put some steam into this business," Paul said to me. I liked the idea of a challenge, and I could see Paul was a man of integrity. Still, the unsanitary state of the operation and small-time nature of his company weighed heavily against me quitting my nice corporate job and uprooting my family. At the end of our meeting, he gave me a bag of dog food to sample. We shook hands and agreed to talk again. I drove back to Napoleon, more certain than ever of two things: I wanted to be my own boss, but I didn't want to pin my future on Iams Food Company.

At the time, we didn't own a dog, so I gave the bag of Iams Plus to my dad, who had a scruffy old collie-mix farm dog named Queenie.

About six weeks later, when we visited my folks, a beautiful animal with a sleek, shiny coat bounded out of the barn to greet us. "Say, Dad," I asked, "did you get a new dog?"

His reply stopped me cold in my tracks: "No, Clay, that's the same dog I've had for eight years. I've just been feeding her that food you gave me."

The transformation floored me. Queenie's coat glowed with good health. If anything could make a dog look like that, I figured the market for it had to be big. I started digging to find out more about Paul Iams and his company. I talked to Frank Pachin again and contacted others within the pet food industry. Then I called Paul and asked for another meeting.

This time, Paul showed me his books, which he kept meticulously in green folders. Revenues hovered at $600,000, including about $100,000 from consulting fees for work Paul did with mink farms and from sales of mink food. Paul's little company had no debt and made a steady, handsome profit.

"I don't believe in liabilities," Paul explained. He had no accounts payable, no deferred payroll. With only four employees and precious little overhead, he paid himself a good salary and made a nice living from the business. We spent half a day on a mink ranch he co-owned. Through my inquiries, I knew that in some quarters Paul was regarded as a fringe player, bordering on eccentric. But as he explained the careful processes he'd gone through to create his special formula, everything he said made sense. By day's end, the quality of the product and Paul's fervor sold me. When we parted company late that afternoon, I drove home to Napoleon, fully converted to Iams and confident that I'd nailed the interview.

I waited for his phone call. Days passed. One Saturday morning in May, as I puttered around the house, Mary saw that I was agitated about something.

"What's on your mind, Clayt?"

"Remember that Paul Iams I told you about?" I replied. "Well, it's been almost two weeks since I interviewed with him again, and he still hasn't called."

"Are you still interested?"

"Yes," I said.

She came back with one of the most important pieces of business advice I've ever gotten: "Then why don't you call him, Clayt?"

I did, and I learned that Paul Iams loved tests. He had waited to see if I'd call, which to him indicated aggressiveness, perseverance, and guts. If I hadn't picked up that phone, he never would have hired me.

Business is like a poker game, Paul often said, and he intended to hire the person with whom he would least like to play poker. "Who would I have to keep my eye on? Who is going to run a bluff? Who's raising when he doesn't have a hand to win?" he asked himself. He picked me out of the dozen candidates he interviewed. Ironically, I've never liked gambling, at least not at a gaming table. I don't like playing someone else's odds.

Later he told me, chuckling, "You were definitely the one I'd keep an eye on the whole game."

On June 1, 1970, I became Iams Food Company's seventh employee. Mary supported my decision completely, because it represented a giant step toward owning my own business. My parents, on the other hand, couldn't understand why I'd left Campbell. After all, I wore a suit and tie every day and worked in an air-conditioned office. Dad thought I had it made, and Mom was deeply concerned that I was making the mistake of my life. "A dog food company, Clayt? What are you thinking?" she sniffed.

We had three kids to feed, $500 in our savings account, and only a used station wagon to our names, but for the first time in my career, I felt like I was moving in the right direction. Paul hadn't made any promises, but he had hinted ownership might be a possibility. I figured that at the very least I'd gain valuable experience that would help me with my own company someday.

We rented a small house for $200 a month in a Dayton suburb. Paul paid me $1,000 a month (20 percent less than what I had been making at Campbell), and I had to buy my own health insurance for $60 a month, but I got a company car: Paul's two-year-old, mud-brown Oldsmobile, which he had on a four-year depreciation schedule. Like his office, the car's interior was covered with

> *Clay had this burning desire to be an entrepreneur. Until he accomplished that, he wouldn't be able to be who he really is. For me, it was really important that he be fulfilled. I wasn't a demanding person materially. I didn't worry. His happiness was far more important to me. I wanted him to take this chance. If working for Mr. Iams didn't work out, I knew Clay would land on his feet.*
> MARY ANN MAAS MATHILE

cigarette ashes. We agreed that I would get 5 percent of any profits at the end of the first year, 10 percent the second year, and an additional 5 percent every year until my bonus capped out at 35 percent of the profits.

"Pick any title but president," Paul instructed.

I decided not to have a business card with a title on it.

## CHAPTER 5

# The Old Dog and the Young Pup

P aul and I quickly established a strong working relationship, which is remarkable considering that putting two maverick entrepreneurs in the same company usually works about as well as placing two alpha males in the same dog pen. But my new employer and I shared many core values: conservative political views, a strong sense of integrity in business dealings, and commitment to producing excellent products.

Neither of us put any stock in fancy degrees or titles. In fact, we both relished proving self-declared authorities wrong.

A rugged individualist and intellect, Paul did everything his way for nearly a quarter-century. He was never satisfied with blindly following the current school of thought regarding dog nutrition. In fact, he was always telling me, "Distrust the so-called experts."

He trusted the results of his own experiments far more than he trusted research done by the "experts." Consequently, much of what he did during the formative years of Iams ran counter to what textbooks taught on animal nutrition. Paul recorded his formulas in a small spiral notebook that he kept on a bookshelf in his office. He also wrote them on construction paper on which he'd carefully drawn lines. He gave the construction-paper copies to the guys in the plant to refer to as they were mixing batches of product.

Throughout my life, I've sought out mentors. In Paul Iams, I found one of the best; in me, he found an eager student. From Paul, I learned the value of completely immersing myself in a topic. Paul spent hours in his office each day, reading everything from *The Wall Street Journal* and *Scientific American* to business books and nutritional textbooks. He viewed continuous learning as an essential part of his job, and in his mind, sending me to the library to study pet nutrition was every bit as important as any work I was doing at the plant.

I have always regarded Paul and what he built with the utmost respect. Everything he ever told me about dog nutrition worked in the field. Because he sensed that respect, I won his trust relatively early in our relationship. Paul knew I had the good of the company at heart when I made any decision or suggestion. His whole life had been spent seeking constant improvement and new ideas, so he encouraged me to pump all my creative energy into the business.

But Paul had one quality that I definitely didn't emulate: a blatant disregard for diplomacy, particularly in the delicate area of customer relations. Although he was an excellent conversationalist with a dry sense of humor, Paul didn't particularly enjoy dealing with people. In fact, he could be pretty prickly. His attitude about customer service was simple: As long as the customer behaved, he'd sell that customer Iams dog food.

There was a single phone line into the company with one phone in Paul's office, one in my office, and one in the plant. If I could reach it before the fourth ring, I'd answer the phone, but our agreement was that Paul would answer on the fifth ring.

One afternoon, I heard Paul pick up the phone. Within a matter of seconds, he slammed down the receiver, bellowing, "Lady, I don't care if you ever buy our product again!"

It seems an unhappy customer had called in to register a complaint. She had purchased a 20-pound bag of Iams Plus and, upon opening it, discovered a greasy old checkered golf cap at the top. Sure enough, we discovered our employee Vanderbilt "Bill" Hart's cap was missing. The irate customer mailed the cap to Delphos Avenue to prove her point.

I shuddered. There was no telling how much Paul's charming telephone manner had cost the company in terms of customer satisfaction and potential sales. Drastic action had to be taken! When I came on board, we offered limited distribution in a few Midwestern states and had one customer in northern California. Far from concerning himself with expanding his customer base, Paul decided it was time to clean house, especially when it came to slow-paying customers. A stickler for paying his own bills in a timely fashion, he told me to collect the money when I delivered the dog food.

Before I joined the company, Paul had divided customers into three categories: A, B, and C. Customers in the A category got a nice letter thanking them for their loyal business. B customers got a letter explaining Iams was changing the way it collected its funds and that all orders would now be payable on delivery. "If you want to find out how to be on our A list, contact me," he wrote.

Customers who rated Cs were simply "fired." Paul curtly told them Iams

> *Paul was the old dog and I was the young pup, yet I considered his venerable company to be the youngster, viewing it through the visionary lens of experience yet to come.*

no longer wanted their business. When I asked him about it, he growled, "Five percent of those no-account customers take up 75 percent of my time, chasing after money they owe me. They give our drivers fits, and I'm tired of it."

Paul's militant strategy sometimes worked. A few customers, it seemed, just needed a little bawling out to shape them up. On my next trip to Columbus, Ohio, I looked up one of the guys who had been chiseling us and had gotten a C letter. He pulled out our unpaid invoice and wrote me a check on the spot. I drove straight to the bank to cash it to make sure it was good.

Paul lacked the territorial nature of most entrepreneurs, which renders them incapable of surrendering a shred of control. He wasn't interested in building a monument to himself. What drove Paul wasn't ego but the thrill of building a better mousetrap. As a result, he eschewed organizational structure and never dictated to any of us. He always gave me the latitude to do what needed to be done.

Still, we both recognized we were approaching the business from very different viewpoints. Paul was motivated by science, not money. He figured he had more than enough of the latter, thanks to his consulting success in the mink industry, and he believed in living simply. The classic, quiet multimillionaire next door, he never bought fancy cars or anything flashy. Growing his company into a massive moneymaking machine never figured into his thinking. "You can only eat so much steak and drink so much fine liquor," he liked to say.

In contrast, I was a classic early baby boomer, thriving on risk and viewing challenges with optimism. Running a business that made a lot of money was important to me, not because of the things money could buy, but because, for me, money represented the poker chips in a high-stakes game. The more chips you have, the longer you can stay in the game and the more exciting the game becomes. I longed to build a big, successful company, and the dog food industry provided the perfect outlet for my competitive nature.

One afternoon, during our customary 4 P.M. coffee break, Paul puffed thoughtfully on his pipe, then declared, "All the hard work at this company has been done." To him, gaining recognition as a scientific expert in pet nutrition and all the breakthroughs he'd accomplished in the field meant that he'd reached the pinnacle of success with the company that bore his name.

But in my mind, Iams Food Company hadn't grown out of the puppy stage. It was an ironic role reversal: Paul was the old dog, and I was the young pup, yet I considered his venerable company to be the youngster, viewing it through the visionary lens of experience yet to come.

Initially, Paul's long-time employees viewed me suspiciously. They saw me as an interloper, especially Willie Watson.

Willie was huge, strong, and not the sort of fellow you wanted to mess with. Once I watched him lift a three hundred-pound electric motor out of my car after it had taken three guys to put it in.

After firing his driver for stealing from the company, Paul wanted Willie and me to do interim service as deliverymen. Willie's work as a part-time security officer entitled him to a license to carry a gun. On our first delivery run, Willie placed his gun on the seat between us with the barrel pointed in my direction. I nervously eyed the weapon as we rolled along, finally saying, "Willie, would you mind moving that gun away from me?"

At the plant, Willie kept his gun close by in case any of us ran into trouble in the neighborhood. I'd been at the company for about a year when I finally got fed up with Willie's attitude. On one occasion I asked him to do something, and he flatly refused. "Willie," I said, "you have three choices: One, do what I ask you to do. Two, leave. Or three, use that .38-caliber on me, because I'm in charge."

After I called his bluff that day, Willie showed me grudging respect and eventually became an excellent worker. In fact, I've often thought I would be dead if it weren't for Willie Watson. Many mornings on my way through the parking lot, I stepped over shell casings from shots fired overnight, and our metal storage building was riddled with bullet holes. But I believe crooks and thugs generally left us alone because they knew Big Bad Willie worked at Iams, and they valued their lives enough to steer clear of him.

Finding a good truck driver proved to be difficult, perhaps because in those days, background checks weren't even considered. During one hiring episode, we advertised in the newspaper for a driver and eight candidates showed up. I hired a candidate named Leroy, then rode with him the next day to help him get acclimated to the routes. We left the plant at 6 A.M. Halfway to Cincinnati, I noticed him rubbing his eyes. "What's wrong, Leroy?" I asked casually.

"I forgot my contact lenses," he replied.

"So what?"

"Without them, I'm legally blind."

I couldn't believe it. I had hired a blind truck driver, and I was sitting in the death seat.

Our next truck driver turned out to be an ex-con who had shot somebody in a bar fight. So Willie and I took turns running routes until we finally found a suitable driver.

By 1972, Iams was generating $100,000 in annual profits, creating a $5,000 bonus for me that I used as a down payment on our first house.

Two years after joining Iams Food Company, I had largely taken responsibility for running the business, handling research and development along with marketing and sales.

I still didn't have a business card or a title. As companies get bigger, they often slide into stagnation. Many corporate leaders forget to question why something was done a certain way in the first place. The biggest battle a company faces is overcoming the inevitable reluctance to keep changing.

One of the things I most appreciated about Paul was that he never argued with me about trying new things. An innovator himself, he staunchly believed in experimentation.

In 1973, I hatched a plan to win over the toughest customers in the dog world: owners of show dogs. Our marketing programs were relying completely on word of mouth, so why not start a buzz with the folks who could influence dog lovers all over the country?

Every weekend, I'd drive our family's 1967 Ford station wagon to a major dog show somewhere in Ohio, Michigan, Indiana, or Kentucky, since the materials for the Iams booth wouldn't fit in the company car. I put twenty thousand miles on that station wagon in one year going to dog shows. All weekend long, I would talk about nutrition with dog owners, giving away samples and telling them how to get our products.

Sales of Iams Plus steadily climbed, and one of Paul's pet projects caught my attention. Four years before, he had developed a premium pet food he dubbed Eukanuba. Paul got the name from a friend in Minneapolis who used to say, "U-kanuba!" for anything superb—a pretty girl, a good steak, or a dazzling car. Not only was its name unusual, so was Eukanuba's makeup. The product contained 24 percent protein and 16 percent fat, similar to Iams Plus, but more palatable and digestible. We sold Eukanuba, packaged in 32-ounce purple and green milk containers, in limited quantities.

Paul explained that through one of his gentleman's agreements (in other words, a handshake deal), he'd arranged for the Ross Wells Division of Beatrice Foods to produce Eukanuba, since we didn't have the capability to make it in pellet form. He had formulated a dry mink food for Ross Wells in return for the manufacturer producing Eukanuba in its Berlin, Maryland, facility. Ross Wells then shipped Eukanuba back to us for distribution. Compared to the leading premium pet foods of the day that sold at $5.45 for 50 pounds, Eukanuba's wholesale price was three times more expensive.

I saw a big future in premium pet foods, so I introduced the product to several local pet shops, breeders, and commercial kennels. We started offering it in 50-pound bags with a wholesale price of $15 per bag. At first, the effect Eukanuba had on dogs wasn't striking enough, so I played with the formulation, increasing the protein level to 30 percent and the fat level to 20 percent. At the time, university veterinary schools were teaching students that such high levels of protein and fat would "burn out" a dog's kidneys and cause fatty liver. But by midyear, Eukanuba's palatability and stool control made the product a hit with breeders and kennel owners. At one show, a Doberman pinscher with a reputation for being finicky chewed through the carton to get at the food.

Production of Iams Plus topped three thousand tons that year, and I really wanted to sell more of it, since we maintained complete control over Iams Plus manufacturing while we farmed out manufacturing of Eukanuba. But Eukanuba's more palatable pellet quickly pushed it ahead of Iams Plus in popularity.

Independent distributors began contacting us about carrying Iams products, spurred by grassroots demand. We didn't recruit distributors according to any grand plan; I just signed them up one by one as I encountered distributors I thought would do a good job selling our products. Most of them distributed Wayne's or Hill's products and picked up our products only because customers were requesting them.

Then came the oil and gas crisis precipitated by the Arab oil embargo. Lines snaked away from gas pumps across the country during the broiling summer of 1973, and fuel prices catapulted skyward, goosing our shipping costs. Worse, when President Nixon imposed nationwide wage and price controls, a loophole exempted certain agricultural commodities, including lard and meat and bone meal. So, although we were legally bound to freeze pet food prices for our customers, we were paying triple and more for our key ingredients. Prices for meat and bone meal soared to an all-time high of $450 per ton, $250 a ton more than the soybean meal our competitors used. Lard prices shot up as well, and Iams plunged headlong into disaster.

That year, for the first time in the company's history, Iams lost money. We faced a painful dilemma. Should we change the formulas we'd worked so hard to establish, knowing quality would drop and dogs wouldn't thrive? Many of our competitors, whose products contained much less meat and bone meal than ours did, shifted even further away from meat-based products and bone meal and resorted to soybean meal, which was under price controls. Or should we stay true to our commitment to produce higher-quality products and try to ride out the crisis? At one point, we were paying 50 cents more to produce a bag of Iams Plus than we were getting for it wholesale. We sold a minimal amount of Eukanuba during that period, and we could scarcely afford to make it.

Paul and I came to a decision. The formulas would remain the same, and we'd gamble that the price freeze would end soon. We knew our company's future rested on customer loyalty, and we could not violate that trust even in the face of heavy losses.

Our gamble paid off in unexpected ways. The pet food industry had been born of the desire of meat and cereal companies to rid themselves of their meat and cereal by-products. Companies including Swift, Armor, Kraft, General Mills, Quaker Oats, and Kellogg had sideline dry dog food businesses, but none of them was selling nutritional science. The only other company going after the premium pet food segment was Hill's Pet Nutrition.

The first Hill's Prescription Diet® product was developed by Mark Morris, a veterinarian in Topeka, Kansas, who believed certain diseases could be managed through carefully formulated nutrition. Hill's produced the products for Dr. Morris under a long-term cooperative agreement, while the veterinarian and his son, Mark Morris, Jr., promoted the products to the veterinary community.

Faced with the crisis generated by wage and price controls, most of our competitors capitulated and altered their formulas, filling their products with cheap ingredients such as corn gluten and soybean meal. Breeders whose lifeblood depended on how good their dogs looked and the quality of puppies they produced immediately deduced that many of the companies had pulled a switch. The proof was in their dogs' appearance.

Throughout 1974 I handed out samples and literature at every dog show in Indiana, Ohio, Illinois, Michigan, and Kentucky. Our products were on everyone's lips and whiskers. The wage and price controls finally lifted in April 1974. Our reputation for quality had been etched into the minds of key players in the pet industry.

After two painful years, we regained the freedom to price our products at a margin that allowed us a profit. And we resumed introducing Eukanuba, selling it in two-pound milk cartons and 50-pound bags.

On New Year's Eve 1974 Paul stood glumly by the stove in my office, warming his hands. Everyone else had left for the day. He looked tired, and I could tell he was in a rare contemplative mood. "What's on your mind, Paul?" I asked.

"Look, I've spent my whole life in this thing. I'm pushing sixty," he said. "I've got plenty of money, but I'm not willing to lose what I've worked so hard for. I hate to keep pumping money into the business, because I'm not sure if it's worth it. I don't know whether I want to keep operating or not."

At thirty-three years old with a wife, three kids, and a fourth on the way, I depended on the year-end bonus to make my house payments. Yet our bonuses had evaporated for the second year in a row, thanks to the wage and price controls. I realized I might lose my house.

The founder of the company stood before me, declaring that we might be at the end of the line. Even then, I never thought about quitting. Instead, I saw a shining opportunity. When I first interviewed with him, Paul had hinted at the possibility of selling me part of the business one day, but he'd never made any promises. Now the time had come.

"I like the business; I believe in Iams and in the future," I told Paul confidently. "I want to buy half the company."

We quickly settled on a fair price. The company's book value amounted to $200,000, so in January 1975, I signed a personal note to borrow $100,000 for the purchase price from Paul. A one-page buy/sell agreement spelled out that if I died, my stock reverted to Paul. If he died, I had the right to buy his share of the company from his wife Jane. That was the only piece of paper we signed. Paul and I split the company stock 50-50, and I finally got a title: general manager. Far more importantly, I became an employer. I had reached one of my primary goals.

I continued my routine of working all week and devoting every weekend to telling the Iams story to potential customers. I loved having a purpose, and we had a great story to tell. Just as Gerber did for new moms, Iams relieved pet owners of a tremendous amount of worry. Our products eliminated the need to add extra oils and vitamins to an animal's diet to ensure good health.

Because I was traveling so much, the work of raising our family fell squarely on Mary's shoulders. Our kids were growing up, and our fourth child, Jennifer, was born in 1973. Yet I was often too busy with our "other child," Iams Food Company, to attend their baseball or football games, read to them, play with them, and simply be there with and for them. Whenever one of the kids complained about my absence, Mary staunchly defended my actions. "Dad's sacrificing for all of us right now," she would say. "He loves you, and he would love to be here, but he can't be two places at once."

Missing those special times in our kids' lives remains one of my lingering regrets, but I am indebted to Mary for never criticizing the choices I made in front of the children.

We believed in the importance of a strong united front. I can proudly say that despite the mistakes I may have made, my kids are fantastic, intelligent individuals who have given Mary and me our greatest joy. They're the successes I point to with the most pride.

When developing a product, a manufacturer must ask certain questions. The most important and seemingly most obvious is, "Who are my customers and what are they looking for?" Countless market analyses have been created to help gauge the answer to this most critical issue. After all, if you make a product your customers don't like, you're dead in the water.

Unfortunately, marketing strategists have yet to develop a survey for direct responses from dogs. Had there been such a survey, Iams Food Company could quickly have addressed some of the unforeseen problems with the world's best dog food.

When I started at Iams, I immediately saw a serious problem: Our primary audience members were turning their noses up at our product. Although we made nutritionally sound dog food, dogs often refused to eat it because it came in meal form, which stuck to their whiskers and got up their noses. It looked like potting soil. Dogs are sensitive not only to the way food smells and tastes, but also to the way it feels in their mouths. They prefer crunchy foods, so the meal forms of both Iams Plus and Iams 999 failed to appeal to their senses.

Making matters worse, dog owners hated the mess our products made. When dogs did eat Iams 999 or Iams Plus (sales were about 50-50 between the two products when I joined the company), the meal often was spilled out of feed bowls and tracked all over.

Still, hard-core customers, including breeders who recognized the phenomenal results Iams Plus produced in their dogs, put up with those hassles. No other dog food could match the performance of Iams Plus in delivering shiny coats and firm stools, the hallmark of a healthy animal, without added vitamins and minerals.

Iams Plus, in particular, with its higher protein and fat content due to the refined meat in the product, won fans among owners whose dogs needed a more digestible, palatable food. People who raised puppies or owned show dogs and working dogs readily overlooked the problems with Iams Plus because they wanted the performance it delivered.

The weekend of our thirteenth wedding anniversary, on July 7, 1975, I was gone as usual, missing my beautiful wife as I stood under an umbrella, desperately seeking some shade from the broiling one-hundred-degree heat at a dog show in Buffalo, New York. Many potential customers bypassed our booth. By the end of the weekend, we'd scarcely seen any action. As I suffered in the heat, rejected and dejected, our distributor, Bill Smith suddenly said, "Put it in a pellet, Clay, and you'll have the world by the tail."

Years earlier, Paul had tried to do exactly that, but after abysmal failures decided the combination of ingredients that made Iams so special also made pellets impossible. He shelved the project. On the four hundred-mile drive back to Dayton late that Sunday, all I could think about was how to make it work.

The first thing Monday morning, I strode into Paul's office and said, "I've been out all weekend, and all I heard from the few people I could convince to stop at our booth was that consumers want Iams in a pellet. Furthermore, our packaging isn't right, and we've got to start advertising."

"Go for it," Paul said.

We continued to reap the benefits of standing pat on quality during the wage and price controls era. Orders were pouring in from all over the country for much larger quantities of the food than we'd ever sold. We splurged with a $15,000 advertising campaign developed by Jackson-Ridey Advertising in Cincinnati. The agency placed monthly Iams Plus ads called Brag Bags in *Dog World* for $1,000 a pop. The ad showed a sketch of a bag of Iams Plus and simply gave the company's address, so customers could find us. The agency also designed brochures and our booth for dog shows.

We were delighted by the response, but totally unprepared for the mailbags full of fan letters we began receiving. Breeders, children, and dog lovers of all kinds wrote to tell us how much they liked our product, to find out where they could get it, to ask questions, or to simply say,

"Thanks." Photos of much-loved pets, sparked by the Brag Bag ads, often were tucked inside the envelopes. Now we had absolute proof we were barking up the right tree with our product.

We direct-shipped Iams Plus to many customers. We could put two 20-pound bags in a box and ship it via United Parcel Service without exceeding the shipper's 50-pound weight limit. As word spread about our products, customers pooled their orders.

We soon developed enough business to stimulate interest from independent distributors and began regularly shipping product to distributors in Derby, New York; New York, New York; Cleveland, Ohio; Chicago, Illinois; San Jose, California; Atlanta, Georgia; and Detroit, Michigan. We were guaranteed extra visibility with our distinctive purple Iams delivery truck, painted to match the product bag, which blared down the highways of Ohio, Indiana, Kentucky, and western Pennsylvania.

I spent most of my first year as an owner concentrating on rolling out Eukanuba at dog shows in cities where distributors sold the product. By the end of the year, we had reached $1 million in sales, double the company's performance when I came on board in 1970. Paul was ecstatic; never in his wildest dreams had he thought Iams would reach that milestone. But I looked at the overall market and estimated our sales accounted for less than 0.01 percent of the premium pet food category. To competitors such as Purina and Hill's, we were the equivalent of a flea on a Great Dane.

One pet shop owner in Cleveland sent Eukanuba to a well-known breeder in Kansas who supplied Doctors Pet stores with puppies. In those days, once puppies were weaned from their mothers, they were fed cooked hamburger and rice, and they often didn't do well during delivery to pet stores. Word quickly spread among kennels in Kansas, Nebraska, and Missouri that weaned puppies fed Eukanuba arrived at pet stores in good shape. The news led to our first order for one ton of Eukanuba. Then pet store owners started ordering Eukanuba because puppies became used to eating it. Once again, word of mouth worked in our favor, and orders began trickling in from all over the country.

I was shocked to see that, with only word-of-mouth support, Eukanuba tonnage surpassed Iams Plus volume that year. Dogs overwhelmingly preferred Eukanuba, which contained poultry products and high fat levels, to the competitive soy-based products that were dominating the market.

Whenever I overheard competitors snickering about "the kook selling the $30 bag of dog food" at dog shows, I'd just smile. My gut told me Eukanuba had the potential to transform Iams Food Company to "best of class" in the pet food industry. Even though a bag of Eukanuba was 50 percent more expensive than other dog foods, consumers realized the real value far exceeded the cost. I made the Eukanuba bag smaller—dropping it to 40 pounds, so it would fit neatly into a shipping box and come under United Parcel Service's 50-pound limit. Reducing the size also allowed us to charge less per bag and helped soften the sticker shock.

We began having difficulty keeping up with demand. Distributors kept close tabs on when new shipments would arrive, since many of them had customers who would meet delivery trucks and railcars at loading docks to ensure they could snag enough Eukanuba to feed their championship dogs.

Paul's handshake deal with Loyal Wells to co-pack what was rapidly becoming our premier product had always concerned me. Paul and I held completely different opinions of the man. Paul is the type of person who makes up his mind about you within the first minute of meeting you. Once you're in with Paul, you're in. He liked Loyal, a tall, handsome guy who presented himself well, and trusted him implicitly. But I had a feeling Loyal's parents had picked the wrong name for him. He reminded me of the used car salesman who sold me my first car, which turned out to be a lemon.

Seeing how successful the Eukanuba brand was rapidly becoming, Loyal, who had sold Ross Wells to Beatrice Foods in 1968, started pressing Paul for a piece of the action. Although we owned the brand, Paul and I knew our position was weak, despite the fact that Paul had fulfilled his original agreement with the company by formulating a mink food in exchange for Ross Wells manufacturing Eukanuba.

After all, our co-packer knew most of Paul's unique formula for Eukanuba and had always produced it for us. The only part of the formulation we held onto at the Delphos plant was the vitamin and essential oil premix that we shipped to Ross Wells to add to the Eukanuba mix. On top of the co-packer's inside knowledge of our product, no agreement existed on paper. Hoping to keep the co-packer happy for a while, Paul agreed to give Ross Wells distribution of Eukanuba along the Eastern Seaboard from Philadelphia to Florida.

"It's a big country," said Paul, who was trying to reassure me and refused to view the situation as being as serious as I did. "We still have plenty of room to grow."

Short term, Paul's reasons for ceding such important distribution territory to one outfit made sense. But I could see our efforts to appease Ross Wells were growing more desperate. War was coming. I didn't know when or where, but I felt it as surely as a farmer knows a storm is brewing. I quietly started trying to figure out how we could make Eukanuba ourselves.

## CHAPTER 6

# Bigger Dreams

The crucial difference between Paul and me was that he was generally content to keep the status quo at Iams, while I was determined to make the company a multimillion dollar success, not by cutting corners but by ratcheting up the quality for which Iams had become famous.

After I became Paul's partner, and well before that, Iams Food Company became more than just a business to me. It was a dream, a vision, on a variety of levels. It represented the achievement of my first big goal, to own my own business, and it offered the opportunity to reach my second goal: real wealth and financial independence. Beyond the personal success, however, Iams was my chance to contribute something important to humanity and the animal kingdom: I could not only deliver the best dog food in the world, but also the message that keeping quality and integrity as primary goals always pays off in the end.

Meanwhile, my stress level was soaring. I had my hands full answering phones, hand-writing bills of lading, pecking out correspondence on an old manual typewriter—all the duties I should have had a secretary to handle—overseeing production and distribution, troubleshooting, problem-solving and...well, you name it, I did it. On top of my seventy- to eighty-hour workweeks, I was burning up the road every weekend, visiting kennel owners and traveling to dog shows, often two in a weekend, to promote our product and increase our market.

On one hand, it was sheer madness. After my grueling workday, I just had time to get home, eat dinner, spend a little time with my family, then put in a few more hours wrestling with company issues I hadn't had time to resolve at the office. Yet this was no more than any other small business owner must do to keep his operation going and, with luck, perseverance, and God's help, take it to the next level. In business, insanity is often sanity. As that mad racing champion, Mario Andretti, once observed, "If everything seems under control, you're just not going fast enough."

We were going fast enough for Paul, but not for me. I had big dreams, all right. I wanted full quality control over Eukanuba, and I had plans to develop yet another product, Iams Chunks, all of which would eventually require us to build another plant. In the realm of superior quality dog food, I wanted Iams to lead the pack, not just in the United States, but all over the world.

In order to accomplish this, however, I desperately needed help with sales. One day a young man named Rob Easterling walked through the door at Delphos Avenue to interview for a sales position with Iams.

Like most people on our home turf of Dayton in 1976, Rob had never heard of Iams Food Company, until he happened to have a conversation across a fence with a schoolteacher in our middle-class neighborhood. "I'm not quite sure what Clay Mathile does," the teacher commented, "but he leaves every morning at 7 and gets home around 6:30 at night. He doesn't wear a tie, but he says he's going to be a millionaire someday, and somehow I believe him. I think you should go check it out."

Rob, a wiry, fast-talking chain-smoker with a quick wit, graduated high school and then supported himself selling everything from insurance to Bibles. He showed up at Iams at just the right time. I desperately needed help with sales.

Rob drove a spanking-new, triple-white Mercury Montego and strode into the interview in the mod colors and style of the day: a perfectly pressed, three-piece mustard-colored linen suit with a wide, dark knit tie and patent leather shoes with suede tops. He made an interesting contrast to me in my uniform of khakis with a blue button-down shirt and work boots.

"Come on in," I said, motioning to one of the old chairs in my office. He good-naturedly plopped down, sending a little puff of dust up into the air. Well-read and a good conversationalist, Rob was thoroughly engaging. I could see that he'd be good with customers. I hired him on the spot, at a salary of $1,000 a month, the same figure I was paying myself.

With some of the pressure off me in sales, I turned my attention to finding a part-time secretary. In October 1976, I placed a blind ad in the newspaper for a secretary, offering $5 an hour and a flexible schedule.

Jan Dinges answered the ad with a beautifully handwritten resume. I was immediately impressed by her striking penmanship, and her work history looked good.

In thirty years of doing business, Paul had never employed a woman. I don't know the reason for that, but one fact was painfully clear: The Iams facilities were definitely not going to win the Good Housekeeping Seal of Approval.

The morning of Jan's interview, I became acutely aware of how the more fastidious opposite sex might view our surroundings. In the gravel parking lot, everybody's car was covered with a thin layer of gritty black beet pulp dust. At the front of the building, a small reception/break area was littered with used coffee cups and overflowing ashtrays. The pungent odor of meat meal lying in open bins wafted through the facility.

I prayed Jan wouldn't need to use the "powder room," because none of the twelve males at Iams ever thought to clean the bathroom.

The plant was really two plants pasted together. Paul built one and then acquired the other. My office was adjacent to the plant at one end; Paul's was at the opposite end of the building, away from the plant. Four loading docks sat in between, with a big open middle room that held finished product. The manufacturing equipment cranked away in Paul's original plant next door. In other words, it was something like a ten thousand-square-foot bachelor pad.

Jan proved her mettle from the moment she walked in the door. The Queen of Clean might have run away screaming, but Jan was as calm and pleasant as could be. Dressed neatly in a camel suit that set off her brilliant blue eyes, she carried herself with dignity and class. I was impressed that she was a college graduate with a business degree. I could scarcely believe we were lucky enough to get somebody of her caliber for $5 an hour.

Ultimately, I believe what caused Jan to sign on with Iams was the same force that enabled us to assemble the foundation for a winning team at Delphos Avenue. How the place looked didn't matter. The joyful mood at the plant was obvious; you could feel the energy. Everyone shared the feeling that the day was coming when the Iams name would make people sit up and take notice. Everyone likes to be a part of the magic surrounding a winning team, and we all knew we were part of something revolutionary.

Jan's first duties involved processing the growing shipments we were making to customers all over the country. When I'd go to the dog shows or when Iams advertised in *Dog World*, we received hundreds of sales leads from dog owners who lived in places where we hadn't set up distribution. Everyone had the same question: Where do I buy the food?

Soon after I started meeting people at dog shows, I realized we urgently needed a way to get the food to these people at a reasonable cost to both of us. Of course, Iams Food Company had to make money on the product, but it couldn't be priced so high that it didn't make sense for the customer.

I divided the country into seven regions based on United Parcel Service's shipping regions. Next, I came up with a published price list for each region for dog food orders, ranging from 40 pounds, which we shipped via UPS, to 2,000 pounds. Trucking companies such as Yellow Freight, Roadway Express, and Consolidated Freightways took the bigger shipments. The freight cost was built into the product price. Price reductions kicked in when a customer ordered 300 pounds or more.

At a dog show, I would hand a customer prospect the published price list with terms for his or her region, along with a brochure that gave detailed information about the food and the company. The pricing structure had been a bear to work out but was a key point of difference for Iams. Competitors would get asked the same question, then potential customers would walk away because the companies hadn't figured out a neat system to deliver their products.

With our system, customers simply sent us a check. They didn't have to pre-pay the trucker or file claims with the trucking company for damaged bags. We delivered the food right to their doors, eliminating hassles. We were the only regional company in the high-end pet food business with a direct-ship program.

Direct shipping built up our following throughout the United States with breeders, kennels, and pet stores. It was a win-win strategy, since the published prices included enough margin that if we later found a distributor, we could both make a profit. If a pet store bought a ton of food, we sold the product to them at a wholesale price so the store could sell it at retail and make a profit. We signed many of our distributors as a result of our direct-shipment program. Once each distributor contract was signed, we gladly turned over all of our customers in that area. The strategy started us on the road to national distribution.

By the time Jan joined the company, about eighteen months after starting this program, it had mushroomed to the point where every single day we were selling at least half a truckload of product in these less-than-truckload shipments. She would open the mail and checks would flutter out of the envelopes.

The independent distributors who clamored for our products in different regions across the country were largely small, family-owned operations. Some had evolved from feed stores and had branched off into pet food. Others supplied pet stores with a range of products. Topeka, Kansas–based Hill's Pet Nutrition had developed several of the distributors. Hill's had its start in 1948, when a veterinarian formulated Hill's Science Diet® to treat a guide dog's kidney problems. So, while we targeted dog breeders and kennel owners, Hill's' sales force peddled its prescription diets primarily through veterinarians.

In the early years, I had approached some of these same distributors about carrying our products, but they displayed little interest. Typically, kennel owners and breeders would start using Eukanuba or Iams Plus exclusively, and then the same distributors who had turned us down flat came knocking on our door.

Jan typed out each invoice in carbon copies and the bill of lading, then called the trucks. UPS deliveries took about a week. She also took on filing any claims with the carrier, and she answered the ever-increasing volume of phone calls. The sheer number of letters we received each day increased so dramatically that Jan soon resorted to taking them home at night, along with a copy of the U.S. map divided into the seven regions. She handled a good deal of the company correspondence after her kids were in bed.

Heroically and incredibly, Jan managed to do her job with only our ornery old manual typewriter to assist her. For a full year, every Monday morning I'd find a nice note penned in her distinctive, flowing script in the middle of my desk. "Clay," it read, "I could really use an electric type-writer. At your convenience." Finally, I gave her $500 to purchase a used, top-of-the-line IBM Selectric and told her to buy a new copy machine in the same week. I thought Jan would faint.

One day I received a call from a feed store owner in Fairbanks, Alaska, asking for a shipment of Iams Plus. "What's going on up there?" I asked, intrigued that word had spread so far, so fast.

"Rick Swenson, who races the Iditarod, saw your ad in *Dog World* and wants to feed Iams to his sled dogs," replied Dick Underwood of Alaska Feed Company.

Soon I received a letter from Swenson, who had run his first Iditarod in March 1976. He said he had fed his team Purina Hi Pro with unsatis-factory results, placing a disappointing tenth. Then Rick met a malamute breeder from Michigan who happened to have our flyer explaining why Iams Plus was better than other foods.

Swenson's letter outlined the problems he was having and his dog team's nutritional requirements. He said he was planning to use our food as a base, then add beaver meat, fish, and seal meat to ensure his dogs ate plenty of omega-3 fatty acids.

I relish challenges, and I knew that huskies are more difficult to feed than other dog breeds because they have a shorter gut. While an average-size dog of thirty-five pounds may consume about one thousand calories per day, a sled dog racing one hundred miles a day can consume up to ten thousand calories a day. Plus, the wear and tear of running a 1,049-mile race from Anchorage to Nome stretches the animals to their limits. The subtlest change in their nutritional status shows up almost instantly.

I saw the benefits of working with Swenson, a raw-boned redhead of Norwegian descent, who impressed me with his knowledge of dog nutrition and love for his dogs. Not only could we help his dogs, I thought, we could put our product to the test in the harshest conditions imaginable. It was a golden opportunity.

In January we loaded a Sea Land container with ten tons of Iams Plus and shipped it by train to the feed store owner for Rick to try. In the loading process, the purple ink overprinted on the Iams Plus bags rubbed off all over our clothes. When we finished loading, our shirts and pants had a faint rosy glow. We not only felt in the pink, we were!

By the end of 1976, I had spent a good deal of time developing a product I planned to call Iams Chunks. I'd been looking for a company to co-pack the new product our customers had been demanding for so long. It would use essentially the same formula as Iams Plus but be produced in a more palatable chunk form.

I settled on King of Sports Mill in Hollansburg, Ohio, which had a small Anderson extruder that I believed could work to make the product. Unfortunately, the feed mill's owner, whose main business was making cheap feed, made it abundantly clear that he didn't have much regard for our formula.

We took 100-pound bags of the meal mix prepared at Delphos Avenue, dumped it into the extruder, and ran it through. We didn't want to reveal anything about the product, and I didn't trust the owner to add any ingredients without hurting quality. The resulting product resembled three-inch-long, mini-cigars, causing the crew to joke that the food looked the same when the dog consumed it as it did on its way out. The mill owner couldn't control the length of the chunks, because he regularly got surges in his extruder. On occasion, flipping the extruder's switch would dim hundreds of lights across town.

I educated the plant owner on sanitation, and he begrudgingly made a few changes to his dryer and crude packaging equipment. By the holidays, the first successful production run of Iams Chunks had been completed. The new product came in 20- and 40-pound bags with a purple-and-green label.

Although I was far from satisfied with the appearance of the Iams Chunks, I was reassured that King of Sports Mill could at least produce enough product for me to do a rudimentary market test.

I put it right next to Iams Plus and charged a 25 percent premium for the new Iams Chunks. I figured if consumers would pay more for Iams Chunks, I could be pretty certain we had a winner on our hands. I planned to test Iams Chunks for a year to be certain demand justified the cost of building our own plant. Sales for Iams Chunks took off like a rocket, while Iams Plus' sales stayed flat.

The new co-packer owned only one small extruder and a small dryer, plus his bagging equipment sorely needed updating. When I saw the burgeoning demand for Iams Chunks, I decided against investing more time in further explaining our business to the co-packer. I had no intention of getting in the same predicament we were experiencing with Eukanuba.

The Delphos Avenue plant was swiftly being outstripped of its capacity to produce Iams Plus, Iams 999, raw ingredient mixes for Iams Chunks, and the vitamin mix for Eukanuba. Unless we built a new plant, and soon, there would be no way we could produce enough dog food to meet the growing demand. The plant already was running twenty-four hours a day, seven days a week at top speed.

I was even more determined to build, because I hated having so little quality control over Eukanuba, which was still being co-packed in Berlin, Maryland.

The final straw came when I got a call from one of our distributors, informing me that small chicken feathers were sticking out of Eukanuba pellets. "Some of this stuff looks like it could fly, Clay," he complained, justifiably frustrated. Although we both knew a few feathers wouldn't hurt a dog, the revolting pellet appearance could quickly kill our reputation, especially since we targeted the crème de la crème of the dog world. Word of any problems with the product would spread fast.

"I'll talk to the folks in Berlin," I promised. "Sounds like they've got a problem with an ingredient supplier."

What goes into making pet food is considerably less attractive than the packaging. I'm sure most people would rather not know the grisly truth about meat rendering and the fact that some plants are known to dump all kinds of dead and diseased animals into their rendering machines, then pass the not-fit-for-human-consumption result off to dog food companies. At Delphos, if a supplier tried to dump bad product on us, we rejected the company without a second thought.

Our formulas called for the highest-quality protein. For Iams Plus and Iams Chunks, we used our proprietary method at Delphos to remove undesirable materials from poultry meal. The Maryland plant used a pre-selection process, which meant that chicken heads, feet, and feathers were all supposed to be pulled out, leaving only high-protein chicken entrails. Although each plant went about it a different way, we both ended up in the same place, using a purer high-protein poultry meat and meal.

The process of rendering separates fat-soluble from water-soluble and solid materials and kills bacterial contaminants, but we knew all too well that too much heat or the use of chemicals during the rendering process could also destroy the valuable proteins and natural enzymes vital to dog nutrition. Paul's pickiness over our protein sources ever since hexane appeared in the pig pancreas from Eli Lilly and Company, coupled with my experience with meat renderers at Campbell Soup, meant that we knew which suppliers to avoid.

Now the star product we'd worked so hard to build over the last several years was spiraling out of control. Even worse, there was little I could do about it. I knew extrusion was the key to being able to produce Iams in pelleted form and to being able to produce Eukanuba on our own. I reasoned that if the Berlin, Maryland, plant could produce Eukanuba, we could figure it out.

The challenge with extrusion, a process developed in the early 1950s by Ralston Purina, was getting the protein in fresh poultry meat cooked properly without destroying it. If the protein became compromised during the cooking process, the dogs wouldn't have the shiny coats and good health that our product promised.

At the same time, we also needed the corn to bind the chunks by turning glutinous. If the cornstarch were not converted to sugar, dogs fed the new Iams Chunks would suffer loose stools.

No other company had tried to integrate so much high-protein, high-fat poultry meal into a dog food pellet. The idea sounds simple, but getting the half-meat, half-cereal mixture to hold together during the cooking process without destroying the protein and winding up with an indigestible mess was monumentally difficult.

There are two tricks to making a high-protein dog food pellet. You cannot overheat the ingredient mixture or you risk destroying it. At the same time, you have to heat the mixture just enough to convert the starch into a sugar, so that it sets up properly and holds the pellet together and dogs can digest it. Dogs metabolize the sugar into energy.

We were able to buffer the protein by adding enough water and steam and by extending retention time in the extruder, so the food was able to cook properly. One caveat: A pellet that holds together doesn't necessarily mean the starch is properly cooked. Knowing when the pellet is exactly right is something of an art. We achieved it only after numerous trial runs and trying many testing methods.

A sales representative for Wenger extruders heard through the grapevine that I'd been looking at extruders. So the next month, on my way to visit kennels in Kansas, I dropped by owner LaVon Wenger's office in Sabetha.

"I've been waiting for someone like you," said LaVon, a second-generation feed mill equipment manufacturer, shaking my hand vigorously. His father and uncle, German immigrants, happened to make an extruder when they were trying to expand capacity of their pellet mills. All pet food companies except Ralston, which made its own extruders, now used Wenger equipment. "This industry needs a good dog food," he said. "Without one, I'm worried pet food is going to become a commodity. I'll do everything I can to help you make a value-added product."

Most other pet food companies buying from him were primarily concocting corn- and soybean-based products with the same basic formulas, competing solely on price. He was intrigued that our products used so much meat protein.

I soon learned that LaVon raised bird dogs and had been frustrated by the poor quality of dog food on the market. I explained what I wanted to do with Iams Chunks. "I've got an extruder in the pilot plant," he offered. "Use it as long as you like."

Since my days at Campbell Soup, I've always believed a relationship with a supplier should be a partnership. I was delighted to find that LaVon shared my belief. We set up a test, experimenting with different flow rates and various extruder configurations to find the right combination. Because the pilot plant extruder was so small, we had to slow the rate of the ingredient flow considerably to achieve the right cook on the chunks. Within a few months and multiple runs, we finally produced enough product to know it worked. We fed LaVon's prized bird dogs, living at a large kennel in Kansas, and Iams Chunks fed beautifully.

Once LaVon saw what we needed, he put his engineers to work on building a longer extruder, so that we could get a faster flow rate. LaVon had established a reputation for integrity, and I trusted him. We spent a good deal of time together that winter and through the spring, working on adjustments to the machinery.

The new extruder, X-175, was designed exactly to our specifications. The custom-built model we eventually ordered called for a ten-head, double-conditioning cylinder, which meant the barrel of the extruder was about fifteen feet long. The double cylinder, which the company routinely put on its X-200 extruders, but not on models this size, became extremely important, since it allowed a 50 to 60 percent longer cook time, a feature that emerged as vital to our future. To this day, LaVon has never revealed to anyone outside our two companies the adjustments we made to the extruder to develop our unique process.

In March we received exciting news: Rick Swenson had won the Iditarod with a record-breaking time. His dogs had been fed Iams Plus for more than a year. This was a major coup for our company, because it lent credibility to our claims of better nutritional value. Of course, all the other mushers started clamoring for Iams Plus, so this time we loaded a railcar with forty tons of Iams Plus and sent it up to Alaska.

By the time the shipment arrived in Fairbanks, the friction had worn through the bags and broken several of them. The meal had frozen into a solid block. The feed store owner took an axe and chopped it into blocks for Rick and the other mushers.

Meanwhile, word-of-mouth sales for Eukanuba blazed like wildfire. Breeders praised its long-term benefits of reduced stools, weight control, and improved coats. The Berlin, Maryland, plant simply couldn't fill all the orders for the high-performance, poultry-based pet food, so we were forced to put distributors on allocation. When breeders found out Eukanuba was in short supply, the product's mystique grew. We started hearing of "Eukanuba riots" breaking out between customers in stores and on distributor loading docks.

We had reached a critical juncture for a small business that was out-growing its operation. It was time to take out a loan and expand. While I eagerly forged ahead with plans to build a modern facility with room for expansion, Paul grew increasingly edgy. In the company's thirty-year history, Iams Food Company had never incurred debt. Paul always paid cash. Going into debt so late in his career flew in the face of his conservative nature. Over a matter of weeks I marshaled all my skills as a salesman to prove to my more conservative partner that this move wasn't foolhardy.

Paul's biggest concern remained protecting the science of the Iams brand. I had to convince him the new product fed well and was palatable and digestible. After I showed him documentation of how well Iams Chunks fed, Paul softened and reluctantly agreed to proceed.

John Young, a long-time friend of Paul, owned a strip of land outside Lewisburg, Ohio, that he planned to develop into an industrial park. John forged his relationship with Paul by supplying him with brewery-quality corn for our dog food. Breweries only use the best grains in beer and liquor. Since a dog's sense of smell is nine times stronger than a human's, Paul always insisted on using grain that would meet brewery standards.

The small rural community John toured me through lies in southwestern Ohio, twenty miles from Dayton, near Richmond, Indiana. It is situated near an interstate highway but is far from the influence of unions. Carl Akey, who had started a nutrition and feed business for swine, had already built his plant on one side of the railroad track. John drove me to an adjacent cornfield and announced, "Here's the perfect spot for your plant."

By June we'd settled on the gently rolling, ten-acre site. John introduced us to a local contractor who ran his own small construction firm. We started working on plans for a state-of-the-art facility that would be equipped with the new Wenger extruder.

To get our financial house in order for our bank presentation, we hired the accounting firm of Haskins and Sells to audit our books. The young accountant sent to do the job was Marty Walker. He had a shock of brown hair and a ready laugh, and we clicked immediately. Three years later, Marty left Haskins and Sells and became a devoted, valuable member of the Iams team.

Marty pronounced Iams fiscally fit and our balance sheet strong. In 1977 we produced $3.3 million in revenues.

Rolf Brookes, senior vice president of commercial lending at First National Bank of Cincinnati asked many questions and demonstrated a good basic understanding of our business. The next day, he came to visit us at Delphos, then talked to our suppliers and customers. I was surprised but pleased at the interest he showed in our company.

Two days later, we secured the $400,000 loan on a 90-day revolving note. I signed personally for the loan, but Paul didn't sign. I didn't believe it would be fair for him to be at risk at that stage in his career, and I thought, "The bank can't get blood out of a turnip, so what do I have to lose?"

Every month, Rolf drove to Dayton to check on our progress. He took the time to learn our business, and his keen interest made him one of my most trusted advisors.

For the first time, I began thinking in terms of concrete future goals. First and foremost, our products should provide the best nutrition available for dogs. Next, I wanted to create an enjoyable work environment where employees felt valued and part of something special. Third, I wanted the company to make a great deal of money, so my family would have financial freedom. It was the beginning of my formal vision for Iams Food Company and for me.

As soon as local entrepreneur Charlie Zumstein and his son Ed heard about our decision to build a plant in Lewisburg, they were on my doorstep. They owned a small trucking company just off the main street in downtown Lewisburg. A World War II veteran like Paul, Charlie launched Zumstein Trucking the same year Iams Food Company started. I liked Charlie and Ed immediately, and I especially liked the idea of giving a fellow entrepreneur my business. When we cut our first deal, they owned three trucks.

## CHAPTER 7

# The Year of Fire and Ice

Sooner or later, I suppose, everyone has one of those awful years when whatever can go wrong does. Queen Elizabeth II coined a great term for this blight of bad luck: "*annus horribilis.*" My *annus horribilis* was 1977 into 1978, the year that pushed me to my limits and threatened to dash every hope I'd ever had for Iams Food Company and my future. One by one, like a row of dominos, every area of our operations was hit by a major crisis.

On the heels of the Ross Wells fire, Ohio began experiencing record-breaking snowfalls. Construction on the new Lewisburg plant had already been delayed several months when the crew finally began work in late October. But before they could get the foundation poured, the deluge hit. Huge snowflakes covered the construction site, making further work impossible.

With Ross Wells incapacitated, we badly needed the Lewisburg facility to get up and running again. All hands were on deck at Delphos Avenue, desperately holding onto the hard-won momentum generated by the New Iams Chunks. We ran the plant 24/7 with three shifts to make the mix for Iams Chunks and to produce Iams Plus and Iams 999. Since Rob Easterling couldn't promote Eukanuba, I pulled him out of sales and put him in charge of local distribution routes and the Delphos plant whenever I couldn't be there, which was most of the time.

When I wasn't up at King of Sports Mill dealing with crises with the Iams Chunks co-packer, I was in Kansas, working with LaVon Wenger and his engineers to put the finishing touches on our specially designed extruder, or on the road visiting distributors, training their salespeople, and fighting to keep them pumped up about Iams until the Lewisburg plant came online and we were back to full capacity. The fire that halted production of Eukanuba spelled disaster for several of our distributors, who had based their businesses almost entirely on Eukanuba and its stunning 30 percent profit margin.

Our phones were ringing off the hook with customers frantically trying to secure the remaining bags of Eukanuba. It was the most frustrating situation any expanding business can experience: skyrocketing demand and no supply. All we could do was produce a bare minimum of Eukanuba at the Berlin, Maryland, plant and pray for an early spring thaw.

But the bad luck continued. Just as we'd taken on a loan to build the plant, interest rates hit record highs, soaring up to 22 percent. We were paying $110,000 a year in interest alone. Add to that the extra $25,000 we would need in the spring to re-dig open footers in the new plant. The footers, buried under months of snow, were filled with dark, sticky mud, which would cause another big delay in finishing the facility. I felt like a dog paddling in the rapids. We were all in for a rough, white-knuckle ride, and although I didn't reveal any insecurities, I had no idea how it would all play out.

I have always liked my own version of Goethe's declaration, "Dream no little dreams, for they have no magic to move men's souls." But dreaming isn't enough. To be a successful entrepreneur, you must have unwavering faith and commitment to those dreams, no matter how many obstacles are put in your path. One of the most important lessons I learned from my experience at Iams was that when we have a mission, we will always have to prove our devotion to it. What looks like bad luck is actually a test, to see how committed we are to our dream.

In 1977 and 1978, I was slammed against so many rocks and whisked into swirling waters so many times that by all accounts, Iams Food Company should have drowned. Yet by the end of that *annus horribilis*, we had topped $5.6 million in sales, a record growth of 26 percent over the previous year.

A number of factors accounted for our doing the impossible, but the critical one was my refusal to give up, my total belief in our product and our mission. I knew we had products that excelled. Iams was the nutritional leader of the dog food pack, and I never doubted in my heart that we were going to survive this battle against the elements and circumstances. The dogs of the world were my proof. Those fed Iams or Eukanuba were healthier. Bitches were delivering more and larger puppies per litter. I was determined to give every dog the chance to have a beautiful coat like my dad's dog, Queenie.

Just one of the curveballs thrown at us that grueling year would have been enough to send any business reeling. God must have really wanted me to prove my dedication to the noble cause of canine health, however, because there were still more challenges ahead.

One of the ultimate tests came on a hot Friday afternoon that sent me spinning and Paul crumpling into one of the old oak chairs in my office. Our bank notified us that $78,000 in checks from our Chicago distributor had not cleared, confirming my worst fears about the state of their business.

There had been indications of the distributor's cash-flow problems when its receivables built up to the point that we insisted the owner pay his invoices before we shipped him any more product. Although I cashed his checks every Monday, if a check bounced, our bank put it back through for payment. Three checks had bounced, but the distributor's bank had held them.

*I have always liked my own version of Goethe's declaration, "Dream no little dreams, for they have no magic to move men's souls."*

*But dreaming isn't enough. To be a successful entrepreneur, you must have unwavering faith and commitment to those dreams, no matter how many obstacles are put in your path.*

Without that crucial piece of information, we continued shipping product to him. Now, instead of the $20,000 worth of product I thought we had with the distributor, we were caught with $78,000 in unpaid product sitting in his warehouse.

Here we were, behind schedule and in debt up to our eyeballs for the new plant. And now, one of our most important markets was threatened. This distributor had represented us in Illinois since 1974. Many specialty pet stores competed in that market, and one of the largest dog shows in the country was held in Chicago each year. We could ill afford to lose ground in that critical territory.

Until that fateful morning, I had too many of my own fires to put out to keep tabs on our distributors beyond making sure we were paid. I always kept an eye on the receivables, but this snafu with the bank came out of left field and hit me hard.

Now I was faced with a big dilemma. I didn't want any of the other four distributors in Chicago to represent our products. They had too much allegiance to our competition. Besides, the way I'd just been burned, I couldn't afford to rely on another distributor unless I could trust that company completely.

So, on this fateful morning I made a decision that ultimately had a tremendous beneficial effect on the Iams distribution system. I decided we would run our own distribution center in Chicago.

I enlisted the help of Tom Rowe, a former distributor employee and sales rep for the Chicago area. I had known Tom since 1974, when we met while attending dog shows and working sales promotions, and felt secure about his undertaking distribution.

But Paul couldn't see the sun at the end of the fog bank. Although my relationship with him had always been rock-solid, the unexpected delays in the plant construction, double-digit interest rates, and the disaster with our Chicago distributor frayed his nerves and strained our relationship to the breaking point.

His biggest area of concern revolved around the extruder. I was betting the company on this plant and making a pellet with the new extrusion process. Until that moment, I didn't realize the extent of Paul's prejudice against an extruded product. Paul had tested extruders back in the 1950s and determined that due to the extreme heat generated by the friction in the process, the machines obliterated all-important proteins. To him, the quality of the product was tantamount, and he had long associated extruded products with the cheap dog foods produced by our competitors.

"It's going to happen, Paul," I said confidently. "We're going to get this plant built; we're going to make great products; and the company will be profitable. The feeding tests of the products we've made with the Wenger extruder have all been excellent. We've got great palatability, and the protein's fine. I need your support, because I'm right in the middle of the bridge here, and I can't jump off now. I want you to come to me if you have any questions about the new plant."

Paul agreed, and I went out to the plant to find Rob. I felt like Desdemona in *Othello*, betrayed by the sneaky Iago, whose false whispering turned the king against her. As soon as I found Rob, I blew up. "Stop blowing in Paul's ear about the Lewisburg plant," I yelled, jabbing my pointer finger in the air for emphasis. "You're here to help me, not hurt me."

"Now, Clay, I didn't mean any harm," he said.

"Just cut it out, Rob," I shot back. "The last thing in the world I need right now is problems with Paul."

That summer I spent most of my time burning up the road between Delphos Avenue and Lewisburg. At last the construction project appeared to be going smoothly. Mack McClain, sturdily built like the football great Dick Butkus, was in charge of building the plant, and he kept the project humming along. As the summer drew to a close, I could watch my dream taking shape. At long last we would be free to pursue our own destiny, rather than relying on other manufacturers.

It was a perfect time for another disaster. On Labor Day 1978, I turned on the local evening news just in time to see a report about a spectacular fire in a feed mill plant. It was King of Sports Mill, our co-packer of Iams Chunks. Even though I could see the flames shooting into the night sky on TV, I simply couldn't believe it had happened to us a second time.

The next day I got in my Ford Bronco and made the hour-long trip to where the plant had stood, in a small Ohio town that wasn't much more than a few houses. I drove by slowly, taking in the scene. I was happy to learn that no one had been hurt, but I was in too much of a daze to talk to the owner or the throng of people hanging around the smoldering ruins.

Back in my office, I called the owner. "How did the fire start?"

"It started in the drier and spread to the whole plant before the firemen could do anything," he replied.

"Are you going to rebuild?" I asked.

"No. It was a total loss. I can't even think about rebuilding."

Once again, I had the nightmare task of telling our distributors we had a problem supplying product, only this time, Iams Chunks would be in short supply. We were just coming off allocation of Eukanuba, and now we were out of Iams Chunks. Though both events were beyond our control, our lack of product didn't say much for our dependability as a supplier. I felt like I was delivering the corporate equivalent of that old excuse: "The dog ate my homework."

But I was always straight with people. I told the distributors exactly what had happened: There had been a fire and the plant wouldn't be rebuilt. "I'd appreciate it if you'd hold out and be patient with us," I said over and over again throughout the day. "We should have our new plant up and running shortly, so we'll be able to supply you ourselves."

Most of the distributors expressed willingness to work with us. The Berlin, Maryland, plant was fully operational again, and the Eukanuba was flowing fairly well, which helped ease their frustration levels.

We were still about a month away from opening the Lewisburg plant, and I estimated that month of not producing Iams Chunks would mean about $300,000 in lost sales. Most of our distributors had competitive products in their warehouses, so when I wasn't shipping product, I was losing sales to my competitors.

As devastating as that second fire was, it served as positive motivation, steeling my resolve to handle manufacturing of all our products, including Eukanuba. I decided we would never use another co-packer for one of our primary products.

With Rob in charge, I left the team at Delphos working to produce the protein we needed for Iams Chunks, Iams Plus, and Iams 999. I asked Jan to switch to full-time as the office manager at Delphos, and I hired a half-dozen fellows from the Lewisburg area to be on standby to run the new plant.

Most of the young men I tapped for duty were barely out of high school and fresh off the farm. I've been teased that my hiring method at that point was to eyeball a prospect and determine whether I could picture him swinging one hundred-pound bags of ingredients.

The Lewisburg facility was much larger than Delphos Avenue and gave us plenty of room for expansion. I'd planned for a production capability of up to $50 million worth of dog food annually.

The 25,000-square-foot facility had three modest offices, a break room, and a quality control laboratory where the food was checked for protein and fat and to verify we were meeting label guarantees. We had a bulk ingredient dump where incoming trucks poured ingredients, including corn and beet pulp. And we had a receiving dock where meat meal was delivered and stored in overhead metal bins.

We started out with one extruder and one dryer. Before building, we learned we could not get natural gas lines installed at the plant, because the current natural gas shortage meant suppliers weren't allowed to sign on new customers. So our dryer used oil-fired steam to dry the pellets as they came out of the extruder. Powering the dryer with oil instead of gas was 50 percent more expensive. A small bagging line required that most work be done by hand.

Almost a full year after we broke ground, we finally fired up the Lewisburg plant on October 12, 1978. There was no fanfare or ribbon cutting; all I cared about that day was getting 40-pound bags of Iams Chunks off the line and out the door. And it was just as well that we'd foregone the traditional inaugural festivities, because at the end of the day there was nothing to celebrate. The kickoff was an unmitigated disaster: absolutely nothing ran right.

I had never built a plant, and I'm not particularly mechanically inclined. The process was a comedy of errors. I was constructing a facility to produce a product I'd never made before, using equipment no one else had ever used. Sure, the extruder had worked in Wenger's pilot plant, but the version we had ordered was much bigger, with a longer barrel and different screw configurations. The changes meant the extruder should, in theory, be able to produce a much greater volume of food in less time, but I knew that just because something worked in testing didn't necessarily mean it would work in practice.

Almost immediately, my mistakes in designing the plant became obvious. Instead of concrete, the entire plant was made of metal, because it was far less expensive. That cost-cutting measure caused two problems: First, the plant was excessively noisy, which was an internal problem from a safety standpoint; and second, because we were out in the middle of a field in a metal building in the middle of a tornado alley, the plant was struck by lightning all the time. The electricity went off with alarming regularity, which shut down the extruder. We'd have to clean it out every time, because the food would set up in the barrel. That meant unbolting the die, cleaning the barrel and the die, and then re-bolting the die on the extruder. The whole process took at least an hour. We eventually installed lightning rods.

Even the lightning rods didn't eliminate the frequent power outages. Because our plant was situated at the outer edge of the area serviced by Dayton Power & Light, whenever a thunderstorm rolled through and knocked out electricity, our power stayed out for an inordinately long time. Because we were in a sparsely populated area, we were a low priority for emergency crews.

I also soon realized we hadn't planned enough ingredient storage space. This left us with virtually no margin for error when it came to supplies. If something went wrong with delivery of any of our ingredients—say, a delivery truck broke down, a load shipped out late, or we failed to order the right amount—it wreaked havoc with our schedule.

Out of necessity, we invented a just-in-time manufacturing process long before it became an industry buzzword. We learned to manage through the challenge of not having enough storage space, largely because most of our suppliers were local. Carl Akey owned a feed plant that was practically at our back door and provided our vitamins, minerals, and amino acids. The corn suppliers were all local farmers, who would deliver at 3 A.M. if we asked them to. Delphos Avenue provided our protein requirements, and we could have a truck at Lewisburg in a three-hour turnaround if needed.

Then there was the faulty sewage system. We'd installed a leach system, which works fine with regular bathrooms. But because we had to dispose of cleaning water that contained fat and meat fragments, the system got plugged up. As a short-term solution, we pulled up a tanker next to the plant, pumped the sewage into it, and regularly hauled the waste out to a landfill. Eventually, we had to install our own full-blown municipal sewage treatment system because we didn't have access to city sewage.

Even the water supply for the new plant came into question!

John Young, the entrepreneur who owned the property the plant was built on, became friends with Paul when he supplied Iams with brewer's yeast and distiller's quality corn. An intelligent, devoutly religious man, small in stature, but big on dreams, John had an agreement with the farmer across the road and down the river valley to supply water to the industrial park. At least that's what we understood when we agreed to site the plant there. We subsequently discovered the agreement was to supply water to a trailer park, which was what John's original permit allowed. The farmer brought suit against him and us, alleging we were cheating him out of water revenue.

Finally, Carl Akey, whose plant also was on John's property and who was also a defendant in the lawsuit, bought the land and water rights from the farmer. We figured he'd drop the lawsuit, but to our dismay, Carl took the position of the farmer in the lawsuit. I still can't quite understand how he went from being a co-defendant to a plaintiff, but it happened. That suit went on for a decade.

When we opened the Lewisburg plant, we faced a crushing backlog of orders: more than 800,000 pounds of product, enough to fill twenty truckloads.

On the day we finally produced salable product, I was running back and forth in the plant like a chicken with its head cut off. Finally, Mack McClain, the builder, who was putting the finishing touches on the building, caught me and pulled me into my office. "Clay, what is the matter with you?" he asked. "If you don't stop running around like a crazy man, you're going to have a heart attack. Is there some sort of problem?"

"I honestly didn't know until today that we could make this product," I confessed. "We thought we could, but we'd never run this specially designed extruder before."

"What?" Mack was thunderstruck. "You built a plant, and you didn't know you could make the product?" He sat down and shook his head in disbelief. "If I'd known that, I never would have agreed to build this plant for you! My reputation is on the line!"

A week after we first cranked up, we finally shipped a split truckload for Buffalo and New York City.

For the first several weeks we worked from 5 A.M. to 10 P.M. seven days a week. I had to teach the first generation of workers everything about the plant from the ground up, and in some cases I was feeling my way along with them. We learned through trial and error how to operate the extruder, hammer mill (which ground the corn and other grains), dryer, and other machinery. I didn't have a desk, but I scarcely noticed, because I never stopped moving. The guys noticed, though, and constructed a temporary desk out of pallets for me.

My days often stretched to twenty hours, and during the course of that critical year in Iams history I worked 364 straight days, only stopping to catch my breath on Christmas Day. Of course, on Sundays we went to church and had Sunday brunch together, but I'd either go to the plant later in the day or work from home.

I basically would never have seen my family if they hadn't chipped in at the plant along with me. They brought me supper at least once during the week. On Saturdays Mary would pack sandwiches for all of us. I would run a production shift and then catch up on phone calls. Cathy, Tim, and Mike would sweep floors, re-bag product that hadn't been sewn properly, help load trucks, and find whatever else they could do to help. Even our youngest, Jen, then six, made herself useful by pretending to be my secretary.

Their presence comforted me greatly. But my crazed lifestyle naturally took a toll on them and became a bone of contention between Mary and me. She longed for my presence at home, but her main concern was for my health. I was a heart attack in the making, a workaholic who had traded smoking for eating and snacked whenever I felt under pressure, which was constantly. Mary became more and more distraught as the pounds piled on, but she stuck with me. A less devoted wife would have thrown in the towel, but I was extraordinarily lucky. Mary never wavered in her support and her faith in my mission. My dream was hers, and it would never have been realized without her.

When I look back on the difficult birth of the Lewisburg plant, I wonder what more could have happened. The deck certainly appeared to be stacked against us. But Paul had picked the right poker player. The only time I become frustrated or demoralized is when I have no options, and I don't remember hitting an obstacle during those years that made me feel like quitting. After all, we'd had some kind of crisis every year, and we had always managed to pull the fat out of the fire.

I firmly believed Iams was destined to come out on top because no other company had an extruded meat product. All the extruded pet food products were formulated from soy and cereals. The young group at Lewisburg shared my confidence in the bright future of Iams because customers and distributors were singing the praises of our product's quality.

And then came the straw—or should I say the needle—that broke the camel's back.

A few months after the Lewisburg plant opened, we finally had one glorious day where everything seemed to be coming together. No shutdowns, all the machinery working well. Could we be out of the woods at last?

Of course not. Late in the afternoon, I noticed the bagging bin was overflowing. Jeff Lawson couldn't pack product bags fast enough.

"What's going on, Jeff?" I asked.

"Well, Clay, the sewing needle broke on the bagging machine, and we can't find a spare to fit it," he replied.

A tiny sewing needle was shutting down the plant? After weathering an entire year of unbelievable stress and strain, I exploded like a pressure cooker. Cursing loud enough for the angels to grab earplugs, I stomped to my office, slammed the door, and sat there steaming.

Jeff, on the other hand, decided to take some positive action. He drove to another feed mill and borrowed a needle for the bagging machine.

When the Year of Fire and Ice finally came to an end, I breathed a sigh of relief. Little did I know the biggest battle I would ever fight, for the Iams brand itself, was just around the corner.

## CHAPTER 8

# Enemy in Our Midst

The year 1979 got off to a promising start. To kick off the new year, I decided to introduce another new product: Iams Mini Chunks. The new food was designed to respond to customer demand for dry food suitable for small dogs and puppies; it was also for dog owners who liked to mix our products with wet food. Iams Mini Chunks contained exactly the same formula as Iams Chunks, just in smaller pellets.

The dog food business is far more complicated than many people realize. Once you have a great product, it might seem as though you could kick back and let it roll out of the extruder while the money rolls in. In actuality, you're faced with an ongoing contradiction. On one hand, you always have to be on the lookout for ways to improve and expand that product to meet new customer demands. On the other hand, when you make a major change in the product, or stop making it, you're inevitably going to upset a segment of your loyal customer base. It's a delicate and continuous balancing act, a little like walking a tightrope and juggling at the same time. You have to keep your old customers happy, bring in new customers, reassure distributors, and keep ten steps ahead of your competition.

A small but fiercely loyal group of customers still favored Iams Plus, but the brand had stopped growing because it didn't appeal to new customers.

Originally, Iams Plus gained popularity because people thought it was an additive. Even though we'd designed it as a complete diet, the meal form made many dog owners consider it a supplement, and no amount of consumer education could convince them to the contrary. Almost everyone who used Iams Plus mixed it with something, despite our best efforts to convince them this was unnecessary—unless, like Rick Swenson, they were racing sled dogs.

I needed to clear the decks, and the Delphos Avenue team needed to turn its attention from making finished goods to supplying Lewisburg with vitally important processed meat protein. Iams Plus was simply not relevant to my game plan anymore, so I decided to discontinue making it. I hoped to minimize the complaints I knew would result by offering Iams Mini Chunks as a replacement.

Adding a new product to the mix complicated our operations. We had to change equipment setups according to which product we were running. Less than six months after opening the Lewisburg plant, I was forced to admit I'd gotten in over my head. Crisis after crisis kept popping up. Living only ten miles from the plant, I found myself hopping in my truck at all hours of the night to put out yet another fire.

One of the most important aspects of running a successful business is knowing when to let go and trusting others to handle the 101 jobs you've been trying to do all by yourself. This may be the most difficult thing for a commander-in-chief to do. By nature, a successful entrepreneur is a control freak. He or she has started a company from the ground up and taken it to where it is. Who knows a business better than the owner? Who but the owner should be responsible for keeping every part of its operation running smoothly and making all the final decisions?

Even though my employees liked me because I never considered myself better than anyone else and was always right there in the trenches pitching in, I fit the mold of the hands-on, micromanaging CEO to a T. It was hard for me to entrust someone else with the enormous responsibilities of running the plant, because I'd had too much unhappy experience with what can happen when you don't have total control over every step of your product's journey, from manufacturing to distribution to sales.

Yet it had become all too evident that if Iams Food Company was going to achieve what I envisioned, we needed to bring someone in to run the plant.

That's when I made my first big mistake. I hired the son of my next-door neighbor, and he lasted about ten days. I had forgotten one of my own guiding principles: Hire professionals when you need them, and let them do their jobs. So I contacted a respected headhunter, who in turn contacted Bob Bardeau, an employee at Wayne Pet Food. Based in Peoria, Illinois, Wayne was enormously successful, doing about $120 million in sales at that time.

Bardeau didn't think he was right for the position, but he told his colleague John Polson about it, completely unaware that John, a production manager overseeing three hundred workers at a high-volume Wayne plant with eight extruders, was looking for another job. Unhappy with the way he thought management was treating employees and, in his opinion, Wayne's lack of commitment to product quality, he had already interviewed with three other pet food companies.

Iams Food Company may have surpassed Wayne in quality, but Wayne was way ahead of us when it came to quantity. The eight extruders John was supervising produced 100,000 tons a year, whereas we ended 1978 shipping the equivalent of 9,800 tons. In fact, we were still measuring our units in pounds.

Nonetheless, John contacted the headhunter and, even though he'd never heard of Iams, agreed to fly down to talk to me.

When I asked him the key question, "What do you think your strengths are?" he answered without hesitation.

"My ability to organize."

This impressed me. To build a big organization and run a big plant, I was going to need people with superior organizational skills. I also sensed John would be good with people, a good leader and a fair manager.

After we'd talked, I took John to see the Delphos Avenue plant and meet Paul, who looked at John's hands long and hard when I introduced him. Paul always said you could tell a lot about a man by his hands, and that the best ones were large and work-worn, with a firm grip. "A strong handshake indicates strength of character," was one of his sayings.

John passed the "handshake" test, but there was another, even more critical exam ahead: the Mary Test.

As I have mentioned, my wife Mary has an uncanny ability to size up a person. She asks questions I wouldn't think to ask. She can detect a phony a mile away and instantly tunes in to someone who has personal integrity. Nobody sneaks past her!

As I drove John to the airport, I told him to talk everything over with his wife and to come and have dinner with Mary and me if he was interested in the position. I knew I was asking a man with a young family to make a three-hundred-mile move to work at a small plant in the middle of a cornfield, for a company that had less than 5 percent of the sales of his present employer.

The following Saturday evening, John and his wife, Sandy, joined Mary and me for dinner at a small restaurant on Dayton's south side. The four of us clicked. The Polsons radiated warmth and, like us, tended to eschew socializing in favor of quiet evenings with their family.

After they left, Mary turned to me.

"I like him a lot, Clay," she smiled. "He's truthful and strong-minded. He's got what it takes to stand up to you, but he's also respectful. He'll be a good leader and a good example. I think he's exactly what you need."

John accepted my offer of plant manager, even though the move to Iams would mean a 60 percent drop in their household income. He told me later that when he informed his boss at Wayne about his decision, the man scoffed. "I've never heard of Iams, Polson. Those little operations come and go all the time."

John just smiled and replied, "I think Iams is going to be around."

John immediately noted some of the bad habits I'd allowed the crew to slip into. By the time he came on board, we'd caught up on demand and didn't have enough orders to justify running the plant at full steam. As a result, most of the employees drifted in late. By the time I decided which products to run and the crew had set up the machines accordingly, it was often 9:30 A.M. We'd typically shut down at 3:30 P.M. I'd installed a basketball goal inside the roomy warehouse, like my dad had for me inside the barn, so we could shoot buckets during downtime. Since we only had enough business to run for three days a week, I'm happy, though not exactly proud, to say the guys learned how to play great basketball on the Iams' clock.

Basic manufacturing rules were being ignored as well. Walls were still being painted, so flammable materials sat around. Everybody, except John and me, smoked inside the plant. Since we hadn't provided a break room or even a microwave oven, people were eating their lunches at their workstations. It looked like an industrial campground. Curt habitually heated his egg sandwich, wrapped in foil, with the steam that came out of the conditioning cylinder on the extruder head. Once he even fried an egg on the extruder!

Two weeks after he started, John asked me to lunch at Buffalo's, a modest little restaurant, popular with truckers, across the road from the plant. Never one to waste words, as soon as we sat down, he got down to business.

"I don't know exactly how to say this, so I'll just say it: Clay, when do you plan to let me do the job you hired me to do?"

"What kind of things are you going to do?" I asked.

"For starters, I'm going to have dog food rolling out of the extruder every morning at 8 A.M.," he replied. Then he handed me a list of things he wanted changed immediately. He explained the rationale behind all his suggestions while I looked over them. He wanted to decide in advance what we'd run the next day. Smoking in the plant and eating at workstations would be verboten, and the basketball hoop in the warehouse had to go.

He was absolutely right, of course. For so long, I'd been trying to make everything happen on my own strength. Although I was used to being the center of the wheel, inwardly I felt relieved that I'd finally found someone whom I could trust to take on a lot of the load. John's willingness to confront me so quickly proved I'd been right to hire him. I wanted a plant manager who was willing to take me on, and I got exactly that.

"Go to it," I said. "It's all yours."

Soon after he joined the company, John suggested that we should count our units in tons rather than pounds. "Someday soon, we'll be doing ten thousand tons a month, instead of ten thousand tons a year," he said confidently.

At that moment, I couldn't quite wrap my brain around that one. Ten thousand tons a month sounded almost unattainable. But I certainly wasn't averse to dreaming big, and after Paul's reticence to expand, it was nice to be working with another visionary.

By Easter I felt confident enough in John's abilities to take a family vacation, something we hadn't done in years.

I don't think I really understood until that moment just how exhausted I was. I felt like I'd been running a nine-year marathon. My fuel tanks were completely empty. John was a godsend in more ways than one. For the first time in years I was able to unwind with Mary and the kids, to recharge my batteries, and to act like a husband and father once more.

And I was about to become a father again. A couple of months later, we adopted an eight-year-old girl named Tina from Allen House, an orphanage in Cincinnati. Mary fell in love with the ivory-skinned, strawberry blonde little girl at first sight. We brought her home for the weekend to see how she got along with everyone. Our youngest, six-year-old Jen, was thrilled at the prospect of having a sister closer to her age. The two girls traded clothes in the car, and when we got home, Jen took Tina into her room, spread her arms wide, and said, "All this can be yours if you decide to become my sister."

Shortly after Tina came into our lives, we had another addition to the Iams family. Marty Walker, the young accountant who'd been handling our books through Haskins and Sells, one of the Big Eight accounting firms, called. He had contacted me a year earlier, asking for a position, but I didn't want to hire anyone at the time, because I wasn't sure we would get the new plant off the ground.

"Clay, I've made a decision," he said. "I don't want to go back to work for the firm. I want to work for you. But even if you turn me down this time, I'm going to be leaving Haskins and Sells. I'm ready to do something else."

Marty had previously passed the Mary Test, so after some discussion with her, I hired him as our controller. He gave the CPA firm his three-week notice. I thoroughly believed everyone who came to work for us needed to learn the business from the ground up. I told Marty he'd need to start in the plant, just like everyone else. The escapee from the CPA world took my rule to heart and dutifully showed up for his first day on June 11, 1979, wearing work boots with his three-piece suit.

People have asked how we came up with our distinctive Iams Food Company paw print logo. It came out of a new product, Iams Puppy Food, which we started making in 1979. Working with Adriane Ridey of Jackson-Ridey, our advertising agency in Cincinnati, we designed a logo that featured the distinctive frankfurter-type style on the new Iams Puppy Food label. The logo used one large circle drawn on a tangent and four smaller circles angled out from the larger one. I thought it was brilliant, but when I showed it around, nobody else got that excited about it. They found it too simplistic, yet it was precisely that innocent simplicity that drew consumers to it. Today, twenty-six years later, that distinctive paw print still symbolizes The Iams Company and its products.

In late May 1979 Paul and his old friend and partner Bill Kelly were invited to a Denver meeting with the head of Ross Wells, who had also become a vice president of Beatrice Foods, following the smaller company's acquisition by the foods giant. After the meeting, I got a grim phone call from Paul.

"I've got really bad news," he said. "Ross Wells has given us a ninety-day notice that they're stopping production of Eukanuba."

I was stunned. "Do we have any legal recourse?" I asked.

"No," Paul replied. "And you know how I feel about lawsuits."

Paul vehemently objected to legal battles. He was a man of integrity, who had started his business in the days when a handshake and a man's word constituted a contract. He'd attempted to explain to the Beatrice VP that he had a long-standing agreement with Ross Wells to produce Eukanuba in exchange for several services he had performed for the company. But a handshake deal with Loyal Wells made ten years earlier didn't impress the behemoth Beatrice Foods. As long as no written contract existed, Beatrice had no intention of honoring it. The company's lawyers knew they had us, giving Ross Wells the golden opportunity to pull the plug on Iams Food Company.

We immediately contacted our attorney, but with nothing committed to paper, he warned a legal battle would be fruitless. My inclination being to concentrate on the future and the positive, I decided that wasting energy on such a negative endeavor didn't make sense. You don't get into a stink contest with skunks.

Besides, this was yet another opportunity disguised as a loss. The time to separate from Ross Wells was long overdue. I wanted control over our product and had been investigating how we could produce Eukanuba ourselves. The timetable had simply been moved up. Still, it was a body blow; our entire business hinged on how rapidly we could figure out how to make Eukanuba in our new plant.

Three months. Ninety days. No matter how you sliced it, the task ahead seemed impossible. Although we owned the formula for Eukanuba (after all, Paul had created it), we had no strategic plan. The problem was how to get fresh meat into it. Eukanuba called for 20 percent more protein than Iams Chunks. Now that we were being forced to reinvent the wheel, so to speak, I decided to push for even higher-quality protein than we'd been using.

Ross Wells used chicken entrails and chicken by-products in their processing of Eukanuba, which meant that we could not call it "chicken meat" on the label. I decided a label advertising chicken meat would be far more appealing to dog owners, but I hadn't heard of anyone in our area producing good-quality de-boned chicken meat at a price that made sense for us. Even if we were to find a supplier, our next challenge would be how to keep the fresh meat protein nutritionally sound and palatable through the cooking process, a trick that would prove far more difficult than I had ever dreamed.

The pressure to solve our dilemma was increased by the knowledge that Beatrice wouldn't have lowered the boom on us if they didn't have their own game plan in place. It didn't take a crystal ball to predict they would shortly be introducing their own premium dog food. After all, they'd had access to our formula and many of our outlets since we'd handed Ross Wells distribution rights to Eukanuba on much of the East Coast a few years earlier.

I was worried. But I was determined not to lose the brand we'd worked so hard to build. Feeling like Spartacus leading the motley slave revolt against the Roman forces, I rallied our small band of workers to do battle with the massive Beatrice Foods conglomerate.

"We're going to figure this out," I declared. Everyone was behind me, because their faith in and devotion to Iams Food Company was as strong as mine.

The day after Ross Wells dropped the bomb, Noel McDonald, an agent who had been selling me vitamins and amino acids, walked in my door.

"Clay," Noel said, "American Dehydrated Foods has started experimenting with some mechanically de-boned chicken meat. Are you interested?"

If American Dehydrated, a small outfit owned by Bill Darr, could pull this off, it would answer my most fervent prayer.

An hour later, Bill Darr called me.

"I understand you might have a need for our comminuted chicken meat," he said. "Why don't I come see you?"

In contrast to his competitors, Bill Darr wanted to provide USDA-approved, good-quality chicken meat to the pet food industry. He had excellent relationships within the poultry industry.

Satisfied that Bill's de-boned chicken meat would fill the bill, I turned my attention to our lack of refrigeration at the plant. Bill planned to ship us the chicken meat frozen in 50-pound blocks wrapped in cardboard.

Unfortunately, we had no way to store or thaw the meat to keep it fresh before we used it.

Mack McClain, the contractor who built our plant, told me about Tri B Meat, a small, family-owned meat packing plant that was just starting up in Greenville, Ohio, twenty miles from Lewisburg. Tri B mainly produced sausage and bologna and had refrigeration and grinding machines where the thawed chicken meat could be prepared for our extruder. I contacted one of the owners, Dick Buchy (pronounced "Beeky"), a colorful character who gleefully set about devising a pump to get the thawed chicken meat into our extruder. We worked out a deal with his company to deliver the chicken meat to us in refrigerated trucks.

Tri B turned out to be a short-lived operation, but it came along at exactly the right time for us. In that brief time period, I had already seen that having a middleman in this process was too unwieldy. Bill Darr bought a refrigerated truck that kept the chicken meat chilled appropriately as it was shipped to our plant directly, and in July I hired Dick Buchy to help us with maintenance. A self-taught wiz when it came to anything mechanical, Dick rigged up a grinder and a way to pump the chicken into our extruder. By that time, American Dehydrated had developed the capability to deliver the chicken meat chilled but not frozen, which eliminated the need for double handling.

After we started making Eukanuba ourselves, our leach field for sewage clogged up because of all the fresh meat we were using in the product. Dick rigged up a skimmer that allowed us to pull off the meat and fat that floated on top of the wastewater. Then we would pump the solid waste material into a tank truck, and Dick hauled it to his farm and fed the high-energy waste product to his hogs. Dick was proud of how his jury-rigged system was working.

One day Dick invited John Polson and me to his farm to show off his hogs. As we walked into the pen, I noticed some seemed to be awfully docile. Others were almost staggering. I asked Dick to let me sniff the holding tank. It smelled like a brewery. The waste materials were fermenting in there and, although he had no idea, Dick was making alcohol. Those hogs were three sheets to the wind!

Later that same month, we successfully produced the first bags of our own Eukanuba. It looked fine and test-fed well, so we shipped it out, despite the fact that because of the ninety-day deadline dealt us by Ross Wells, we didn't have time to do long-term feeding tests through the independent lab we normally used before introducing new products.

It didn't take long for the complaints to start coming in. Don Laden, a young man Tom Rowe had hired to work in the Chicago distribution center shortly after it opened, called me soon after we made the first shipments. "Clay, a Great Dane breeder just called me, saying that her dogs have loose stools from the new Eukanuba," reported the nineteen-year-old. "She was furious. She demanded that I come over and help her clean out her kennels. What should I do?"

"You call her back and tell her that's the best food her dogs have ever been fed!" I bellowed, slamming down the receiver. Nobody had ever produced a dog food with that much fresh meat in it. Polson, Buchy, and I were working practically around the clock on Eukanuba, and I was in no mood to hear any criticism.

But breeders from all over the country were soon calling me, complaining that their dogs had loose stools. Distributors screamed that the new Eukanuba wasn't as palatable as the old formula. Some even quibbled about the different shape of the pellets.

It turned out that we still hadn't gotten the right cook on the meat and starch. The higher protein content and fresh chicken meant that in order to maintain the integrity of the protein we had to slow the extruder and give that fresh meat a much longer cook time. Otherwise, the starch in the corn was failing to convert properly, resulting in loose stools for the dogs eating it.

We had initially cranked the extruder up to 85 revolutions per minute (rpms). On a broiling hot day in August, John, Dick, and I kept setting the extruder lower and lower, until finally at 55 rpms, a full 35 percent slower than before, the product looked just right. "Stop!" I yelled. "It's perfect! Nobody touch anything."

After the Eukanuba fiasco was resolved, I took my family on another vacation. The year before, we'd become friends with the Odio family from Costa Rica when we hosted one of their sons, Manrique, in a student exchange program. Harry Odio, a charming and exceedingly bright man, held the position of chief financial officer for one of the local paint manufacturing companies owned by H.B. Fuller. He asked many thought-provoking questions about my business and was shocked to learn that even though we were approaching $7.7 million in sales with a 37 percent growth rate, I had neither a budget nor a business plan. Harry convinced me I had to have both a budget and a board of directors, something I'd never taken the time to think about.

Iams Food Company was clearly at a turning point. We had to make the jump from a small, seat-of-the-pants operation to a large company. This fact was brought home when John Polson and I visited the owner of Pass Pets in St. Louis, who had a chain of fifteen pet stores. John wanted to know his story.

"He's been asking us for product for five years, but I don't have it to give to him," I explained.

For years I'd been turning away new business because I operated the company from a production-bound standpoint. After two plant fires at our co-packers, I was gun-shy about making any promises I couldn't keep when it came to delivering product.

"What?" John exclaimed. "This man has been waiting for our product for five years! Clay, we've got more than enough production capacity now. You don't have to turn customers away anymore."

By mid-summer, my suspicions about Ross Wells had started to come true. Long before the ninety days were up, I got a call from a distributor who sold a lot of Eukanuba for us.

"A funny thing just happened, Clay," he said. "A Ross Wells salesman came by with a new product that sure smelled and felt like Eukanuba, just in a different package."

"It's a long story," I replied, trying to keep the rage out of my voice. "Before I get into it, why don't you tell me all about this new product?"

CHAPTER 9

# Waging War

The Lewisburg plant had not quite reached its one-year anniversary when the ninety-day deadline to begin producing Eukanuba ourselves came to an end. Sure enough, Ross Wells officially rolled out its new premium dog food called A.N.F., which stood for Advanced Nutritional Formula.

Imitation may be the sincerest form of flattery, but I was anything but flattered as word trickled in regarding what Ross Wells was doing. Backed by big bucks from Beatrice Foods, the Ross Wells team could afford to do all the things we couldn't. They hired an enormous sales force. Their reps carpeted every dog show with samples of A.N.F., which they touted as the original Eukanuba. Their reps carpeted every dog show with samples of A.N.F., which resembled the original Eukanuba that they used to make for us.

Meanwhile, our new Eukanuba looked and smelled different from the old product. We were using fresh chicken, while A.N.F. was formulated from chicken by-products. The pellets were shaped differently, too. Ours looked like little pillows about $3/8$ of an inch square, whereas the A.N.F. pellet was longer and thinner.

Ironically, we were fighting the Eukanuba legend and mystique we'd built. We'd done such a good job convincing dog show people and breeders that Eukanuba was the best dog food around that some were reluctant to stick with us since the A.N.F. formula so closely resembled the original Eukanuba.

Immediately after introducing the new Eukanuba in the summer of 1979, we had lingering difficulties with consistency. A.N.F. made big gains, especially on the East Coast where Ross Wells was deeply rooted.

Ross Wells simultaneously deployed its own sales and service centers, which quickly became nationwide distribution centers for A.N.F. Our former co-packer pursued many of our distributors, including our independent distributors. Salespeople boasted about the technology in the dog food, the same exact technology we had helped the company develop.

But Ross Wells seriously underestimated our little regional company, a mistake many of our competitors made in Iams' growing years—and an error in judgment that I discovered could be a great advantage. If the big guys don't think you're worth watching, you can accomplish a hell of a lot while they are doing business as usual and laughing at you or, better yet, asleep at the wheel.

What Ross Wells failed to understand was the powerful connection we'd forged with influencers, kennel owners, dog show people, retailers, and breeders across the country. Our customers understood that we cared passionately about the product and their dogs, and you just can't fake passion.

Re-establishing ourselves with these key influencers became vitally important to the survival of Eukanuba as a premium brand. Whereas the Hill's strategy depended on veterinarians recommending Science Diet, we and several other dog food companies targeted breeders and kennel owners who raised puppies. Breeders focus on how their dogs look and perform as a result of what they are being fed.

Dogs can be finicky, however; and once they get used to a certain type of food, switching them can be tough. We reasoned that if we got the dogs on Iams products when they were puppies, the puppy breeders and retailers would influence the dogs' new owners to continue feeding Eukanuba.

We had transformed the lives of kennel owners. Until Eukanuba came along, they were forced to mix wet foods, cook fresh meat, and go through all kinds of gyrations to try to improve the health of their litters. Before our complete diet was formulated, kennel owners would spend hours every day cooking fresh meat mixtures for their pups. Our dry product produced stronger, more successful litters, and it simplified the kennel owners' lives. As a result, many of them felt that they owed us a debt of gratitude. Plus, I made amends for the new Eukanuba and our manufacturing hiccups by offering an unconditional guarantee on our food. We owned up to the problems that had existed, offered our sincere apologies, and replaced food or refunded their money, no questions asked. We explained that we had worked out the problems and now had a great new product. Many were willing to give us a second chance.

No business asset is worth as much as well-earned goodwill among a company's stakeholders. A large number of our customers remembered that we had resisted the temptation to cheapen Iams Plus during the wage and price controls fiasco, even when holding firm on high-quality ingredients almost bankrupted our company. They had seen us zealously guard our product's quality when the easy solution—and the one many of our competitors chose—would have been to substitute less costly ingredients.

Was refunding customers' money and replacing initial runs of Eukanuba with bags that had been properly extruded a costly decision? In the short term, yes. It probably cost us more than $100,000. Was it the right call to make? Absolutely. A company owes it to its customers to step up and pay for its mistakes. I was willing to absorb the cost, no matter how high, to reassure our customers we were committed to giving them what they deserved.

Customers will forgive you if you make a mistake. But they won't forgive a company that tries to be slick and finesse the situation at their expense. Although Ross Wells may have had the edge in terms of money and sheer numbers of troops, our strongest assets came under the category of "invaluable intangibles": trust, integrity, concern for pets, and concern for people. We had something incredibly important, we had the kennel owners' trust.

We had invested years on the road telling our story and explaining our commitment to the well-being of our canine customers. And I'd never been less than honest. When we'd run out of Eukanuba or run low on the product, I had always been completely upfront with everyone about what had gone wrong.

Ross Wells was living proof of Napoleon Bonaparte's wry observation, "Never interrupt your enemy while he is making a mistake." But we couldn't simply sit back and enjoy the show. We had to capitalize on those mistakes, with every ounce of strength and determination we possessed.

Business is war, and I personally led the charge, if you can call it that, since there were only two of us to take on our adversary's intimidating sales force. Rob Easterling and I hit the road, calling on all our key customers to tell them we were continuing to improve Eukanuba and that our modern plant had more than enough capacity to keep them well supplied with Iams products.

While Rob concentrated his efforts on kennel owners, breeders, and key retailers, I vigorously defended our hard-won inroads with our regional distributors, who numbered fewer than twenty (including our company-owned operation in Chicago) and our sixty-eight local distributors. Even though we were badly outnumbered and forced to divide our efforts, Rob was a great salesman and relationship-builder. I couldn't have had a better man in the trenches with me.

On the home front, John Polson and his team were cranking out our products at an unbelievable pace, while Marty Walker was fielding calls from our distribution managers, customers, and distributors in my absence.

If you're a history buff, you know that although it's good to anticipate your enemy's response, it's more important to maintain your own strategy. My favorite book at this time was Sun Tzu's *The Art of War*, a slim volume based on the translated writings of a Chinese philosopher-turned-general who lived 2,500 years ago. I used many of his observations in my battle against Ross Wells.

Take Sun Tzu's tenet, "What the multitude cannot comprehend is how victory may be produced for them out of the enemy's own tactics." Ross Wells managed to anger and alienate many independent distributors by indiscriminately placing its own distribution centers in major markets. In the process it made two major tactical errors. First, it hired people with minimal operating skills to run the centers. Second, it started competing with important distributors in some of the most lucrative pet food markets.

At Iams Food Company, we took great pains to avoid making any of our independent distributors feel threatened. I have always put great value on people and on the human equation in business. I recognize the tremendous role that satisfied and energized employees and associates can play in a business's success, and I genuinely care about them as individuals.

> *What the multitude cannot comprehend is how victory may be produced for them out of the enemy's own tactics.*
>
> SUN TZU, *THE ART OF WAR*

As an entrepreneur, I valued the fact that these independent distributors were small, mostly family-owned businesses, and I wanted them to thrive with us, not be worried about competing against us. They understood their local markets better than we could, and we looked to them as partners. Our competitor's missteps paved the road for Rob and me to strengthen our relationships with our distributors and enlist their help in fighting the new common enemy of Ross Wells.

I viewed our distribution centers in Chicago; Bensalem, Pennsylvania; and Hollywood, Florida, as special operations forces that assisted us in better understanding our distributors and the pulse of the local market. Our distribution managers attended trade shows and handled booths on our behalf, but we clearly told independent distributors we didn't mind if they took our accounts, the area retailers, and breeders to whom we'd sold products.

Here's how it worked: In the Chicago area, for example, we sold products to five independent distributors (sub-distributors) who worked different parts of the market. One sold to feed stores, another to pet stores, another to kennels, and another to veterinarians. The fifth sub-distributor, south of Chicago in Springfield, served rural feed dealers.

We published our price list with volume prices for 500 pounds of food, 1,000 pounds, 2,000 pounds, and 5,000 pounds. We adhered strictly to that price list. Customers could buy from us directly, or a distributor could step in. The distributor might choose, for instance, to give a customer 2,000 pounds at the price per pound that was normally reserved for a customer purchasing 5,000 pounds.

Doing so still allowed the distributor to make a tidy profit. Meanwhile, our new customers got serviced, and the distributors loved it because we were generating new business for them. At the end of the day, our distribution center strategy gave us what we were after: increased market share and expanded distribution.

I worked hard to turn the tables on Ross Wells, calling on and successfully converting a handful of its independent distributors on the East Coast, in the mid-Atlantic area, and the Southeast, especially in the Carolinas and Florida, the territory Paul had ceded to Ross Wells in a futile effort to keep parent company Beatrice Foods at bay. My time in the field spent getting to know independent distributors was paying off. They trusted me far more than the hired guns Ross Wells was trotting out to service their accounts.

Armed with a product that was finally right and a plant with ample capacity, I turned my energies toward establishing national distribution. Curiously, the fight with Ross Wells probably pushed that need to the forefront of my agenda. The distribution strategy we created under duress became a vital ingredient in our recipe for growth.

Another of Sun Tzu's dead-on pieces of advice was, "In the enemy's country, win people over by kind treatment and use them as spies." Although I wasn't much of a joiner, I learned I could pick up a good deal of information at industry association meetings, where I could handily fly under the radar because we were still viewed as a fringe company. At Pet Food Institute meetings, the competition's salespeople invariably greeted me with, "Are you the guys charging $20 for a bag of dog food?" My affirmative reply would be met by derisive laughter.

The snickering didn't bother me a bit. In fact, I used our reputation for being on the edge to my advantage. I purposely avoided volunteering or being drafted for duty on any committees. Instead, I hung around the technical people and scientists, all largely ignored by the marketers and salespeople. The scientists were delighted to talk about industry trends and the latest advances in nutrition, and I was more than happy to listen to anything and everything they wanted to tell me.

The marketing people typically ran the pet food companies, dictating to the research and development department what it could and couldn't do. At that time in the late 1970s, it was commonly thought there was nothing new left to be discovered in the pet food industry. Instead, the companies were striving for cost advantages. The marketing people nixed most suggestions from the researchers, since improvements cost money and they didn't want to add to the manufacturing cost of their products.

I took the scientists out to lunch. "We tested your product," they'd say wistfully. "It's great." We treated each other with respect, because we were speaking the same language, and they recognized I knew what I was talking about when it came to animal nutrition.

By 1981, our employees numbered eighty and sales jumped another 27 percent to reach $12.8 million. We were up to 20,544 tons in annual sales. Suddenly, John Polson's prediction of 100,000 tons didn't seem so far away.

In the spring of 1980, we introduced Iams Puppy Food with the new paw print logo. It was an immediate hit, and I was delighted because it helped us increase our product line. On Friday afternoons, if we finished early and the plant was cleaned up, John and I sent out for pizza and beer for the guys at the plant to celebrate how well everything was going.

Unlike some manufacturers, we always guaranteed our people forty hours a week and paid them for forty hours. We never cut labor costs by docking their pay if we didn't have enough work for them or if they finished their work early. I see that as a huge breach of trust between an employer and employee. Sadly, many companies resort to those tactics because they view employees as a cost rather than as an asset. I've especially seen entrepreneurs guilty of treating hourly workers like that. Then they wonder why their employee turnover rate is so high and complain about lack of loyalty in the workforce.

The plant was going like gangbusters. All the pistons were firing, and we were bringing good people on board. My dream was coming true. Everyone clearly felt they were participating in something special.

I always told our employees, "If you aren't making mistakes, you aren't busy enough." If somebody was genuinely doing his or her best and blew it, I never punished that person. After all, in those early days we all made our share of mistakes.

Sometimes we hit big speed bumps. One night John left Dick Buchy in charge of a second-shift run of Iams Chunks. Although the chunks Dick ran that night looked great, for some reason they weren't dense enough. Kenny Bowers, a young, skinny, redheaded fellow who is still with the company as a maintenance manager, came into the production room and told Dick he was having trouble closing the bags. "Just bounce the bags on the floor so the food settles and you can sew 'em up," Dick said.

Thinking he could fix the problem, Dick kept making Iams Chunks and making it and making it. Pretty soon, he'd run eighty tons of the too-light stuff. But he never got the density quite right, and there was no way the bags would close. It was 4 A.M. before the crew got everything cleaned up from the mess. John came in just as the guys were hauling the last of the open 40-pound bags to the back with a skid-steer loader. When I arrived the next morning, I couldn't believe what I saw. The bags were stacked to the rafters. We had to re-grind all of it to use as an ingredient in future batches.

When Dick came slinking in early the next afternoon, I could tell he was wondering if he still had a job or not. "Dick, I was pretty livid this morning when I saw what happened on your watch," I said. "But, hey, we all make mistakes. Just don't do it again."

Dick told me later that exchange had set the tone for his career at Iams, giving him the confidence to make decisions, trusting that I really meant it when I said mistakes weren't fatal.

No one outside the dog food business can imagine the crazy things that can affect production. Everything went relatively smoothly with Iams Puppy until the weather started turning cold in November. Because our demand was steadily increasing, we were often running a second shift. When Iams Puppy was manufactured later in the day and into the evening, we started noticing the pellets, which had holes stamped out of the middle, looked like frosted Cheerios.

Since the plant was constructed out of metal and we didn't have heat, it was extremely cold inside. After puzzling over the problem, we discovered the cold outside air being taken in by the dryer was compounding the frigid conditions. The additional blast of icy air was causing the fat in the Iams Puppy formula to congeal on the outside of the pellets rather than being absorbed. The simple solution was to add heaters to warm the air as it entered the dryer.

In 1981 we came out with Iams Cat Food, a dry food that used the same extrusion process as Eukanuba.

I'm often asked why we didn't enter the cat food business earlier. In the early years, I suspect it had something to do with the fact that Paul Iams wasn't particularly passionate about cats. Later, we were focused on producing nutritionally complete dry diets, and most cat fanciers preferred to feed wet food to their cats. Plus, we had our hands full with two brands of premium dog food, which represented a bigger opportunity for us.

The company was growing at such breakneck speed that everyone except John moved offices to a hastily constructed metal building on a hill overlooking the plant. We expanded the plant's practically nonexistent warehouse space and reconfigured the extrusion room to accommodate a second extruder.

Instead of sitting in the office, I much preferred to be out in the plant, talking to employees, sometimes working side by side with them, loading trucks, or whatever. Without knowing it, I was employing a couple of management techniques that later were popularized in Tom Peters' 1982 masterpiece *In Search of Excellence*: "management by wandering around" and "the open door policy."

Wanting to encourage the valuable flow of information between our employees and me, I told everyone to call me "Clay." I'd encountered CEOs who didn't even deem it necessary to say "Good morning" to employees. That elitist attitude made absolutely no sense to me and went entirely against my goal of establishing a fun, open workplace that people would look forward to coming to each day.

Allowing myself to be perceived as "one of the guys," however, turned out to be a big mistake. At summer's end in 1981, when the National League pennant race was coming down to the wire, we continued a tradition I had started the previous year. I rented two buses to take the plant guys to Cincinnati to watch the Reds play. We had several cases of beer, and very soon, all decorum, including mine, went out the window, along with something else. Some of the guys mooned another passing bus, thinking it was carrying our other employees. Unfortunately, its passengers happened to be a group of nuns.

After a few more beers, one of my guys hit me in the face with a sandwich, and I retaliated by grabbing him by his shirt and slamming him into the seat in front of me. That incident marked a turning point. I realized that I was in danger of losing the respect of my troops. I could no longer afford to be one of the guys or to let my temper get the better of me. Every interaction with an employee was an opportunity either to gain ground or to go backward. I wanted to march forward.

"How are things going? How can I help you?" I asked almost everyone I encountered at the plant. And I meant it. I love to "match-make" people with the job of their dreams.

Human beings don't achieve greatness unless they are working in an arena that speaks to their hearts. Marty Walker stood out to me as a man of many talents. Although he was an adequate accountant, I could not envision him rising to the top of that field. I felt certain he had another destiny.

At his previous job with the CPA firm, Marty had brought in a tremendous amount of new business and demonstrated good selling skills.

He excelled when he was interacting with our distributors, customers, and distribution center managers.

I called him into my office. "I don't think your strength lies in being a controller," I said. "How would you like to be in charge of sales and marketing?"

Marty eagerly accepted his new post, hiring his own replacement, and Rob reported to Marty in his new role.

The better everything was going at the plant and the bigger my plans got for our future, the more I sensed Paul's increasing discomfort. Whenever I tried to engage him in a discussion about the long-term future of the company, he would hedge or change the subject. After he turned sixty-five in August 1981, Paul became uncharacteristically quiet. I couldn't figure out what was going on in his mind.

Paul and I had reached an impasse for two reasons. First, neither of us trusted the other one's lawyer. Paul's attorney was his cousin, who had little experience handling issues common to small businesses. I hadn't been much more selective in hiring my counsel, whom I met when he was coaching my kid's soccer team.

The other bone of contention was the debt I'd incurred. The company easily gobbled up all the capital we were bringing in to fuel growth, but Paul had reached the stage in his career where he wanted to start taking cash out of the business. He pushed to pay down debt, but I argued we should keep rolling over our short-term loan and use incoming cash as working capital to service the debt.

Complicating matters was the fact that Marty's former boss told Paul he could extract whatever cash he wanted from the business. That made me angry. I had grown progressively disenchanted with the CPA firm because I'd found our contact there to be less and less available when I had questions.

At length, Paul and I agreed to find new advisors. Rolf Brookes, our banker, recommended Dave Phillips, a managing partner in the Cincinnati office of Arthur Andersen & Co. When I put in a call to Dave, he answered his own phone on the first ring, in stark contrast to how I was being treated.

Dave immediately made an appointment with me, drove up the same day, and met me for lunch in Dayton. We left our table that night at 10 P.M., when the restaurant staff finally signaled it was closing time. We covered every topic from business philosophy to family. Our value systems were virtually identical. Like me, Dave grew up poor. "Our family lived next door to a janitor," he told me. "The difference between him and us was that he owned his house and we rented." I felt like I'd known him all my life.

Paul and I both went to work on finding new legal counsel. By chance, Paul's mother lived in an apartment next door to a senior partner of Smith and Schnacke, the most prestigious law firm in Dayton. "Who is the top young up-and-coming attorney in your firm?" Paul asked the man during a visit to his mother. He was given Dick Chernesky's name.

Ironically, I knew about Dick. My sister had briefly worked for him before her husband asked her to quit because of the grueling hours her job required. His client list included several of the firm's largest clients and some of the largest corporations in Dayton, including Dayton Power & Light Company, as well as several large family-owned businesses. I figured if those companies trusted him to handle their legal issues, ours would be easy by comparison. I checked him out with several of my sources, including my sister, and all the feedback was positive.

Dick met me at the Lewisburg plant. "You need to know a couple of things before we decide if we're going to do business together," he said. "Number one, I used to employ your sister, and it didn't work out due to the demanding schedule. Number two, I'm going to do a legal audit of your company. You'll pay for it, and it will cost you $10,000. Once I'm done I'll decide whether I want to do business with you or not."

"Fine by me on both counts," I replied, impressed by his straightforward approach.

The fact that he required that we do a legal audit signaled that he only wanted to do business with ethical companies. The audit also would give me insight into any legal problems we might have lurking in the wings. What he told me about my sister dovetailed with her account of the events that had transpired, and I appreciated his willingness to bring a touchy subject out in the open. Dick didn't hesitate to deal with tricky issues. He had the key quality I look for in every business relationship: integrity.

I told both Dave and Dick that their first assignment as advisors was to help me figure out how to buy out Paul's half of the company. "That's easy, Clay," said Dave. "The company can buy his stock. You just need to figure out what Paul wants."

Dick, who was astounded to discover the original agreement between Paul and me existed on a single page spelling out our buy-sell arrangement in plain language, agreed there would be no legal problem with such a deal.

A quick call to Rolf Brookes confirmed what they'd said. With the company's strong performance, the bank would easily approve the deal. Both Paul and I were ecstatic. That's when I finally discovered that Paul had wanted to sell me the company all along but thought it was impossible since I didn't have much money to my name. I'd misinterpreted his resistance to discuss selling his stock as a lack of confidence in me, when it was actually due to frustration at what he saw as an insurmountable obstacle. So much for communication!

Assessing what Paul wanted for his 50 percent share was relatively easy. Dave and Dick simply asked him. As usual, Paul was Mr. Simplicity. All he wanted was a payment of at least $100,000 a year for perpetuity and a new Buick.

I balked at the Buick. I wanted to buy him a Chevy. When I told Dave, he snorted. "This conversation is one of the dumbest I've ever had with an entrepreneur," he snapped. "I've got news for you, Clay. You're not going to buy a Buick or a Chevy. You're going to buy him a Cadillac, and you're going to be happy about it. If you want that man's goodwill for the rest of your life, you'd better exceed his expectations."

I was shocked at Dave's suggestion, since he drove a Gremlin. (Later, he told me he'd vowed never to drive a better car than any of his clients.)

But I took his advice and told Paul to pick out a Cadillac. For a man who'd lived as unostentatious a life as Paul, he lit up like a marquee. Pleased as punch, he ran right down to the Cadillac dealer and drove back to the plant to show me his new cream-colored Eldorado. I guess if you're going to splurge once in your life, you'd better do it by the time you hit sixty-five!

On January 4, 1982, a week before I turned forty-one, I became the sole owner of Iams Food Company.

For more than a decade I'd dreamed about having a business I could call my own. I thought back to that day in 1970 when I began working for Paul Iams and refused to put my title on a business card. Suddenly, I began to laugh. At long last I could lay claim to a title that summed up everything I'd always envisioned: owner and CEO. Maybe it was finally time to print up business cards.

## CHAPTER 10

# Learning How to Run My Company

Paul and I agreed not to make a big deal about the buyout. There was no formal announcement of the change in command. Paul came into the Lewisburg office every day as he'd always done, and he kept his small office at Delphos Avenue as well. Marty Walker phoned the companies and distributors who needed to know, and I conducted business as usual.

I could have pretended that nothing had changed. That was a fantasy I almost toyed with, because, to be honest, I felt overwhelmed. Owning a company that was making $12.5 million in sales every year, yet was further in debt than I'd ever imagined possible, was daunting. Perhaps the most unsettling revelation of my new position was my weakness as a manager.

Even though I had made major decisions for years, I was woefully deficient when it came to understanding and implementing the principles of enlightened management. One of the reasons for this was that Paul thought the management philosophies of the day amounted to so much hot air and considered management education a waste of time. Another was that when I was still playing fire chief and putting out daily blazes at the plant, I didn't feel I could take time to attend seminars or join business networking organizations.

One evening, Mary looked at me with concern. "I've noticed that you've been very tense lately, Clay," she said. "What's bothering you?"

Suddenly I had to unload. "I'm scared to death, honey," I confessed. "I own this company, and I don't know how to run it."

"Well," Mary calmly replied, "I guess you'll just have to learn."

Shortly after this invaluable conversation, a flyer came across my desk from the American Management Association® (AMA), advertising its weeklong course for CEOs and presidents at Wigwam, a luxury resort in Carefree, Arizona. The agenda looked exactly like what I needed to learn: the basics of how to run your own company. I signed up to go with Mary, who agreed to take the accompanying course for spouses of entrepreneurs.

From the first session I was hooked. For the first time I heard others talk about how to run a company in a formalized way that made sense to me.

Along with thirty other CEOs and presidents of small entrepreneurial firms, I soaked in everything the speakers had to say. You couldn't argue with their credentials; they ranged from a bank chairman who had run his own family business in banking and oil to consultants and successful CEOs. I particularly admired the chair of the event, Gene Engelman, chairman of Texas Commerce Bank of Forth Worth, a dynamic thinker and leader whose youthful energy belied his seventy-plus age. A successful entrepreneur and family businessman in his own right, Gene exuded optimism and a great sense of humor. I'll never forget his reassuring observation: "One good thing about not planning is that if you don't know where you're going, you can't get lost!"

Gene maintained that empowered employees could make all the difference in a company's success or failure. I'd read a lot of management books, but many of the popular theories of the day appeared fatally flawed to me. They were too concerned with numbers and control. By contrast, the AMA course emphasized the need for participative management, and their consultants' ideas meshed perfectly with the vague notion I'd started developing back in 1977, shortly before we built the Lewisburg plant. When I thought about my dreams for Iams Food Company, I'd jotted down that I wanted to create a workplace where people felt respected and enjoyed being part of a mission. Most successful corporations I admired operated with an articulated set of principles. A mission-driven company is driven by those principles, not the rules, regulations, and procedures I had found so stifling during my short stint in corporate America.

I read a great deal and had begun to find my own entrepreneurial heroes to emulate. Take Ray Kroc, for example. The legendary founder of McDonald's focused on just four goals: quality, service, cleanliness, and value. He knew that if McDonald's could deliver those four simple things, success was inevitable. To make sure everyone else in the company understood the critical importance of these goals, Kroc visited his restaurants all the time. The first place he inspected during his famous unannounced visits was the restroom. He'd hit the roof, and the Golden Arches, if the restroom failed to measure up to the company's established standards of cleanliness. Next he walked around the parking lot, looking for trash and constantly monitoring things that quickly telegraphed whether that location was delivering the McDonald's promise of consistency.

Sam Walton, another one of my business heroes, flew his own plane to visit his Wal-Mart stores around the country. Walton didn't weigh down his employees with a lot of rules and regulations. In fact, he believed each store's manager understood the community far better than corporate headquarters could and, as I did with our distribution managers, Walton trusted local managers to make the right decisions for their stores. Like Ray Kroc, Sam Walton's philosophy was simple but irrefutable: Do what the customer wants. As long as a Wal-Mart employee was working to accomplish that mission, Sam was satisfied, and employees were given a great deal of leeway to do the right thing for customers.

At the AMA course, I realized my ability to take the company to the next level hinged on how well I could learn and apply six basic principles that were each covered by a different expert:

- Planning for the long term and setting objectives
- Organizing our company's structure and hiring the right people
- Maintaining control while delegating authority and responsibility
- Implementing decision management by developing plans of action

- Creating a climate to achieve a positive corporate culture
- Implementing leadership that inspired others without being autocratic

Even though I'd hired great people and given them substantial responsibility, I was used to being a one-man band. Now I was being told not just that I didn't have to do everything, but I shouldn't do everything. What an energizing revelation!

Implementing my newfound knowledge was easier said than done, however. As I've observed before, entrepreneurs are control freaks. We keep a finger in every pie, because we're always worried we'll miss out on something. That's one of the reasons so few entrepreneurs make it to the next level of professional management. They won't give anybody the responsibility to do a job, much less the authority to get the job done.

This was a critical obstacle I knew I had to overcome. As the week progressed, I made a paradigm shift. To make the transformation from a classic entrepreneur to leader of a professionally managed organization, I needed to change roles. Instead of focusing totally on making and selling our products, I needed to concentrate on building the organization and managing people within that organization. I could no longer afford to be chief salesman and marketer.

The "climate setting" facilitator introduced what was a hot concept of the day: DISC, a behavioral formula asserting that people basically fall into four quadrants:

- Dominant
- Influential
- Steady
- Compliant

Testing showed that I was a Hi-D/Hi-I, which means that I typically liked to tell people what to do and would wield my influence to get them to comply. If they didn't, I would then try to "sell" them on my idea. In other words, I was a friendly dictator, but a dictator nonetheless, with a reputation for lacking patience.

The information explaining the behavioral negatives that go along with my personality type stated that Iams employees most likely felt unsupported and undervalued by me. The test results warned that I had likely created a climate where employees waited for me to tell them what to do and then were given little feedback to let them know if their performances met my expectations. That atmosphere naturally bred frustration that would ultimately lead to discouragement.

During that week in Arizona I had to face a hard truth: The self-confidence, excessive drive, and sheer force of will that had allowed me to push Iams Food Company past incredible obstacles were the very qualities that could undermine my leadership. I needed to change my behavior and stop steamrolling my way to success. Until then, I rarely gave much thought to how my behavior affected other people. I thought of myself as a good leader, but the fact was that I rarely let other people make any key decisions. I was strangling initiative and good ideas by arrogantly assuming my way was the best way.

I could hardly wait to get back to Dayton and transform Iams, but to my surprise and disappointment, we were cautioned not to change a thing when we returned to our respective companies. Instead, we were advised to report what we'd learned to our management teams and then decide if we as a team wanted to make the vital changes necessary to become a professionally managed company. The sobering news was that the process of implementing professional management would take a minimum of three years, a tough dose of reality for an audience that was raring to go after a weeklong dose of inspiration.

The old me undoubtedly would have barreled back into Dayton, issuing marching orders. Practicing constraint and allowing others to come to their own conclusions was my first big test. As soon as I returned, I met with Marty Walker, John Polson, Rob Easterling, Jan Dinges, and Dale Lundstrom, who had taken Marty's old position as controller. I explained what I'd learned and told them to take a course for executive managers. "Go hear what I heard," I said. "Then let me know if it's something you agree we should implement."

When they returned from the course, they all agreed we should move ahead. My next step was to hire George Bickley, who had presented the planning segment of the AMA course. George worked as a management consultant and boasted an impressive client list that included Sun Trust Bank and several midsized manufacturing companies. When I checked all his references, he got rave reviews.

George charged a $20,000 retainer for the year, paid quarterly. His fee included up to three two-day sessions with our management team. If he felt that the team wasn't applying what he taught, he could fire us as a client and keep the money. If we felt we weren't getting the help we wanted, we could fire him, but his fee was nonreturnable. It sounded like a lot of money with too many one-way conditions, but I was convinced that by hiring a good consultant I could expect at least a 1,000 percent return on my investment. I've since learned that a good consultant is often worth far more than that.

I rented a conference room at the local Holiday Inn for our first two-day meeting with George. John, Marty, Dick Buchy, Rob, Jan, Dale, and I all stayed overnight so that we could spend some rare social time discussing major issues that came up during the sessions and get a taste of team-building and participative management.

At 9 A.M. sharp, George, a tall, thin man who perched on a stool and reminded me of a giant praying mantis, introduced himself as our new "vice president of heresy."

"I'll be telling you things you've probably never heard," he said, surveying us with a keen eye, "and things you've probably never wanted to hear."

George then asked us to think about our top three operating problems in doing our jobs. He wrote each problem down on a big white piece of paper and mounted it on the wall of the conference room. By the 10:30 A.M. coffee break, the walls were papered with problems. That was bad enough; what was worse was that I was smack in the middle of about 75 percent of them.

I was livid. I could feel my face flush and my jaw start to ache from clenching my teeth. Before I fired George, however, I decided to get a consensus from the others and find out if they shared my dismay. During the break, I milled around the hallway quietly gathering feedback. Everyone was enthusiastic about how much they were learning.

I was dumbfounded. My team saw the session in a completely different light. I decided that a prudent man would bite his tongue and go back for more. Returning to the session and keeping my mouth shut was the beginning of a new me.

"Ongoing problems are symptomatic of underlying weaknesses," proclaimed George from his watchful post on the stool, looking me square in the eye. I girded myself for the painful process of peeling the onion layer by layer to get to the core issues facing our company. For the next two days, we explored the company's strengths and weaknesses. George didn't pull any punches. He was brutally honest and demanded the same from us. If any of us fudged on an issue, he would catch us red-handed and call our bluff.

As layers were stripped and masks discarded, the discussions often became heated. I wasn't used to being challenged. We were in uncharted territory. Intellectually, I understood my authoritarian behavior would eventually squelch our growth. But becoming a team leader willing to listen and learn from my management team proved to be a long, slow, painful journey.

One of the biggest traps companies can fall into when they start strategic planning is that executives come up with a grand plan without a clearly designated way of integrating it into company operations. We scheduled regular review meetings to make sure everyone was on target with the strategic plan and to ensure that ours didn't wind up in an impressive-looking binder gathering dust on a shelf.

Submitting to George Bickley's regular interrogations was an exercise in productive masochism. He asked penetrating and sometimes embarrassing questions and had the unnerving habit of nailing you to the wall if you said something stupid. Although his tactics were often annoying, they served their purpose: to force us to rely upon real information instead of the gut feelings and emotions that had guided the company in the past.

One of the problems John Polson put on the table was how we handled "holds," product held because it didn't meet specifications.

"What do you do when you've run product, and you find something that indicates you're out of spec?" George asked.

"Well, we check the product, then go back to the production line and fix it," John replied.

"How much time has elapsed between the time you detect the quality problem and when you fix it?"

"About four hours."

"What happens to all the product you ran prior to discovering the problem and that you weren't certain met specifications?"

"We ship it out."

George perked up and said something that set the room on fire: "Then don't sit here and pretend you believe in quality!" he thundered. "Your priority is production, or you wouldn't ship another pound of product until you knew for sure it was in spec."

We had thought we were doing a good job on quality, but now we were caught breaking what we claimed was a core belief.

"And while we're at it," George continued relentlessly, "let's talk about housekeeping. I'm presuming you have cleanliness standards in each department. How often do you clean up a dirty area?"

"We clean it when we get a chance," said Dick Buchy.

George looked unimpressed. "If you're running this high-quality product in a dirty plant, you run the risk of sucking dirt and other foreign materials into the product."

We decided right then that whenever we discovered a problem, we would shut down the plant. We also decided to give our quality-control people *carte blanche* to do a housekeeping inspection in any department at any time. And we scheduled regular cleanup shifts throughout the week.

The new order reminded me of the unspoken lesson I'd learned from Grandpa Good and the pristine state of his tool shed. People from miles around came to him to sharpen their tools because they trusted his deep commitment to excellence.

Our new commitment sent a powerful message to our plant employees that when it came to quality, we meant business. If the product wasn't right or if the plant wasn't clean, whoever caught the problem had the authority to stop production. Every person who worked for Iams now knew that quality was more than a slogan at our company. Short term, we'd make more money shipping out product no matter what, but in the long run, taking shortcuts and skimping on quality always comes back to bite you, especially if you're banking on a healthy slice of the premium segment of the pet food market.

"What's the size of the premium dog food segment?" George asked at one point during the meeting.

"Nobody tracks those numbers," I replied, embarrassed.

George was appalled. "How on earth do you expect to plan for future growth if you don't even know how big a market we're talking about?" he exclaimed. "We can't even have an intelligent discussion without that data."

Then he posed another embarrassing question: "If you were in a management meeting at Hill's today, what do you think you'd be talking about?"

Whoops. I had violated one of the key tenets of *The Art of War*. We didn't know ourselves, and we didn't know the enemy.

Until George poked us in the ribs, we had never made a major effort to gather market information. We had no idea how much business our competitors were doing. We knew we were growing at about 20 percent a year, but we didn't know how much market share we had.

As a result of that first meeting, John Polson hired an engineering consultant to find out how big Hill's was. The consultant knew how many plants Hill's had, how many and what type of extruders the company used, the number of employees at each plant, and the approximate size of the company's finished goods warehouse.

Everyone took responsibility for coming up with information prior to the next meeting, including sales numbers, tonnage, and personnel issues. We all agreed to be accountable for our assignments. Jan began taking minutes at the strategic planning meetings and distributing them to the team before the next meeting.

When we started looking at our strengths and weaknesses, another startling fact came to light.

"Who is responsible for purchasing?" George asked. "How do you negotiate price?" Twenty-year-old Jerry Nill, who is now a manager at An-Pro, was in charge of buying all meat products for our company at a cost of $7 million a year. That meant that 60 percent of our costs was in the hands of a kid. He wasn't doing a bad job, but obviously we'd put him in way over his head. A role that represented such a significant part of our expenditures required experience. One of our new objectives became setting up a protein division and hiring or developing experienced executives who could run the operation and develop suppliers.

Still another important change came out of that meeting. With the massive hiring effort we were undertaking, we desperately needed written, fully thought-out job descriptions, along with standards of performance for each position. People have a chance to shine when they understand your expectations, but without direction they tend to flounder.

Just getting the job descriptions and requirements right turned into a two-year process that Jan and I worked on diligently.

Soon after I bought Iams, Dick Chernesky came to me with two important pieces of advice. First, as Harry Odio, my friend from Costa Rica, had done some years before, he urged me to establish a board of advisors. I'd been so busy in the trenches I had neglected to put one in place, and I assured Dick that a board would be my next priority.

But I balked at his second piece of advice.

"Clay, you've got to get a distributor agreement," he said.

"Oh, no," I shook my head. "I'm a handshake guy. I cut deals with all these distributors, and I'm going to honor my end of the bargain."

Dick was adamant. "You're going to be sorry," he warned. "Someday you'll end up in a lawsuit. You'll find yourself in court in the distributor's backyard with a local judge and no contract to back up your position. Mark my words, Clay. You're going to get hammered."

When I thought back to the horrible experience of almost losing Eukanuba because of a handshake deal, I could see the wisdom in Dick's words. Our distributors were playing a critical role in our plans for national expansion, yet they were an independent breed, and hardly any of them sold our products exclusively. In fact, the majority of their sales came from Wayne's or Hill's, not Iams products. Thank goodness I went ahead and let Dick draw up agreements defining our relationship with our distributors. Sure enough, as the years progressed, disagreements inevitably arose with some of them.

I went about putting a board together the way most entrepreneurs do: all wrong. I tapped Dick and Ralph Heyman, a senior partner in the firm Dick worked for; my friend Harry Odio, who was working in Costa Rica; and Bill Borchers, the fellow who handled the company's insurance. Of course, these men were stellar professionals, but they were also either paid consultants or friends, which almost guaranteed eventual conflicts of interest. Unwittingly, I'd made the common mistake most entrepreneurs make when they populate their boards of directors with golfing buddies, their bankers, their lawyers, and their accountants. As a result, you lose the outsider's perspective on your business that makes a board so valuable in the first place.

Nonetheless, we were on our way to becoming a truly professional outfit. We scheduled quarterly board meetings. At the first one, we tackled the issue of package color and how to make our expanding line of products more appealing to customers. Then one of the board members asked, "Who buys your products?" I was thrown for a loop. Once again, I didn't have the answer to an obvious question.

"I'll find out," I said.

We were amazed to discover that more than 70 percent of the people who purchased our products were women. We ran consumer panels to find out what colors they liked. The colors of the rainbow won out, with red, green, and yellow ranking the highest.

Iams Food Company was overdue for a radical image makeover. Along with the new packaging, the company needed a new name. I'd never liked

"Iams Food Company" because we were a pet food company. Paul put the word "food" in the name because he made both mink and dog food. He also wanted to differentiate himself from the numerous feed mills that made cheap dog food as a sideline. However, I thought the word "food" caused confusion for people who would assume we were making food products for human consumption.

When Rolf came up with the same suggestion, I set up a meeting with Stockton West Burkhart. Before we hired the agency, its young creative staff came up with impressive proposals that would greatly improve our hopelessly outdated graphics, which was my primary goal.

I told the creative team we hired, Stockton West Burkhart, that I planned to change the name of the company to The Iams Company. They immediately worked up packaging and logo changes incorporating the best elements from our old packaging: the memorable paw print and the distinctive frankfurter-type style, which had been used on the Iams Puppy materials. The repositioning called for these images to be used on our packaging across the board, giving our brands a more unified look. I loved the new look and approved the paw print as a permanent part of our logo.

During a July distribution center meeting in Lewisburg attended by the employees, our distributors, and members of Stockton West Burkhart team, I introduced the new, rainbow-colored bags: rhodamine red for Eukanuba, glossy green for Iams Chunks and Iams Mini Chunks, golden yellow for Iams Puppy Food, and orange for Iams Cat Food. All were emblazoned with the paw print. The old purple Eukanuba bags didn't bear the Iams name anywhere. Now at a glance, consumers could easily recognize that the same company produced all the products, while the packaging made it easy to differentiate the formulas.

Then I made the name-change announcement. "We're not a food company. We're a pet food company, and the old title is misleading," I said. "From now on we'll refer to ourselves as 'The Iams Company.'" After more than a quarter century in business, we had a new name, a new look, and a whole new direction. At the AMA conference, Mary and I had bonded with Jack and Laura Cobbledick, a couple from Canada. I'd told Jack, the managing director of a Toronto franchisee group, about my plans to eventually take The Iams Company international, and he'd offered to investigate the best route to introduce our products to the Canadian market.

In September, we spent the Labor Day weekend with the Cobbledicks and Darcy and Jenny Sweeney, another Canadian couple we'd met at the AMA conference. At the Sweeneys' summer home on Lake Muskoka, north of Toronto, I turned to Jack. "Why don't you consider being our distributor up here in Canada?" I suggested. At the time Wayne Pet Food dominated the Canadian premium market segment, and hardly anyone in Canada, except for hard-core dog show people who occasionally bought Iams products from our Buffalo distributor, had heard of The Iams Company. I offered to give Jack extended terms for a year, and he agreed to become our first foreign distributor.

In October, Jack opened a modest two thousand-square-foot warehouse with a truckload of food and no customers. "Don't worry," I said. "Soon people will be calling you, begging to carry these products."

On December 1, Jack called me with the grand news that he'd already met one of his goals: He'd sold his first truckload of dog food in less than a month. We had staked the Iams flag in Canada. I smiled at the sheer glee I heard in his voice.

"We're just getting started, Jack," I said. "You just wait."

CHAPTER 11

# Superstars, Stars, and Rising Stars

In that critical phase of a company's development when its product is competing with many others and risks being overshadowed in the marketplace, I can't overemphasize the importance of creating a network of strong, loyal distributors who can make the difference between moving up and going under.

We were finding the Texas market for premium dog food tough going. For one thing, Hill's Science Diet had gotten a good five-year head start on us by winning the allegiance of veterinarians and large kennels. And the Hill's product was less expensive than Iams and Eukanuba. We quickly learned that price was a big factor in the Texas market. It was small consolation that our nemesis, A.N.F., also trailed Science Diet, or that Wayne Pet Food, a once-strong competitor in the premium dog food segment, was steadily losing its grip as well.

Then we had a problem with our Texas distributor, which actually operated as a passive sub-distributor. The distributor picked up only about ten tons of Iams and Eukanuba each month with an open flatbed truck and sold it to kennels and pet stores. The company management obviously believed our products would never outsell its competitors. The last thing any company needs is a distributor who doesn't believe in its goods. You might as well shoot yourself in both feet.

At this stage, we'd made our mark from Chicago to the East. A.N.F. had demonstrated its strength in Florida and the mid-Atlantic states. The

143

Hill's Science Diet stronghold started in St. Louis and stretched to the West Coast.

The battlefield was laid out before us. Like a general sticking strategic pins on a war map, I determined the time had come to concentrate on building a national presence. Since Texas buyers were such hard sells, I picked the state as the battleground where I'd roll out the sales strategy I planned eventually to deploy throughout the country.

Our distribution system had sprung up organically over the previous decade. The more dog shows we attended, the more kennels and breeders clamored for our products. Invariably, after working those shows, we got calls from distributors wanting to represent our products.

At first I accepted whomever happened to call first. As time went on, however, I began getting on airplanes and meeting with potential distributors in person before signing them on. Knowing the vital long-term role they would play, I wanted distributors with a strong entrepreneurial spirit, who believed in our products and our emphasis on nutritional science, and who shared our love of animals.

We simply weren't comparable to cereal-based dog foods, a commodity product sold solely on price, and any distributor of our products had to understand that.

A good example of the kind of distributor I valued highly was Warren Kirkley, an excellent veterinarian who claimed a large clientele of breeders. He started out as one of our direct-ship clients in Denver, eventually becoming our largest customer in that market. A brilliant man with wide interests (he frequently judged rose festivals), Warren's knowledge of animals was astounding. Eventually, I offered him the Denver distributorship, which covered Colorado, Wyoming, and New Mexico.

We had signed a dozen or so independent regional distributors, including a few who had relationships through long-standing handshake deals with Paul. They were an eclectic group of characters. A charismatic young man represented us in six western states, including California and Hawaii. A colorful promoter who handled all of New England and eastern Canada with his Pet Nutritional Services Company. One of our earliest distributors was the partnership of Ira Slovin and Shawn Bader of Fauna Foods Corporation, which handled Manhattan and its boroughs, Long Island, and northern New Jersey. While still in their early twenties, Slovin and Bader started selling Iams in 1973 out of a cramped store on York Avenue and 59th Street, in the shadow of the Queensboro Bridge.

Our distributor in upstate New York, Andy Hmura at Gaye-Dell Pet Shop sold our products to the monks of New Skete. The monks bred and raised German shepherds to earn money, and they loved our product so much we were featured prominently in a book about the dog-breeding business written by Brother Job Evans.

One of the most rewarding aspects of building the distributor base was the personal bonding that grew out of professional relationships. For instance, Bill Smith of Lab Animal Diets and Supplies covered Buffalo and western New York state. Bill was a devoted family man whose wife Doris always insisted I stay for one of her wonderful meals when I was in town. Through the years, I developed personal friendships with many of the people who not only got our products into the marketplace but also became an integral part of the Iams mission and spirit.

While we represented as much as 90 percent of the business for most of our regional distributors, few of the sub-distributors sold our products exclusively. In fact, our products usually represented no more than 10 percent of their sales. In several markets, the sub-distributors passively took orders and paid scant attention to our products. I didn't have a problem with their lack of commitment to our products, because I believed over time we would convert their hearts and minds.

To accomplish that feat, however, I had to get even closer to them. So, I arranged a series of meetings with our independent distributors. I brought in groups that I dubbed superstars, stars, or rising stars, with the objective of getting them all to the superstar level. We spent two days brainstorming on different subject matters. I facilitated the meetings, and by the end of the two days the walls were once again papered, à la George Bickley, with strengths, weaknesses, opportunities, problems, and challenges. My purpose was to gather information about the distributors' respective markets and formulate appropriate strategies for success.

The pet food industry had started out as the stepchild of the feed industry and had experienced relatively little change in basic operations for almost half a century. In that era, most pet food distributors were small, unsophisticated mom-and-pop operations that had their roots in the feed industry and were content to conduct business in the same fashion year after year.

But by the early 1980s the pet food industry was growing up. The economy was burgeoning, and people had more money to spend. They were also becoming more aware of the importance of nutrition for their pets and were hungry for quality products and premium brands.

Although the term "yuppie" hadn't been coined yet, we recognized this new quality-oriented consumer as our ideal customer. Pet "lovership," as opposed to ownership, was on the rise. Dogs were going from the backyard to sleeping inside. Most families had a dog, often a purebred, pedigreed animal, that was treated as part of the family. We were selling to the breeders who were producing these puppies and who, in turn, were recommending our food.

A good marketer understands his target audience, and I was the prototypical Iams and Eukanuba customer. I was making good money and living in a nice house. Our family owned two pedigreed dogs, a recently acquired giant Schnauzer named Schotzie, which means "treasure" in German, and Muffy, our miniature Schnauzer. I wasn't about to feed our high-class canine "kids" any less than the best, and neither were many other owners like me.

These discriminating consumers weren't likely to shop at their local feed and seed store or buy bulky bags of generic pet food. They frequented the clean, brightly lit pet store chains, many of them franchised, that were replacing crowded, dark, and smelly pet stores run by hobbyists. We were on the crest of prevailing macro- and microeconomic factors; the trends were all converging in our favor. We had developed the right products at the right time. Now we needed to get them in front of the right customer.

I decided that working with a loose confederation of distributors wasn't getting the word out fast enough. We needed a regional sales force overlaid at each of our distribution centers. So I began hiring our own regional sales managers to oversee the sales forces.

Even though we were striving to increase sales, we were still extremely protective of our brand, which had earned a certain reputation, a mystique, if you will, in the marketplace. As a result, we never backed down on price. Back in the old days at Delphos Avenue, when potential customers would sometimes try to haggle with Paul about price, he would indignantly reply, "If you want a cheap product, go down to Landmark [the Ohio Farm Bureau stores] or Cargill. We don't sell cheap feed." Then he'd get up and show them the door.

That philosophy had been ingrained in all of us. One day, for instance, Rob got a call from the owner of Petland in Chillicothe, Ohio, the first franchised pet chain in the country and the second largest at the time. The owner had heard from the kennels supplying Petland with puppies that they were feeding Iams Puppy and Eukanuba with great success. Rob drove to the company's headquarters to meet with the owner and the buyer for the stores. The buyer asked him for a free 20-pound bag of Iams Puppy to do some test-feeding.

"We'd really like you to carry our product," Rob assured him, "but I'm not going to give it to you for free or at a discount. Iams and Eukanuba work, and we've proved that over and over. Ask any breeder."

The buyer agreed to purchase two 20-pound bags at the retail price. Two weeks later, he ordered two tons. Petland ultimately became a big Iams customer. Can you imagine calling on such an important outlet and not giving them free product? But Rob wanted Petland to know we had respect for our products. We weren't interested in just any kind of business. We were interested in the right kind of business at the right price.

When my assistant Jan went on vacation in February 1983, a young woman named Joanne Weaver filled in for her. I was, as usual, insanely busy, and Joanne kept interrupting me with batches of letters that needed to be signed. Finally, I asked her, "Joanne, how does this work usually get handled?"

"I prepare the letters, and Jan signs them," she replied.

"How many of these requests and questions do you know the answers to?"

"Oh, probably 95 percent," she answered.

"Why don't you go ahead and sign them then?"

Joanne was confused. "But what do I put for my title?" she wondered.

"Customer service," I answered.

And so our customer service department was born. It immediately became a full-time job for Joanne, and it was an important one, because we were generating a lot of sales through customer service. In fact, before long, Joanne needed to hire staff to help her.

A successful company not only talks, but listens. Our new customer service department played a key role in ferreting out what our customers were telling us. The message was, "We want someone who will be responsible for feeding and care of our dogs and cats, and we want it to be a company that will care about our pets as much as we do."

I built the business by exceeding customer expectations and delivering the best nutrition and technology available in pet food.

One day I asked Joanne, "How many times a week do you run into a situation where you have to give away a bag to satisfy a complaint?"

"Less than one or two," she replied.

We discussed offering a 100 percent satisfaction guarantee during our next planning meeting, and subsequently became the first pet food company to stand behind our products and offer to replace the product or refund a customer's money in full. Our new policy made a strong statement about our commitment to quality. Shortly after that, we became the first pet food company to put a toll-free phone number on our product bags, and we established a dialogue with our customers. In my mind, we weren't just selling dog food; we wanted to enhance the animal's life by educating the consumer.

With this approach we gave careful thought to what happened to our product after it left our plant. We needed to be sure our distributors and retailers were handling products properly, a real challenge because the industry itself was not conducive to stringent quality control.

More than once, we took the unprecedented step of pulling our product from a retail customer if the store wasn't kept clean or the retailer wouldn't pay bills on time. We expected the Iams name to be treated with respect, because we'd made quality the bedrock of our company.

Several of our distributors had warehouses in seedy neighborhoods, where rent was cheap, and they'd been in those locations for years. I drove to Detroit to meet with Stan Watkins of Watkins Brothers, a distributor Paul had done business with for many years, and noticed evidence of mice and rats all around the dirty warehouse.

"Times are changing, Stan," I told him. "Either clean up this place or move."

Stan started to make excuses about the age of his building and how the neighborhood had changed around him, but I waved him off.

"Look, you've got six months, or we're pulling the product." Stan ultimately moved his warehouse to a new place in the suburbs.

A priority for me that winter was finding the right person to run our protein division. Tom Weinkauf's name surfaced. Tom had worked in production for Doane, the nation's largest private-label dog food manufacturer. One of Doane's major customers was Wal-Mart. Tom knew low-cost manufacturing about as well as anyone in the industry.

Tom joined the company in February 1983. Strong and honest, he and John Polson worked well together. Shortly after he moved to Dayton, Tom married his longtime girlfriend Dori on a Saturday. The following Monday I had scheduled an intensive strategic planning meeting with George Bickley and had assigned Tom Peters' watershed book, *In Search of Excellence: Lessons from America's Best-Run Companies*, as required reading. Tom dutifully spent the weekend on his reading assignment. Then he holed up with the executive team at the Imperial Hotel for four days, during which none of us made calls out or accepted them unless it was an emergency. His new bride might not have appreciated that kind of dedication, but I did. Any man who could give The Iams Company priority on his honeymoon weekend deserved respect!

I viewed strategic planning as a major tool in our arsenal. As we introduced new products, built new plants, signed on new distributors, and added more retailers, strategic planning gave us a road map to ensure we had enough working capital on hand; research and development knew the priority of new products; and plant managers knew how many tons to produce.

When we hired Tom, I envisioned having him run a separate company called Protein Blending Incorporated, which would be located in Iowa, since we were using a lot of pork in our products at the time and that would put the operation near good supply sources. So at the first planning meeting he attended, I asked Tom to put together a business plan for the proposed new venture.

During the meeting, I announced a five-year plan for $100 million in sales, up from our current $32 million. Tom later asked John if he thought my numbers were right.

John replied, "If Clay says it will happen, he might miss it by a year or two, but he'll make it happen."

I spent my forty-second birthday saying goodbye to my mother, who died two weeks after Christmas of advanced pancreatic cancer.

Losing Mom hit me hard on two levels. First, having her taken away when she had just begun to enjoy life was terribly painful. My parents had finally started to travel, wintering in Hanes City, Florida, and seeing us frequently during the rest of the year. Mom loved to have the grandkids underfoot, and sometimes we spent the weekend at the farmhouse where I grew up.

Second, I was just starting to be successful, and I felt cheated of the opportunity to share the fruits of my labor with this proud, ambitious woman who had loved me with such fierce devotion and had used sheer will to propel me toward the American Dream. I was grateful that she'd seen me get this far but devastated that she wouldn't be here to share the joys, struggles, and triumphs of the important years ahead.

When Woodrow Wilson's beloved father Joseph died, his forty-six-year-old son wrote, "It has quite taken the heart out of me to lose my lifelong friend and companion. I feel a great emptiness. No generation exists ahead of me. I am now directly in the line of fire." It is painfully true that as long as our parents are alive, we somehow feel insulated from mortality. Three years later, I lost my father as well, forcing me to take stock of my life and my priorities.

> *It has quite taken the heart out of me to lose my lifelong friend and companion. I feel a great emptiness. No generation exists ahead of me. I am now directly in the line of fire.*
>
> WOODROW WILSON

My mother's death left an aching void inside me. And yet, from the pain came a renewed sense of purpose, to become all that I could be for her.

Clay, left; Bruce Byrnes, center, with Procter & Gamble; and Tom MacLeod celebrated the company sale at a Dayton, Ohio, press conference on August 11, 1999.

At the time of the company sale to Procter & Gamble, the Iams board of directors included, front, from left, Cathy Volker, Clay Mathile and Dave Phillips; back, from left, Pete Rhodes, Daryl Schaller, Tom MacLeod, Lorne Waxlax and George Weigand. When Weigand retired from the board, Allen Hill, CEO of Dayton Power & Light, took his position.

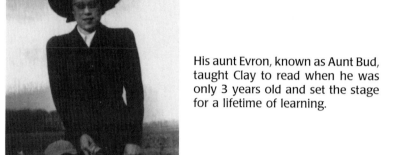

His aunt Evron, known as Aunt Bud, taught Clay to read when he was only 3 years old and set the stage for a lifetime of learning.

Clay's mother's family had a strong influence on his early life. From left, Ahi Good, Clay's uncle; Pauline Winter, Clay's aunt; John Edward Lee Good, Clay's grandfather; and Helen Mathile, Clay's mother.

As a child, Clay divided his time between school and working hard with his family on the farm. Perhaps his empathy for animals began there.

Clay and Mary, dressed for a special high school dance. Clay announced plans to marry Mary on their second date.

Clay and Mary were married on July 7, 1962, in Custar, Ohio. Clay was an accountant with General Motors in Toledo, Ohio, earning a monthly salary of $450.

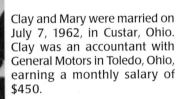

Clay's mother returned to college to earn a four-year degree in education.

Early Iams manufacturing facilities were utilitarian and little different from other small pet food manufacturing sites at the time.

An unlikely partner for Clay, Paul Iams proved to be a valuable mentor, sharing Clay's sense of integrity and committment to excellence.

The unique pink-and-green Iams product bags were becoming well known throughout the pet food industry in the mid-1970s.

A portable, inexpensive trade show space was used extensively in the 1970s to promote Iams products. Rob Easterling (with glasses) and Paul Iams manned the booth.

The tenacity of a Wenger company salesperson convinced Clay to upgrade extruding capabilities, which significantly improved Iams manufacturing results.

The Lewisburg, Ohio, plant, a 25,000-square-foot facility, opened October 12, 1978, after several construction delays.

Developing a respectful, positive, sharing climate for all Iams employees was part of Clay's mission.

With a new role in Iams, Clay took a deeper look into his own beliefs about how a business should be run. It was a precursor to his later interest in entrepreneurial education.

Targeting the Cornhusker State for manufacturing expansion, The Iams Company built a new plant outside Aurora, Nebraska, in 1984.

Moving the home office to the first floor of an existing complex at 7250 Poe Avenue in Dayton supported Clay's growth strategy for his blossoming company. Before long, Iams had taken over the entire complex and began adding on, as shown here.

Iams product display racks were among the first in the industry and were designed to attract consumers to the broad range of products.

The Iams Way became synonymous with quality and a strong sense of mission, all aimed at helping America's dogs and cats.

The Paul F. Iams Technical Center, a $5 million facility, fulfilled a dream for Clay and Paul Iams.

# C.E.O.'s Corner

Clay Mathile introduced Iams University to employees, urging them to never stop learning.

## SCHOOL WITHOUT WALLS

You have undoubtedly noticed the increased activity in the training programs being offered at our Company over the past two years. The last issue of the Iams Times carried an entire page of training classes for the first half of 1989.

I see this as the beginning of what we are calling Iams University. This has been a vision of mine to have a university without walls; a system of education that provides outreach training for all our associates, our distributors, our retailers, our supportive influencers and our customers.

The future depends on knowledge and enhanced skills to meet and master change. Iams University will be able to provide a great deal of the knowledge and skill base that will be required.

We all need to remind ourselves that our individual education never stops. It will be up to each of us to use this resource to grow and keep pace with the times.

*C. H. Mathile*

Iams University continued to expand its offering for employees in all areas of the company.

A new $25 million plant in Henderson, North Carolina, was designed to manufacture products for sale in Europe. Work on the new facility began in 1989.

**Mission**

To enhance the well-being of dogs and cats by providing world-class quality foods.

**Beliefs**

Culture
Customer
Products
People

**Goals**

Double Sales
Maintain Quality
Earnings

**The Iams Company Vision**

Pawprint recognized as the world leader in dog and cat nutrition. ·
Remain privately owned.

**Strategies**

Improve Core Products
New Products
International Growth
Improve Efficiencies

By 1993, Iams pushed distributors to carry only Iams products.

Iams always put on the ritz for its distributors. The annual national sales meeting with distributors was a highly anticipated event. This group met at Amelia Island in 1992.

Raising awareness of Eukanuba products in mainstream marketing in the early 1990s gave Iams two strong brand names and offered pet owners two lines of premium pet foods with many product choices.

Kramer, a rescued bassett hound, became an ambassador, accompanying his owner, Tom MacLeod, to many events and adding humor and personality to his company appearances.

You and Your Dog and Your Cat were launched in 1994 and celebrated the relationship between owners and their pets.

The Iditarod race brought much exposure for Eukanuba when it was reported that the champion musher, Rick Swenson, fed his dogs the premium dog food.

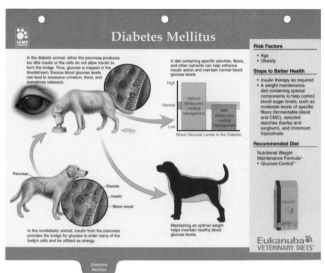

After many years of competing against Hill's, Iams introduced its first in a series of veterinary diets in 1994, offering answers to specific health issues.

Clay often sought insight and guidance from family business expert, Dr. Léon Danco.

The Iams International Nutrition Symposium, first held in 1996, helped make The Iams Company a partner with other researchers to develop better nutrition for animals.

When Iams celebrated its 50th year, the company kicked off a yearlong anniversary bash at the annual sales meeting in Hawaii. A highlight of the celebration was the presence of Jane and Paul Iams, shown here with Clay and Mary.

The Iams team, including employees around the world, were the power behind the company's success.

## CHAPTER 12

# New Horizons at Aurora

W e were running out of capacity at the Lewisburg plant, and it was happening faster than I had ever imagined. I originally thought Lewisburg would fill our needs for at least a decade. Now the two extruders were pumping out product around the clock.

Expanding the existing plant, however, wasn't an option, due to the lack of city sewage lines and our ongoing problems with water supply. Besides, we were shipping more and more product west, and a new site in that direction would yield substantial savings on freight costs. I commissioned a study to determine the best location for a new plant.

Lewisburg is located on the eastern edge of the Corn Belt, where all the raw materials that go into our products are produced. The price of corn and other feed grains is based on the freight-on-board commodity price in Chicago. At Lewisburg our cost for grains was slightly less than the Chicago commodity price.

The study showed that if we built a plant at the western edge of the Corn Belt, closer to our finished goods source, we could purchase ingredients for even less than what they cost to purchase in Lewisburg. Plus, being eight hundred miles closer to our regional distributor in California would save us about $1 a mile on shipping costs.

Eight hundred dollars in savings per truckload adds up quickly. We figured we'd soon be shipping 75,000 tons west, which would be 3,750 truckloads (20 tons per truck). That would mean $3 million in freight savings a year by shipping from a plant farther west.

Building a new plant is a massive undertaking. Constructing one in a new location would cost $10 million for construction and another $5 million for equipment. I was sweating bullets; $15 million was roughly equal to the book value of our entire company.

I called John Polson into my office. "There are only two people in this company who can do this new project: you and me," I said. "I cannot go, and I cannot afford any mistakes on this one. I bet the farm once, and now I'm betting it again on this new plant. How would you feel about moving west?"

After talking to his wife, John took the job. Before he accepted his new assignment, however, he issued a couple of conditions. "You've got to promise me you'll stay out of my hair," he said.

"No problem," I said, making a silent pledge to myself to put a lid on my dictatorial tendencies. "I trust you to do this project."

"Okay. Next thing: Don't nickel-and-dime me. I'll bring it in under budget, but I don't want to constantly be justifying every expenditure along the way."

"Fair enough," I nodded. "You'll have everything you need. I want this new plant to be state of the art." Satisfied, John immediately started laying the groundwork for our most ambitious project to date.

With his new title of vice president of western operations, John, along with Dick Buchy, scouted out potential sites in the four states the study had recommended. John also assigned Dick the task of visiting and interviewing several general contractors. Dick found a family-owned company called Todd and Sargent in Ames, Iowa, that had built a number of impressive facilities. Lee Sargent, a son of one of the founders, was a good engineer, as well as honest and professional. We began a long relationship with Todd and Sargent, who ended up building all our other U.S. plants and continually updating all our facilities.

Nebraska's professionally run and well-organized Office of Economic Development offered John and Dick a generous package of incentives well suited to a company our size. The office had put together a program that showcased a collection of what it called "All Nebraska Cities." Each of these rural towns met standards that made them attractive to prospective companies and had assembled additional incentives, aside from those offered by the state itself, to encourage industry to set up shop.

I'm sure by now you've figured out that neither John nor I like unions. If you're running your company properly and doing the right thing by your workers, you don't need a union. We wanted our new plant to be located in a right-to-work state, which kept Nebraska in the running.

So we zeroed in on the Cornhusker State. Now we just needed to decide which of its towns would be the best match for us.

John and his hand-picked plant management team flew to Nebraska to visit four potential sites: Aurora, Central City, Hastings, and Kearney. Since I was asking these men and their families essentially to turn their lives around and relocate to an entirely new environment, the town we chose needed to be a place where they would feel most comfortable. Likewise, John and I had chosen the team members not only for their skills, but also with an eye to how they would fit into a community. Our plan called for our employees to plant deep roots in the town we selected, as well as to transplant the family-oriented Iams culture to Nebraska.

Whereas most manufacturers hire a construction group to build a plant with no input from operations, we took a radically different approach. Operations people are rarely afforded the opportunity to take part in the design-and-build process because most manufacturers are unwilling to shell out the cash that involvement requires. So operations people are forced to make do with designs created by people who have never run plants. Not surprisingly, manufacturers frequently encounter problems once a plant starts up.

To avoid that hazard, we took some of our best people out of their regular positions at Lewisburg and committed them to the new plant project a full year before we produced a single bag of dog food there. Starting with the site selection, our team slated to run the plant was involved in every aspect of building the new facility and getting it up and running. That strategy represented approximately a $500,000 commitment of resources, but after the $1 million or so worth of mistakes I'd made with

Lewisburg, I was determined to do things right. Although it represented a steep upfront expenditure, putting the operations people on-site would ensure the plant layout was workable and the equipment operated properly as it was being installed. I knew this would save us money in the long run. Penny-wise and pound-foolish is no way to run a business; whatever you have to spend to do the job right will pay off in the end.

John and his team narrowed the potential towns down to three and kept their top choice a secret. The team and I flew out and met with officials in each of the three towns.

I was enchanted with Aurora, a quiet, tidy town with a courthouse square, tree-lined streets, and turn-of-the-century Victorian houses. Settled by Germans and Scandinavians, Aurora brought back memories of my German ancestry, as well as the German influence on the Ohio farming communities. Here was a place where hard work and belief in the Great American Dream was very much alive and well.

The deciding factor for me, however, was Aurora's progressive leadership. "We're losing our native sons to Lincoln and Omaha," Ken Wortman, an upbeat local entrepreneur and community spark plug, told me at our first meeting. "We are seeking a partner who will enable us to win back our young people. We have great schools and a great community, but we don't have anything to keep our youth here."

I liked the forthright nature and the energy level of this small, genial man who, although he was close to retirement age, gave no sign of slowing down. Ken owned the local Ford dealership and the neat-as-a-pin motel where we were staying. He also owned a weighty Rolodex containing phone numbers for everyone from the state's governor and Nebraska's U.S. senators to the CEO of the electric company, and he didn't hesitate to make use of his connections on our behalf.

Along with Chamber of Commerce President Donna Rasmussen; Phil Nelson, owner of the local telephone company; Gary Warren, a local attorney and president of Aurora Economic Development Corporation; Paul Kemling, chairman of the county commissioners; and Bud Pence, a real estate developer, Ken laid out a plan that thoroughly addressed our needs, down to the most intricate details.

For instance, Gary helped us take advantage of an agricultural variance in the price of natural gas. Local farmers got a price break on the natural gas they used to pump water for irrigation. Paying the agricultural price instead of the higher industrial rate would mean significant savings, since we would be using natural gas in the drying process for pet food.

We certainly got the royal treatment. The political leadership, school administrators, local newspaper editor, business leaders, and hospital administrator all banded together to woo us. Local farmers also welcomed us, because our presence yielded another local outlet for a portion of the millions of bushels of corn produced annually in Hamilton County where Aurora is located.

Their collective excitement and civic pride electrified us.

The ultimate success of any business depends to a great degree on how well it gets along with the community.

When we began manufacturing Eukanuba at Lewisburg, we were forced to run a second shift at night to produce the other Iams products. During the summer in that part of the country, many people didn't have air conditioning, so folks left their windows open. One fellow wrote a letter to the editor complaining about the stench coming from our plant, a decidedly unwelcome visitor on hot, humid summer nights. Soon citizen groups got involved and angry newspaper editorials began appearing with alarming regularity.

We had to figure out a way to scrub the air to eliminate odors. I'd never even heard of odor-scrubbers before we started getting complaints. Now we had to do some fast backpedaling. We researched the problem and installed odor-scrubbers in the plant to remove the smell, assuring the community I'd do whatever I could to eliminate the problem. The incident made me resolve to become a known factor in Lewisburg. I made it clear I was open to complaints and suggestions, and I helped form Lewisburg's first chamber of commerce. Eventually, the people of the community learned that they could trust The Iams Company to be a good neighbor and corporate citizen.

After getting off on the wrong foot in Lewisburg, I wanted to be absolutely certain that we'd be welcomed with open arms in Aurora. Local business and political leader support was obviously important, but just as critical to me were three other components:

- *Media support.* From the Lewisburg experience, I had learned the hard way about the power of the printed word and the importance of public opinion. I wound up having to devote a great deal of time and energy to rebuilding community relations and establishing trust with townspeople in the wake of negative publicity that all started with one disgruntled man's letter to the editor.

- *Health care system.* If we were going to be the main employer in town, I wanted to be certain our people had access to excellent health care. Though small, Aurora had a modern and well-staffed hospital and helicopter service to Lincoln for cases beyond local medical capabilities.

- *School system.* Our future workforce would be products of the local schools, so having good education available was important to me. We needed smart people to run sophisticated machinery. Aurora's schools were ranked among the best in Nebraska.

One sticky issue, however, was sewage. We asked the community to supply us with a city sewer inlet at the site, which was 4.5 miles west of town. Unfortunately, Aurora didn't have any sewer lines that extended that far, and the town leaders were reluctant to extend them. Finally, our staunch supporter Ken Wortman found a government grant that would supply half the funds for the Aurora Economic Development Corporation to run a sewer line adjacent to the selected plant site. The development group planned to develop the land in the future, and the grant would allow it to hook up existing businesses in its local industrial park.

The proposed 20-acre site for the plant and infrastructure meshed perfectly with our needs. In addition, a railroad track and Interstate 80 both ran near the potential site, which would aid us in transporting ingredients and shipping finished goods. The farming community's population of 4,200 could readily supply the 100-person workforce we estimated we'd need. I decided that even with the $80,000 price tag of the land, Aurora matched what I envisioned for our new plant.

Aurora was my management team's first choice as well. But one final step needed to be taken before we signed the deal. We invited Aurora's civic leaders to come to Lewisburg to see our facility and assess its impact on the community firsthand. We flew them in and hosted them for two days while they spoke with local suppliers, toured the facilities, and got to know our employees. I wanted the leadership of Aurora to understand fully our commitment to good corporate citizenship. Never again did I want to go through the horrible experience of making an investment in a community where we weren't welcome.

With a new plant coming online to guarantee us plenty of capacity, I turned my attention back to strengthening relationships with our independent distributors, some of whom had gotten too independent. As we established a national presence, I wanted our brands to be represented in a cohesive manner and our message to be consistent. But some of our regional distributors were behaving as if the products were theirs.

The most problematic was an energetic, creative, and enthusiastic distributor from the East. He was a flamboyant promoter, he produced all his own marketing and advertising materials for our products. He was even excited to wear a dark pink shirt and dark pink corduroy pants that matched the rhodamine red of the Eukanuba bags, undoubtedly a fashion first.

One day in 1983, he called me to announce he'd found a distributor in Germany, Helmut Grönemeyer, who wanted to take on Eukanuba and Iams products. He planned to meet with Grönemeyer in Frankfurt at the Sieger Show, a premiere show for German shepherds held each September.

When I mentioned the plan to Mary, who comes from German ancestry, she gave her characteristically on-target assessment: "I think you'd better go to that show yourself, Clay. He is great at what he does, but the Germans tend to be much more conservative in their approach. I have a feeling they aren't going to like his flashy style."

I contacted the Berlitz folks in Dayton, and they set me up with a translator, Lottie von Fahnestock, who happened to belong to our church. When we arrived at the show in Frankfurt, our distrubutor had already set up a large booth and was hawking our samples like a carnival barker. In his blinding attire, he looked conspicuous amid the conservative Germans.

After listening to the reactions of the Germans who were coming by the booth, Lottie quietly told me our distributor was not making a good impression. In fact, the Germans were completely turned off by his theatrical approach.

It got worse. Because it was the rainy season, our distributor had ordered some yellow-colored ponchos, emblazoned with the Iams paw print. Sure enough, late that afternoon it started raining cats and dogs. People snapped up those ponchos, paying five deutsche marks.

The ponchos developed cracks right around the logo and started leaking. Before long our booth was surrounded by wet, angry Germans demanding their money back. It looked like our grand introduction to the European marketplace was an unmitigated disaster. However, we shipped 210 tons of products to Germany the next year.

Although I admired our distributor's drive and spunk, it was time to establish our own international capabilities. We gradually eased him out of the equation, and I gave the job of negotiating all the ins and outs of shipping product overseas to a young woman named Joy Cagle, who had been an executive assistant in sales and marketing and who had handled international shipping for her previous employer.

Like so many early Iams hires, she rose to the challenge.

The other fortuitous connection that resulted from my attendance at the show was with Lewis Tan, a German shepherd importer and breeder from Singapore. After the show, Lewis contacted me about direct shipping to Singapore. Joy sent him twenty tons, and by the next year, he ordered fifteen times that amount. I realized that if our products could transcend the initial international fiasco, we were even better off than I thought.

Bob Bardeau, the fellow we'd first approached for what turned out to be John Polson's position, had grown disenchanted at Wayne Pet Food. For several years he'd been calling John, asking for a job. On November 1, 1983, I finally hired him as our new quality manager.

John assigned Bob the task of managing the formulas for our products. At the time, I would enter each formula on the company's sole computer, which was in my office. I kept track of the pricing and ingredients on that computer and was, for all intents and purposes, the entire Iams R&D department.

Because so many changes were afoot, John felt it was crucial to let the plant workers know what was going on throughout the company. In December of 1983, he and his assistant, Connie Patterson, published the first edition of *The Iams News.* Volume 2 of the newsletter appeared in February 1984 and was called *The Iams Times.* The following month, John and the team moved out to Aurora. The final plans for the fast-track project required engineering on the fly, because we needed to be up and running quickly. For a nominal fee Aurora gave John the use of the chamber of commerce office on the backside of the barbershop in the heart of town. Remember Andy Griffith's Mayberry, where Floyd's Barbershop was the center of all activity, political, economic, and social? You get the picture.

Our first Aurora hire was Teresa White as a secretary. As of 2006, she's still with the company at Aurora. We also started looking for our first production crew and professionals we would need in accounting.

Aurora's business leaders continued to come through in a pinch. One of the many challenges we faced was sourcing the wooden pallets that held dog food during shipping. Trees are in short supply in Nebraska, and we soon discovered that no one for miles around produced wooden pallets. Local businessman Bud Pence took up the challenge and started a small manufacturing company to produce wooden pallets to supply us.

Sadly, I missed the groundbreaking ceremony for Aurora on May 8, 1984, because Mary's father passed away that weekend after a yearlong struggle with cancer. Losing him and my mother within such a short time span hit me hard and took some of the joy out of our Aurora success.

The Aurora groundbreaking stood in marked contrast to the low profile we'd kept while building the Lewisburg facility. Nebraska's lieutenant governor and several people from the Nebraska Economic Development Agency joined the celebration with Iams employees and their spouses. The local media turned the spotlight on us. We felt like celebrities and, indeed, we had finally come out of the shadows and into the glare of pet food fame. Until then, Iams had flown under the radar. Nobody really took us seriously; I was viewed as the nutty guy who charged double what everybody else was charging for a bag of dog food. There was no way for competitors to know how big we really were, since our retail sales didn't go through grocery stores, which reported that data. Because we were privately held and had never tapped into the financial community to fund our growth, no information was available through those sources either.

Our little metal building in Lewisburg had cut an inconspicuous figure. But once we started pouring Aurora's concrete towers, which reached one hundred feet into the sky on that flat land, our competitors jumped up, rubbed their eyes, and began to take notice. We were building our second plant in five years, an impressive multimillion-dollar project, and suddenly the hunt was on for any scrap of information about Iams. It was like wartime espionage; our competitors even went so far as to send planes overhead to take pictures of progress at the plant site.

I had kept my promise to John Polson not to interfere in the Aurora operations. But late that summer, the suspense got to me. Using the excuse that I wanted to show Mary the progress on the new plant, I flew out with her unannounced and drove out to the site. Dick Buchy proudly showed us around, and we chatted for a little while before heading into town, where John had his office.

John registered no surprise at seeing Mary and me. When I started telling him what he needed to be doing with the project, however, he quietly replied, "Clay, you sent me out to do this job. I think you'll be pleased with it when we finish, and if you aren't, you can replace me."

That was a tough one to swallow, but Mary chimed in, "You said you were going to let him do his thing, Clay. John expects you to hold your end of the bargain."

Shortly before 4 P.M., John stood up and shook my hand. "Well, Clay, I've got a meeting," he said. "It's been nice seeing you and Mary."

Feeling like I'd just been handed my hat and shown the door, I realized I wasn't used to being on the other side of the desk. Out on the sidewalk, I grumbled to Mary, "I thought we'd at least go to dinner."

Mary just laughed. "John's independent. You've got to give him the opportunity and let him run this show. I have a feeling you won't regret it."

Everyone worked feverishly to get Aurora operational before the end of the year. If we could ship product by December 31, we would receive a $500,000 investment tax credit. The pace was even more frantic because this plant was the first one John and his team had constructed, and it was the first pet food manufacturing plant the contractor had built, too.

Of course, there was a last-minute hitch. The natural gas lines weren't laid in time, so the dryer would not operate. John worked his way around that by air-drying the product. Thanks to the Herculean efforts of John's new crew at Aurora, we qualified for the tax credit. They managed to produce just enough product on New Year's Eve to ship, invoice, and receive payment. John brought the project in on time and under budget, a remarkable feat.

Around that time, I got a call from Hill's chief financial officer. At Hill's annual planning meeting, management had suddenly realized the company was going to be out of capacity by the following year. Our growth rate and Hill's were neck-and-neck at that time, but while we were working with a five-year plan, our rival only did annual planning.

"Our president would like to see you," said the CFO.

The president of Houston-based Rivianni Foods, then Hill's Pet Nutrition's parent company, was a pleasant man who wanted to purchase The Iams Company and, with it, the enticing plant capacity at Aurora.

I politely declined his offer. He asked if we might be interested in co-packing for Hill's. "Not a chance," I replied. What I didn't tell him was that even with the tremendous capacity boost from Aurora, the new plant was still going to be starting up under a load. Our West Coast distributor was slated to sell a sizable quantity of our products in the new year.

That marked the first of many offers from rival companies looking to buy me out. It looked like The Iams Company had finally come of age.

## CHAPTER 13

# It's All About the People

N o matter what business you're in, one cardinal rule always applies: Ultimately, it's all about people.

A company is its employees. At Iams, I was immensely proud of what our group of 150 workers, many of them young and inexperienced and only a few with college degrees, had accomplished. I often joked that we had more in common with mutts than with purebred show dogs.

In one way, however, we did resemble a purebred. Like a Great Dane puppy, we were growing very large, very fast. And any time a company experiences a huge growth spurt, it has to contend with the growing pains that go along with it. As The Iams Company acquired a new plant and faced overwhelming new demands in every area of operations, the employees experienced a crisis in morale. We were so preoccupied with the sheer volume of information bombarding us from Aurora, Lewisburg, Delphos Avenue, and a new Dayton home office that we barely had time to assimilate the barrage of paper, much less manage the information in a coherent and timely manner. As a result, we simply couldn't give the employees at each plant the attention they needed to get them through this critical phase in our development.

But as George Bickley reminded us at our planning meeting, "The people who are the hands-on doers and make the company run are just as important as the managers." The last thing we could afford was to lose our employees' enthusiasm, faith, and trust. As the Aurora plant swung into operation, we faced three crucial tasks: managing a vastly increased information flow, handling the staggering production demands of a rapidly expanding business, and becoming better managers for a better company.

By the time 1985 rolled around we were bursting out of our corporate offices at Lewisburg. We had twice expanded the metal building, known as "The Hill," and there was nowhere left to grow.

In February 1985, a staff of twenty-three, including me, moved into our new offices at 7250 Poe Avenue in the Dayton suburb of Vandalia, ten miles from Lewisburg and conveniently located just off Interstate 70, five miles from the Dayton airport.

Moving my office to Dayton was part of our growth strategy. With Aurora coming online, I was concerned that having the corporate office at the Lewisburg plant could make the workers at the new plant somehow feel second-class. But I realized that leaving the Lewisburg plant workers behind would likely be traumatic for them and for me. After all, many of those folks had fought valiantly in the foxhole alongside me during the plant's construction and the wild early skirmishes with our competitors. I felt extremely close to my troops and genuinely enjoyed strolling down the hill from my office and walking around talking to people in the plant.

Losing that daily personal contact was going to be tough.

I instructed the staff to refer to the new and purposely unpretentious corporate headquarters as the "home office." I thought that sounded warmer and less pompous. Because I'd worked side by side with employees in the plant, I never wanted them to think we were getting too big for our britches.

Even with this forethought, shortly after our move to Poe Avenue, I caught wind of some grumbling from a handful of Lewisburg workers who had been especially close to me. They were concerned Iams was going "too corporate" and worried that bureaucracy couldn't be far behind. Losing John Polson to Aurora and me to Dayton was a double-whammy for the Lewisburg team. In the workers' minds, leadership at the plant had evaporated.

Although Tom Weinkauf was given ultimate responsibility for both the Lewisburg and Delphos plants as vice president of eastern operations,

I had given John Polson and Tom the additional heavy responsibility of overseeing our four distribution centers in the west and four centers in the east, respectively. That meant both men were forced to leave day-to-day operations of the plants to others.

My purpose in giving John and Tom extra duties was to get our costs at the distribution centers back in line. The centers were having a tough time showing a profit because distributors cherry-picked the best accounts, leaving the centers to act more as service centers. I knew John and Tom could control our costs at those centers because they were stronger managers than those I had in sales at the time.

Indeed, within eighteen months John and Tom helped the distribution centers improve from losing 3 cents on every sales dollar to making 3 cents on the dollar.

John named Lyle Fangman, a former production manager at Ralston Purina, as his plant manager in Aurora. Tom chose Roy Gobbett, who had been the production manager under John, as the new plant manager for Lewisburg. The troops at Lewisburg were already chafing under the new leadership, and the fact that the new plant manager had a very different management style than John's or mine exacerbated the situation. Whereas John rarely blew his cool and I'd forged a strong emotional bond with the employees, Lewisburg's new plant manager focused solely on results. He was excellent at handling technical aspects of the plant but short on people skills and tended to scream and yell when something went wrong.

We also hit a stall with the full-fledged opening of Aurora. After the sprint to produce food prior to the December 31 deadline for the tax-credit eligibility, we found it would be a full three months before the natural gas lines were properly installed at the plant.

At the same time, the Lewisburg plant had been laboring under tremendous pressure, taking on extra volume while the Aurora plant was under construction and ramping up to capacity. For months Lewisburg had been open seven days a week with three shifts operating around the clock. In September Tom approached the workers with a stunning directive: Turn out five thousand tons of product each month. Since that's what the plant had been producing quarterly, it amounted to a 300 percent increase in production. The Lewisburg crew heroically rose to the challenge, shattering previous production and profitability records throughout that fall and early winter.

Despite the intense pressure on the Lewisburg plant, the commitment to quality never flagged. That September, trucks were lined up outside the plant waiting for product when the hourly lab check showed the latest run was 0.02 percent out of spec on the high side in protein content. The new management could easily have put forth a good argument for releasing the product. Instead, they put the product on hold and set the tone for the entire campaign, sending a powerful message to the whole company that when it came to quality, we weren't going to step out of bounds, no matter how great the pressure or temptation.

Traditionally, we closed the Lewisburg plant for four days over Thanksgiving because a number of the workers liked to go hunting. As Thanksgiving drew near, however, it became apparent the shutdown would be impossible. With 87 distributors clamoring for our products nationwide, we could ill-afford a situation that forced us to go on product allocation again. When Tom broke the grim news to the workers, there was silence. Finally, one young man asked, "Would it be okay if we at least take Thanksgiving Day off?" That's the kind of dedication the Lewisburg workers had. By the first of the year, the plant had produced 832 tons that we didn't even have orders for yet. Almost unbelievably, we were ahead of the game. For the first time in our company's history, product supply and demand were in harmony.

Then, on February 14, 1985, the Lewisburg plant received a decidedly unwelcome Valentine's Day present: a ferocious blizzard. Subzero temperatures and treacherous roads covered by snowdrifts prevented third- and first-shift employees from relieving the second shift. Six second-shift employees, Gary Manof in maintenance; Bret Weldy, a mill operator; Dan Garretson, an extruder operator; Jerry Sturgell, a packaging operator; Jim

Sizemore, a lab technician; and Doug Fox, the shift supervisor, volunteered to stay and keep the plant running to avert a shortage.

Tom Mullis, one of the second-shift volunteers who had gone home to check on his family, returned to bring the hungry crew sandwiches midway through their ordeal. He made part of the trip on foot after his truck slid off the highway, braving knee-deep snow and vicious, icy winds.

The dauntless skeleton crew worked thirty hours straight until they ran out of room to store product. Only then did they shut down the plant. Plenty of product was waiting once the six-foot snowdrifts blanketing our drive were cleared away and trucks rolled in again two days later. The record-setting blizzard put a punctuation point on all the pressure Lewisburg was already experiencing in its valiant attempt to meet demanding production schedules.

Physical separation from long-time leaders and the unrelenting work schedule took their toll, however. For the first time in our company's history, morale at the Lewisburg plant began to suffer. Aurora had been a colicky infant, and symptoms of sibling rivalry were evident. The oldest was jealous of all the attention the new baby was getting. We decided to hold an open house at Lewisburg to bolster morale and reach out to the community. To prepare for the event, we cut back on production and gave the Lewisburg crew a rest. Then we tackled some overdue maintenance and spruced up the place with a fresh coat of paint.

We threw a catered barbeque, and for the first time workers were allowed to bring their families to the plant. I made the rounds, personally thanking everyone for the hardships they'd endured and congratulating them on the 300 percent production increase. John Polson came back for the occasion and expressed his gratitude to the Lewisburg team for shouldering the lion's share of the load so he could get the Aurora plant up and running.

One of the most moving moments for me that day was my dad's reaction to the event. He just stood there silently, taking it all in. Finally, toward the end of the party, he pulled me aside and said huskily, with tears in his eyes, "I wish your mother could have seen this, son. She would have been so proud." That was the closest my father ever came to praising my accomplishments, and it was all the more poignant because he had recently been diagnosed with leukemia and would soon be gone. I thank God that he lived to witness this milestone in my life and to express his pride in me at last.

Just before the move to Poe Avenue, we decided to plunge into the computer age. If we were going to meet the aggressive goals I'd set, we desperately needed to get automated. Bob Bardeau and I used a clunky computer to keep track of product formulas, and May Gilman, the plant secretary, ran another monstrosity to enter and track orders. Beyond that, no one at Iams had access to a computer.

I hired Les Pitstick, a former IBMer, who came to us from NCR Corporation, and our first executive with an MBA, to oversee our first major investment in computer systems. In those days, purchasing a computer system was a crapshoot. Not only did we have to determine which system would operate without the constant shutdowns that plagued the early machines, but we also had to sort through the options and hope we had chosen the one that could grow with our company.

At the same time, we hired the consulting firm Arthur Andersen to help find the best solution for our data processing needs. Les worked with the folks at Arthur Andersen and simultaneously facilitated both the move to Poe Avenue and installation of our first full-fledged computer system. Many companies tried to write their own software with varying degrees of success, but Les wisely chose to purchase an out-of-the-box system from J.D. Edwards. Within a few months accounting and sales were computerized with remarkably few bugs.

I soon promoted Les to vice president of administration because he impressed me as one of those go-to guys capable of handling just about any job I sent his direction. He never let me down, and I'll always be grateful to him for the many ways in which he improved our company.

My biggest struggles early in the strategic planning process came under the heading of "people issues." I am by nature a paternal leader, and I was still striving to figure out how to lead without being dictatorial.

Even though I wanted the company to be professionally managed, The Iams Company really operated as a family business on two levels. First and foremost, I was building the business for my wife and children, and the kids routinely spent summer breaks working at the Lewisburg plant.

Iams also was a family business in the sense that I sought to create a family atmosphere for our employees. Professional management and family-style management aren't necessarily mutually exclusive, but combining the best of both worlds takes a good deal of skill.

Overseeing a major computer system installation, Les Pitstick was the first company employee with an MBA.

I had grown frustrated with our inability to fully communicate and push the planning down to the next level of the company. Once again, I received an opportune invitation from the American Management Association to attend a series of roundtable discussions with other CEOs. The first night in Pinehurst, North Carolina, I had dinner with my friend Joe O'Rourke, a facilitator at the conference, and mentioned my problem.

"The best operational planning facilitator in the country is Jim Kingsley," said Joe.

"How do I get in touch with him?" I asked.

"He happens to be standing right over there. I'll introduce you."

I explained my dilemma to Jim.

"You've got to simplify things," he replied. "If you don't integrate the planning process with the operational process, the new and different never gets done."

Jim's down-home, calm demeanor appealed to me. His business strategy was refreshingly uncomplicated; he understood words and slick presentations would do nothing to help the third-shift worker in Aurora, Nebraska, understand our plan. I wanted someone who could help us get everyone in the company on the same page, so I wasted no time. Although I'm famous for sitting on a decision for months, I also have a good instinct for seizing the moment. I hired Jim on the spot as our new planning meeting facilitator.

Ongoing learning and training became a critical factor in propelling The Iams Company forward, not just for me but for everyone. The previous year, I had taken a small first step toward establishing what would later become Iams University by setting up a modest program that reimbursed employees for classes they took to help them do their jobs better.

And I continued to attend AMA sessions. At one session, called "Competency Lab," I learned some uncomfortable truths about myself. The twenty CEOs in the session were divided into groups of five. Each group was told to pretend the CEO of our fictitious company had just been killed in a plane crash. Within our groups, we were asked to hash out who should take over as the new CEO and how the company should be reorganized. The purpose of the exercise was to vie for the CEO spot. Every session was recorded on videotape.

Naturally, I thought I should be anointed, and I maneuvered hard to convince my teammates I was the logical choice. In the end, I won the exercise and was voted the best choice for the vacant CEO slot in our imaginary company.

The exercise enabled our peers to evaluate each of us on our management skills, which were measured according to eighteen management competencies in the areas of goal and action management, directing subordinates, human resources, leadership, and specialized knowledge.

When we returned to our respective companies, we gave people who worked with us and for us the management competency score sheets and asked for evaluations of our management skills. Each of us was videotaped on the job, as well, so the group from the AMA session could see us in action on our home turf.

When we reconvened a few months later in New York City for the second week of workshops, we each gave a presentation on our strengths, weaknesses, opportunities, and problems as a manager. Those sessions brought out my competitive nature. I was confident about the content of my presentation. I told my peers I thought my weakness fell under the leadership category, and I pegged it to logical thought.

"Some of my employees sometimes find it hard to follow what I'm communicating," I said.

One woman, an executive with Kroger who had remained quiet throughout most of the sessions, spoke up immediately. "Logical thought isn't your weakness at all," she said, looking me squarely in the eye. "Your problem is that you use people. You manipulate to get what you want."

I rocked back on my heels and felt my face flush.

Others in the group quickly concurred. They cited some of the tactics I'd applied in the group, as well as some of their observations from the videotape of me in action at The Iams Company, as evidence of my manipulative management behavior.

I was genuinely shocked. I thought I had mastered all eighteen competencies and had become the ultimate well-rounded manager. But from my peers' merciless observations, I realized I'd essentially skipped over the second rung on the career ladder, which was directing subordinates. Never having been in a supervisory role for long early in my career, I hadn't learned the art of developing people. When I returned home, I bravely asked John Polson, Les Pitstick, and Jan Dinges if they agreed with the assessment. What I learned stunned me. They all agreed that I manipulated employees to get them to do what I wanted.

"Sometimes I feel like I'm being used," John reluctantly admitted.

Slowly and painfully, I began to understand my problem. On the surface, I often looked like the good guy because my behavior wasn't overtly coercive and I did care about the people who worked for me. But, like many high-level executives, when push came to shove, I turned the screws to achieve my objectives. I tried to mold employees into a likeness that fit my perceptions and needs. As a result, even though I hired good people in key positions, I never really developed them.

If I was going to build our organization correctly, I had to make a radical change in my management style. Instead of the Pygmalion approach, I needed to encourage and allow my employees to shine according to their individual strengths and capabilities. It was a subtle but dramatic paradigm shift.

In today's vernacular, leading people with their best interests at heart is called being a servant leader. I had always said that I wanted to live by the Golden Rule, treating other people the way I wanted to be treated, with dignity and respect, but I had been blind to my own lack of sincerity in regard to others' welfare.

It's no easy task to let go. Engaging in deep soul-searching and learning to put people above my own agenda was the hardest work I've ever done. But the payoff was worth the rough ride. When I stopped trying to pull the strings like a puppeteer and encouraged employees to become responsible for their own decisions, the positive results were almost instantaneous. When given the opportunity to think and act independently, the employees took ownership of their jobs and started developing at a breathtaking pace. At the same time, I was amazed to discover I could do more when I wasn't trying to control everything.

I've never understood managing by fear. People do their best work when they're comfortable and empowered, not when they feel intimidated. You want employees to feel at home and valued for their skills. There's a lot of power in people feeling good about themselves.

The worst year of my life was working at General Motors. If you found a new and better way to do something, you were handcuffed by a voluminous set of books called the "Manual of Organizational Policy." Before you could change anything, you had to go to headquarters and make the change to the manual. Employees were treated like machines. GM only valued the factual side of the brain; the intuitive side was dismissed.

At The Iams Company, we were not out just to make money. We wanted to build a great company that made great products. You can't do that by procedures and policies. You do it by hiring the right people and empowering them to make good decisions.

When you succeed at that, you communicate a powerful message: "I trust you." I trusted that our employees cared about our mission as well as about my family and me. I also trusted them to make good business decisions. As a result, John Polson could sign purchase orders for $500,000. Bob Meyer, our chief financial officer and vice president of finance, could sign checks for up to $1 million. A team of hourly employees at the plants could purchase capital items up to $5,000 without the approval of anyone if the team unanimously agreed an item was needed to improve quality or productivity. Many of these investments had the highest returns of any I've ever made.

We were on the verge of boosting our sales force from 40 people to more than 200 as we fought for shelf space in retail outlets. We needed to exert greater control in the marketplace and not rely so heavily on our distributors' sales forces to sell our product. By expanding our own sales force, we'd be better able to disseminate product information and train our distributors' salespeople. I needed help on the hiring front.

Midway through 1985, it became clear we needed to concentrate on human resources. After all, if people are a business's most valuable commodity, the HR department is a company's most valuable department. Les Pitstick convinced me to bring in the big guns and recommended Dick "Boomer" Baumhardt as a consultant. Boomer, a highly decorated captain in the U.S. Marine Corps and a World War II veteran, specialized in union avoidance, one of my priorities. During his career in labor relations, he didn't lose one of the forty-four union elections that came up for vote on his watch.

Boomer immediately began to review our personnel policies and procedures. The reality at The Iams Company was that "policy" didn't exist. My deep distaste for bureaucracy had resulted in a lack of clear directives committed to paper. Boomer set to work writing our first policy manual and instituted a human resources program that represented the kind of company I wanted to build. Once again, I found myself in the hot seat. My paternal instincts, Boomer warned, could get us in trouble. Over the years, I had made personal loans for cars and houses to various employees. "The law says you must treat all your employees equally," he said. "You have to avoid even a hint of favoritism."

Eventually, with Boomer's guidance, we established extensive performance reviews and an innovative bonus system.

We handed out an attitude survey and discovered that the major bone of contention among our employees was lack of communication. Boomer immediately bumped up *The Iams Times* from a quarterly publication to a monthly, and we started sending it to employees' homes. "You want the entire family to feel connected with the company," he explained.

Boomer also advocated quarterly meetings at every location. The top executives carefully rehearsed for these meetings, and we finished each one with a question-and-answer session that became popular with employees. At Boomer's suggestion, I started having lunch with a small group of employees a few times a week. No topic was off-limits during these lunches. We also instituted staff breakfasts. At these low-key meetings, I would engage in casual conversation that put the employees at ease. Then I would ask everyone to name his or her biggest problem and to make a comment about his or her Iams experience. By the end of the session we had covered important issues that invariably affected more than just the individuals at the meeting.

As we started bringing on more new people, it became apparent that our new employees were more likely to appreciate the quality and care we took in making our products if they were able to observe how they were made. So, we made a blanket rule that everyone who worked for The Iams Company had to spend a week or two working in one of the plants.

Some of our best salespeople came from the ranks of plant workers who started their careers making Iams and Eukanuba products. I'm convinced that happened because they believed in the process. Eventually, many of them earned supervisory positions.

The more committed we were to nurturing that commitment to quality and powerful sense of mission that formed the bedrock of The Iams Company, the more we understood we were looking for a special kind of person to work at Iams. We couldn't hire people wholesale. A company driven by materialism and the bottom line is interested only in good technical skills, but a spiritually motivated company like ours would succeed when it was populated with unique individuals who were willing to become part of not just a company but a dream.

## CHAPTER 14

# Above the Radar

A company knows it has arrived when its competitors start threatening to put it out of business. Shortly after the Aurora plant began operating at full throttle, a letter arrived from Bill Lacey, president of the grocery products division of Ralston Purina Company.

"We've been watching you for some time," he wrote. "I'd like to talk to you."

I called Dave Phillips for advice on how to respond.

"You should meet your competitor," said Dave. "See how he thinks."

So I called Bill and invited him to meet me at my Poe Avenue office.

On the appointed day, I got a call from the receptionist at the Lewisburg plant. "Clay, we have a fellow here who says he has a meeting with you and that you invited him here. What do you want us to do?"

Instead of coming to Poe Avenue, my competitor had taken the opportunity to scout our plant facility. I told her to tell him to stay there; I'd come get him.

As soon as I had Lacey in my car, I let him have it.

"What kind of stunt did you think you were pulling back there?" I asked.

Although he wanted me to think it was an innocent mistake, I knew I'd only given him the Poe address.

"That's real funny, Bill, since you wrote me at my Poe Avenue office and that's the only address I ever gave you," I retorted.

As soon as we sat down at our table with a nice view overlooking the eighteenth hole at the Miami Valley Country Club, Lacey peered at me over his wire-rim glasses and announced, "We've seen the growth in the super-premium segment, and we see it as an emerging sector in the marketplace. I'm here to make you an offer. We're prepared to pay you $75 million for your company."

The fact that he was trying to position my brand as "super premium" galled me. He obviously thought Purina Dog Chow was a premium brand, a stance that I found laughable. And I was amazed that he thought he could waltz in and bully me into selling my company. A Harvard MBA, Lacey represented everything I loathed about monolithic corporations. He used all the buzzwords and clichés in vogue at the time, but I strongly doubted he'd ever been within one hundred miles of an extruder.

I let an uncomfortable silence elapse before answering, then finally said, "Well, Bill, there's a problem with that, since my company's not for sale."

He barely skipped a beat. "We've let you exist to this point, but we know how to make your product. If you don't sell to us, we're going to introduce a new super-premium product that will run you out of business."

"Let me tell you how it is, Bill," I replied evenly. "Ho Chi Minh told the French and the Americans, 'For every ten of us you kill, we'll kill one of you, but even at these odds, you will lose, and I will win.' Mark my words. Before you run me out of business, you'll be out of a job."

About eight years later, at the time we hit $500 million in sales, Bill Lacey left Ralston Purina. And I hadn't even had to use a crystal ball to predict it. Clearly, we were no longer flying under the radar. The Iams Company was now out in broad daylight, its growing success prompting our competitors to gird for battle and move in for the kill. I decided it was high time to expand our retail penetration broadly and make our visual displays grab the customer's attention.

When I visited retailers, I was invariably dismayed by the poor display of our products. Most pet food retail businesses were still primarily mom-and-pop pet shops and small regional chains. Many stores didn't have shelving to display pet food. I'd walk in a store and see bags of our products stacked on the floor.

I had first put a bug in Marty Walker's ear about a solution when he became director of marketing for Iams in 1982. The first prototype rack appeared that year on Marty's watch but was never mass-produced. It was made out of particleboard, and the shelves buckled under the weight of the product. Besides, the timing was all wrong. We still had too much to do. We were concentrating on filling the pipeline with our products, and we didn't have our distribution system set up or our retailers in place.

A rack with brightly colored, rounded topside panels emblazoned with our name and the paw print, as well as Paul Iams' signature, had been designed in 1984, but no one was pushing to get it out where it would do us any good. None of our competitors had anything like it, but it was only a matter of time before they started using display racks. I saw the rack as a big opportunity to once again get a jump on our competition. I waited for marketing and promotion to step up to the plate...and waited and waited.

Finally, I called Tom Young, vice president of marketing, into my office one steamy August afternoon. "Tom, I want those racks in two thousand retail stores across the country within the next twelve months or you're fired," I said.

I rarely issued ultimatums, but I wanted Tom to understand how critical it was for our brands to get premier placement in stores.

"Clay, I don't know how we're going to get that done," Tom stammered.

"I'll tell you how you'll get it done. Give every salesperson a Black & Decker drill and tell them to hop to it!"

Those first display racks weighed about 180 pounds and were designed to hold 1,000 pounds of dog food, double the amount most retailers carried. The idea may have been simple, but it caught our main competition in the premium segment, Hill's, completely off guard. Retailers clamored for our brightly colored racks and gave us great placement in the stores. In fact, within two years, we installed six thousand racks in pet stores all over the country.

Now we had to address sales. We held our first sales meeting at the Cobb Galleria in Atlanta and invited our rapidly expanding sales force, key managers, distributors, and some plant employees.

Unfortunately, we hadn't put enough thought into what we were trying to accomplish with the meeting, which was completely unrehearsed and had no theme. In short, the event was not one of our shining moments.

In front of my amazed eyes, presenters disintegrated into buffoons and ruffians. To illustrate the importance of pest control, our quality assurance manager paraded on stage wearing mouse ears and calling himself "Dr. Death." The head of the newly formed technical services department gave an uninspiring update on plans for our new research and development facility. Later, he and one of our veterinarians got into a heated and extended argument on stage about animal nutrition. I finally had to step in to break up the row.

The weekend degenerated from there.

Two independent distributors were invited to present at the two-day meeting.

At the meeting, one distrubutor lectured on the virtues of showmanship and showed television commercials he had produced to promote Iams and Eukanuba in his local market. I felt he'd gone too far. I was livid that he would take it upon himself to decide how the brand should be positioned.

The second distibutor was slated to speak about his best practices for working with retailers. He was a mild-mannered, clean-cut young man who had become a distributor early on and built up an impressive operation, accounting for almost twenty percent of our volume and employing fifty people. In fact, his sales in the western region were the primary impetus for building the plant in Aurora. Mary and I both liked him a great deal, and he was widely viewed within the organization as one of my protégés.

But as he grew increasingly successful, something began to go wrong. Rob Easterling had been warning me that this distributor's operation left a lot to be desired, but he had put on such a good show for Mary and me that I chalked up the negative rumors about him to jealousy from other distributors.

When this distributor took the stage at the distributor's meeting, however, I almost fell out of my seat. He came out barefoot and started an emotional speech about the need to be open and honest with each other and to share all your secrets.

It turned out that he had become a devotee to a California "human potential" movement.

To my acute embarrassment, I felt that our most important representative in the West had substantially changed and no longer reflected an appropriate image for The Iams Company. As our regional distributor in the west, he wielded a good deal of influence in a crucial territory. Since our western customers tended to be more health conscious than their eastern counterparts, we figured they would be keen on providing their pets with the best nutrition available. We were banking on that region to be one of the key engines fueling our growth in the coming years.

The following Tuesday, I had the distributor and his management team meet me in a hotel conference room. Anticipating that his staff would clam up if he was in the room, I asked him to leave. Then I turned to the others and said, "I'm going to ask you a bunch of questions, and I want straight answers."

Half of the people in the room were barefoot. Instead of sitting at the horseshoe-shaped conference table, one woman lounged in a beach chair positioned against the wall. I felt like I'd been transplanted to a hippie commune.

"What's your job?" I asked the beach chair occupant.

"I'm the executive assistant," she languidly replied.

"Okay, then can you take the minutes of this meeting for us?"

"I don't take shorthand."

"Can you take notes?"

"No."

It turned out that this laid-back creature was on staff as the masseuse.

I ran the meeting in true George Bickley style, asking about strengths, weaknesses, opportunities, and problems. At first, the group hesitated to speak up, but by late in the day the walls were plastered with problems.

One of the big problems that surfaced was the distributor's apparent blatant disregard for the brand equity of our product as evidenced by his price schedule. He had a price list with ten different levels, starting with the highest price for a 200-pound purchase all the way up to the best price for a bulk buy of 10,000 pounds.

By selling our pet food more cheaply there than anywhere else in the country, he maximized his sales figures in the short-term, but he cannibalized the resources needed to develop the West Coast region and cheapened our brand image in the process. His rock-bottom prices lured customers from as far away as Arizona and Nevada to make the drive to buy our products, creating disruption in those states. He also had been loading up sub-distributors with product, making 20 percent on every trailer we shipped to him. No one had a good handle on exactly who the sub-distributors were, what they were doing to market our products, and what was happening to our brand equity in the west.

In addition, he maintained a bloated stable of forty-eight sub-distributors who sold to retailers. Sub-distributors added cost and confusion to the distribution and marketing system, and we had recently decided to eliminate them altogether. This situation simply sped up our timetable.

When the distributor finally joined the meeting, he blanched when he saw all the issues papering the walls. I faced him head-on.

"The number one issue that has to be resolved is this: What are you going to do to repair damage to The Iams Company's reputation in your marketplace?"

Way back in 1977, during an airplane ride, I had jotted down the words "culture" and "people" as two of the main ingredients important to the Iams formula for success. Since 1983, I'd consciously tried to operate The Iams Company based on the philosophy of doing the right thing for our culture, customers, products, and people: CCPP. I particularly liked the acronym because C and P happened to be Paul's and my first initials. CCPP gradually became identified within the company as "The Iams Way."

That first sales meeting showed me that we could not do business with companies that held vastly different priorities from ours. Although our eleven regional distributors were independent, they represented us in the marketplace. Part of building a national brand with a consistent marketing message nationwide and moving the organization ahead meant weeding out the distributors who did not share the same commitment to CCPP.

Shortly thereafter, Rob and Les flew out to inform the west coast distributor that we'd decided not to renew his distribution agreement. I thanked my lucky stars I had listened to Dick Chernesky and had written contracts with all our distributors.

More than one hundred people on the West Coast were selling our products. In January 1986, I assigned Mike Major the mission of cleaning up the mess and gave him the job of regional sales manager in the west, based in the Los Angeles suburb of Rancho Cucamonga, California.

Mike found our products stored under terrible conditions. Several sub-distributors kept Iams and Eukanuba in stacks outdoors, exposed to the elements and vermin. He tapped a handful of good sub-distributors to become full distributors.

The previous out-of-whack pricing structure came back to haunt us, too. Our new distributors had to adjust pricing, and California customers became furious about the increase, causing sales to plummet. The screwy pricing and lack of appropriate marketing opened a window for a small, regional southern California-based dog food manufacturer called Nutro. Although it had been around for years, Nutro skyrocketed under new management that year. It was a full five years before our former customers forgave Iams.

I decided Mike needed reinforcements in the fall of 1986, so I asked Tom Rowe to relocate from the original Chicago distribution center, where he'd gone to replace a fired manager, to Milpitas, California.

Within a year, Mike and Tom had pared the west coast distribution staff of fifty down to eleven salespeople and one administrative assistant. This miracle was the equivalent of turning a sputtering old clunker into a purring Jaguar. The West Coast distribution system was finally running as smoothly and efficiently as it should have been all along.

A strong distribution system can give you a decided edge against competitors. Smart distributors look at your product and figure out how they can help add value to your business. By the time we paid attorney fees, settlements, and write-offs, the fiasco had cost us a lot of money, but it was worth it. I learned that if The Iams Company was to become truly successful on a national and, one day, international level, we had to make distributors part of both the Iams family and The Iams Way.

We wanted strong business partners who believed in what we were doing and who shared our mission and vision. We were dedicated to helping our distributors make money and feel rewarded in the process.

Creative experimentation was key to strengthening our relationship with our distributors. We had launched Iams University in December 1984 to provide our employees with training programs in everything from specific job skills to career development and effective management strategies. The "university without walls," as I called it, grew to include outreach training for our distributors, retailers, supporters, and customers. As early as 1987, we let independent distributors take courses at Iams University to help them better sell our products. After all, a number of distributors had evolved from tiny mom-and-pop feed stores and needed training in everything from efficient use of a warehouse to CEO development and strategic planning.

After that disastrous but invaluably instructive sales meeting in Atlanta, we decided to hold an annual world-class sales conference for our distributors. We brought all the distributors and their spouses from around the country to luxury resorts in places such as Scottsdale, Palm Springs, Cancun, Hawaii, and Marco Island for four-day meetings. Our meeting planner, Janet Werner, worked exclusively on the distributor sales meetings for a full nine months prior to the event.

Mary attended the conferences with me, along with my entire top management team, each of whom was required to make a presentation. We set up displays as if we were exhibiting at a trade show, with booths dealing with every part of our business and giveaways for the distributors. We brought in inspirational keynote speakers, including famous coaches Lou Holtz and Al Maguire; professional athlete-turned-politician Jack Kemp; and Charles Garfield, author of *Peak Performers*, one of my favorite business books.

At the Saturday evening gala at each distributor meeting, I would give a sort of state of the union address. I never wrote my speech until I had the opportunity to spend time with the distributors. I listened carefully to their concerns and challenges during the days leading up to the grand finale. Then on Saturday, Mary and I spent much of the afternoon sequestered in our suite, where she helped me craft my speech. The focus of these meetings was making the distributors feel important and part of the family. By the end of the weekend, they all left with a good understanding of our plans and how they fit into those plans.

We spent a minimum of $1,500 per attendee, outside of speaker costs, and paid attention to every detail. For example, each distributor found a gift basket waiting in his hotel room. I've never scrimped on paying for the best; my philosophy has always been, "Give the best and you'll get the best." For five years, starting in 1988, our annual budget for the distributor meeting exceeded $750,000. It was a big investment, but the payoff was far bigger. Giving our distributors a strong sense of importance, purpose, and belonging immeasurably strengthened our position in every area of the country.

In addition, we took a cue from the Dana Corporation and its extensive dealer network and from what our board member Ed Wingate had instituted when he was with Toro Corporation and formed a distributor advisory board. This board met twice a year, once after the distributor meeting and then again in the fall, usually either in Florida, where we played golf, or in Lexington, Kentucky, when the changing October leaves formed a breathtaking and invigorating backdrop to our activities. These meetings were valuable on both a personal and professional level; we all had fun together and at the same time were able to discuss issues important to our distributors.

As the 1980s drew to a close, I knew we were going to have to professionalize our distribution system. The mavericks and mom-and-pop operators who happened to get on board early were not necessarily the distributors capable of handling the growth we were realizing.

In some cases, our business had simply outstripped the distributors' abilities. In other cases, the distributors were "harvesting" their businesses, building bigger houses and buying second homes and fancy cars instead of plowing the money into building bigger warehouses, buying better computer systems, and hiring more qualified people—all the things that would enable them to grow along with us.

When the big money started rolling in around 1985, some let their egos get the best of them. In many territories, sub-distributors showed themselves to be stronger than the regional distributor in the same area.

Major retail changes in our industry were also driving our need to rethink and redesign our distribution system. In the early days, when mom-and-pop retailers were the primary places our products were sold, the distributors, who had formed long-term relationships with these retailers, wielded a good deal of power in the market. But starting in 1987, giant pet superstores such as PETsMART and PETCO Animal Supplies began assuming the reins of power. These gargantuan retailers built 50,000-square-foot stores that stocked 10,000 to 15,000 products, including several lines of premium pet food. Because PETsMART and PETCO had set up their own warehouses, they expected us to deliver our products directly to them and sell it to them at the distributors' price. Our main competitor in the premium segment, Hill's, immediately agreed to the retailers' terms.

Since Hill's management came from the grocery store business, PETsMART's and PETCO's demands must have seemed perfectly reasonable to them.

The retailers were essentially demanding that we gut the dis
system we had worked so hard to establish over the past fifteen ye
flatly refused to go along with their plan.

"You are a retailer, so we're not going to sell you Iams and Eukanuba
at the distributor price," I insisted at every meeting we had with representatives from PETCO and PETsMART. "Whether you take delivery at
your store or your warehouse, you're still going to pay the same price, and
it won't be the price we give distributors."

Neither retailer knew how to deal with me. They couldn't threaten
me; I wasn't like those corporate managers who worried about making
their numbers at the end of the quarter.

In the end we won. While our competitors were actually increasing
the cost of distribution for every retailer other than PETsMART and
PETCO, we were decreasing our distribution costs across the board. At
the end of the day, PETsMART and PETCO let us continue delivery to
their stores or warehouses. The industry and the system needed store-
door delivery, and we became the leading brand in both those chains.
Retailers soon began giving us feedback that made it clear they liked the
new arrangement. They didn't have to handle as much inventory because
we gave them better service. We dealt
with complaints faster and more efficiently, and our products moved off
shelves faster.

Our distributors picked up any
damaged goods or broken bags on the
next delivery to make the process of
returns as hassle-free as possible.
Whereas the big retailers typically de-
ducted 1 percent off a sales invoice as
a returns allowance, we didn't permit
that deduction because we dealt with our returns on the spot.

*Together, Iams manage-
ment and a distributor
advisory board hammered
out specific roles for distributors, focusing on
logistics and leaving
marketing to Iams.*

As soon as market dynamics shifted from the distributor to the retailer, we had to change our approach to the market again. Distribution

ng value to the marketing function and more about
managed their warehouses, truckers, shippers, de-
other words, independent distributors relinquished
s and took on logistical roles.

ally happy, but we retained the integrity of our system
ributors more efficient than the retailers' warehouses. I
never wo. out whether customers, meaning the distributors and
retailers, liked me or not. Business is not a popularity contest. My job was
to make sure I was fulfilling or exceeding our promises and that our customers were doing well handling our products. It always comes down to
doing the right thing; if distributors and retailers make money doing business with you and your word is good, they will respect you.

On the international front we were going great guns. We beat Ralston
Purina to the European market, and Mars, the big player in Europe, didn't
have a premium dry product. In fact, premium pet foods were virtually
unknown in Europe when we introduced our products.

Our board of directors advised us to hire a European to guide our
efforts on the continent. Our first managing director in Europe, Marcel
Blok, based in Eindhoven in the Netherlands, was an excellent strategic
marketer and provided us with good packaging and advertising. He knew
how to promote products at the dog and cat shows. He also did most of
the legwork involved in locating top-notch distributors and developing
programs for them.

We applied what we'd learned in the United States to our European
distribution system. We signed dis-
tributors to an exclusive contract up
front. Since the countries are small, one
distributor could handle a whole country. And we courted dog breeders.
That strategy played well in Europe
where breeders have even more influence, since many pet lovers there tend
to be purists. Helmut Grönemeyer in

*A battle of wills between Clay Mathile and large-scale retailers ultimately ended with a better distribution system for the chain stores.*

Germany, our first distributor in Europe, raised prize-winning Alsatians and helped us gain a strong following among German dog breeders.

We hosted our first international distributor strategic planning meeting in London in November 1987. We were beginning to grow an organization that would secure our lead as the primary competition in the sale of premium pet food in Europe.

## CHAPTER 15

# Front and Center with R&D

W hen I became sole owner of The Iams Company, I made a solemn promise to Paul Iams to preserve his prized legacy of scientific research. As part of that promise, I planned to establish a world-class pet nutrition research center bearing his name.

In 1983 we began consulting with Warren Kirkley, the Denver veterinarian who distributed our products, on several important research projects conducted at a handful of universities. At Colorado State University, we sponsored a research project on cat food and the causes of kidney stones in male cats. We also funded a growth study in which kittens were fed our food or our competitors' foods.

The next year I offered Dr. Kirkley directorship of our R&D program. Unfortunately, because the new position would have required him to close his vet practice and move to Dayton, he declined. Recognizing that new product development would be critical to our future, I subsequently hired Tom Willard, a pet food consultant with a PhD in animal nutrition from North Carolina State University, as technical services director. Dr. Kirkley, who was an excellent veterinarian, remained with us as a consultant.

Our strategic plan for the R&D center called for a two-phase project that would occupy a 104-acre site adjacent to the Lewisburg plant. The new center would stand as a crowning achievement and concrete demonstration of our commitment to providing the best nutrition to dogs and cats. I wanted it to be world-class.

The first phase consisted of an animal care center with housing for resident dogs and cats and an on-site veterinary hospital. I wanted the conditions at the facility to simulate as closely as possible the family pet's experience at home. The animals would be socialized and given names. Although government standards for research facilities called for animal cages that measure at least 9 square feet, we used 13-square-foot pens specially designed so animals could live as a family unit. The facility also would include a two-story pilot plant where food would be formulated, as well as offices and a laboratory. The second phase would include a large central laboratory and an expanded animal care facility.

The R&D center had numerous functions. It would enable us to research new products better, achieve long-term quality standards, provide centralized laboratory services to the manufacturing facilities, develop improvements in the manufacturing process, and evaluate how Iams' products stacked up to the competition. Naturally, it would cost money—lots of money.

The first time I told Bob Meyer, our CFO, we were going to spend $25 million on the new R&D center, he looked around for the marbles he figured I'd lost.

"Are you crazy, Clay?" he politely queried. Bob had great difficulty envisioning the value of a sophisticated R&D center. "That's more than it cost to build our two plants combined!"

"Hey, Bob," Les Pitstick piped up, "remember that at Iams, we operate by the Golden Rule. We can all have our say, but at the end of the day gold rules, and it's Clay's gold."

Ironically, I found the special person I was looking for to be the research nutritionist for the new R&D center thanks to the inventor of Purina Dog Chow.

Our executive recruiter called Diane Hirakawa, a PhD candidate in companion animal nutrition from the University of Illinois. Diane was the star pupil of Jim Corbin, PhD, who started teaching after he left

Ralston Purina. All the big players, including Ralston Purina and Carnation, were courting the twenty-five-year-old Japanese-American while she was still writing her thesis that fall.

At the University of Illinois research facilities, students worked with pointers. The dogs couldn't produce good litters because they were being fed a cheap feed. Dr. Corbin asked that the diet be switched to Iams Mini Chunks, but the administration protested because our product was five times more expensive than the food the university was using. Incredibly, Dr. Corbin believed so strongly in Iams that he subsidized the extra cost of our food out of his own pocket.

Soon, Diane witnessed an amazing change in the animals. Before the switch to Iams, the dogs' stools had been so soft that cleaning the cages was an all-day ordeal. But once the animals were put on Iams, their stools were firm and small, and the students had their afternoons free.

Before long, the bitches at the Illinois research facility were whelping healthy litters of six to eight puppies each.

After our executive recruiter approached Diane, she sought advice from her mentor.

"The company has a small plant, it's not a big player, and it has no R&D center," Diane complained to Dr. Corbin. "Their products are sold in stinky small mom-and-pop pet stores. I think Clay Mathile is a shyster, peddling expensive premium pet food."

"Diane, there's only one company you should work for and that's The Iams Company," Dr. Corbin replied. "Those people care about animals, and you love dogs and cats. Clay Mathile will give you an opportunity to make a difference in your field and help you fulfill your goals in life."

Diane subsequently flew from Chicago to Dayton to have dinner with Mary and me at the Miami Valley Country Club. We spent most of the evening discussing nutrition.

Diane wasn't convinced that dogs needed as much protein as Iams contained or that chicken protein was far superior to soybeans or tofu as a protein source. We had a fairly heated argument.

The following day we drove to Lewisburg, where I showed Diane the site for our future R&D center.

"I'm going to build a state-of-the-art facility," I said, sweeping my arms wide to indicate the acreage near the hill where the executive offices had been. "You could be a big part of it."

But Diane was still sitting on the fence.

"Here," I said, handing her a Tupperware container of Iams Chunks. "Take this home and try it out on your dog."

"I don't have one, but I'll try it on our family's dog," Diane replied. Ironically, she didn't have a pet because she was allergic to dogs and cats! But she loved animals so much that she took allergy shots and medication to be able to work around them.

I laughed, because it was so remarkably similar to the exchange I'd had with Paul fifteen years earlier. I was sold on this young woman with such a brilliant career ahead of her, who wasn't afraid to challenge me on anything.

"I want you to be our research nutritionist," I told her. "I'll give you all the tools you need."

"But I haven't even finished my thesis yet!" she replied, incredulously.

"You can work part-time Monday, Tuesday, and Wednesday until you finish."

Diane promised to consider the offer and left carrying that small sample of dog food. I knew she'd be back.

Diane was still unconvinced. But when she took the food home to her mom and fed it to her finicky, pampered ten-year-old miniature poodle named Taffy, the dog sniffed the air and went right to his bowl. The next day, for probably the first time in his life, he had a normal, firm stool. Diane was on board.

When Diane joined the company, I asked her to focus on two things: "Number one, if you're doing the same things three years from now that you're doing today, you're not doing the right things. Number two, you have to figure out how to make our plants obsolete. Around here, we don't allow sacred cows."

Diane soon learned I never let grass grow under my feet. An architect called her on her second day on the job to begin work on the plans for the center. She later told me how shocked she was to get that call so quickly and how much confidence my demonstration of faith in her meant.

With the Aurora plant now up and running for a year, we had more than enough capacity for the first time in five years. Finally, we could divert some of our efforts to rolling out new products. We made Eukanuba Puppy Food—which had been reserved exclusively for puppy breeders in Kansas—available to the mass market in March 1986.

We broke ground on April 2, 1986, for the new research center, scheduling a year of construction for Phase I. That same month we introduced Iams Kitten Food. The new product that stands out to me, though, was created by one of our employees in his kitchen at home. A firm believer that great new ideas often come from unexpected places, and in line with my desire to create a work atmosphere where people were encouraged to take risks, I extended an "intrapreneurial" opportunity to our employees. I offered to provide $10,000 seed money for research and travel to whomever had a new and viable product to test. The offer wasn't limited to R&D; anyone in the company could take the challenge.

Bob Bardeau, our quality control manager at Lewisburg, had noticed feed stores routinely stocked big bins of generic dog biscuits sold in bulk. He was inspired to work on developing an Iams dog treat, which, if successful, could become a great extension of our dog food business.

Bob baked biscuits in his home oven, experimenting with different amounts of meat protein and striving to achieve the right balance of vitamins and minerals. Although his family wasn't too thrilled with the smell of the burnt meat that was a frequent result of the experiments, his devoted shepherd-husky mix Micah wouldn't leave his side.

Finally, Bob hit upon a prototype that satisfied both him and Micah. Even though he could only bake six at a time, and each batch had to bake for thirty-two minutes, Bob produced three hundred of the I-shaped dog biscuits and brought them to work.

I was delighted by Bob's tenacity and creativity. I was further delighted when we tested the biscuits and dogs gobbled them up. Diane Hirakawa helped Bob refine the formulas and, in May 1986, he leased a bakery in Cleveland to bake several test batches. That trial run was successful, too. I asked Bob, who was studying for his MBA, to write a formal business plan for his creation. "It's all yours, Bob," I said. "I want you to treat this project like it's your own new business." I subsequently promoted him to new products manager in the marketing department.

Bob unveiled the dog biscuits at our distributor sales meeting that November in Dallas. Everyone was eager for new product, and his presentation was a big success.

The first Friday in December, everyone received a $275 bonus, so that they could use the extra cash for Christmas shopping. Mary and I were at the Lewisburg plant late that evening to present the checks to the third shift when we saw Bob sitting at his desk looking forlorn.

He was upset because he'd been at the co-packing facility for the biscuits in Michigan all week watching a disaster unfold. The biscuits were coming out like charcoal briquettes.

"I'm getting nothing but trash at the co-packer," he moaned. "I'm scared we're not going to get it figured out in time to make our deadline for the rollout."

We spent the next few hours throwing around ideas. After all, I was the expert in the field of new product hurdles. Finally, I said, "Let me ask you one question: A hundred years from now, is it really going to matter?"

Bob started laughing. Mary said, "You'll figure it out before Monday."

Before we left, I gave him an extra vote of confidence. "Bob, you've done an amazing thing. You've created a company within the company."

Iams Biscuits, in 4-pound and 20-pound red boxes, hit the market in January 1987. In 2003 the product that had been created in Bob Bardeau's kitchen added a considerable sum to the company's sales—I estimated the amount at $40 million.

Opening the Paul F. Iams Technical Center, which initially cost $25 million, on June 4, 1987, marked a milestone in our history and signaled our deep commitment to continuous improvement. As a bonus, it enabled me to honor the man who had dedicated more than three decades of his life to giving us the technological edge in the pet nutrition field. That same year, I became convinced I should entrust Diane Hirakawa with the future of Iams research and development.

Since a dog's sense of smell is nine times keener than a human's, most of our competitors' research centers focused almost exclusively on palatability studies, which measure how well an animal likes a food's taste or smell. In direct contrast, the Iams Technical Center devoted 80 percent of its studies and tests to digestive research and nutritional metabolism and only 20 percent to palatability testing.

We were more interested in figuring out the connections between our products and the animals' well-being than in how tempting our food was to their olfactory sense. Our research honed in on the animals' coats, eye clarity, muscle tone, and the birth weight of puppies and kittens.

Everything was designed with the dog and cat in mind. The facility included a large exercise yard so thirty dogs could play outside together in family units. The dogs got obedience training, played ball, and took dips in the kiddie pool. The pet-passionate caregivers gave the animals personal names. There was piped-in music. The animals got the best toys, gazebos, and play structures. They couldn't have been happier if they'd checked into the Ritz Hotel. And the facility was meticulously designed. All thermostats were installed at the animals' height, so temperature control was geared to their comfort rather than ours. Computerized lighting controlled natural light cycles. In the cat living spaces, enormous windows allowed for a more natural environment. Each dog run was two to three times larger than those of comparable facilities, and they were equipped with swinging doors so the dogs could go in and out as they pleased. We de-ionized the water supply to remove naturally occurring minerals from the local water supply, so mineral studies weren't compromised. And the research rooms featured seamless operating room–style floors designed to eliminate any areas that might harbor harmful bacteria.

In May we issued invitations for the grand opening of the R&D center. The big day dawned without a cloud in the sky. Paul Iams and his wife were there for the ribbon-cutting ceremony and festivities that followed.

Despite my aversion to tooting our own horn, we invited the local media. I thought the center's opening presented a great opportunity to highlight to consumers as well as the pet food industry Iams' deep commitment to research in the pet nutrition field and to the well-being of the world's dogs and cats.

The first dogs that would take up residence at the center came from Rick Swenson, who traveled from Alaska to be on hand for the ceremonies. Rick kept about one hundred dogs in his kennels for his championship dog-sledding teams. He had loaned us his husky-mix dogs in the past for various studies. Most research facilities use beagles, but that is a hardy breed that can tolerate almost anything. Huskies have shorter guts than other breeds, so their digestive systems are extremely sensitive to any change in formula. That made Rick's dogs a good choice for the research that would be done at the center. The center's first cats came from breeders.

I gave a brief speech. Because I was more than a little nervous, I mistakenly welcomed the contingent from "Aurora, Kansas." Although I immediately corrected myself, the good-natured folks from Aurora, Nebraska, weren't about to let my *faux pas* slide by. The next week they sent me a red T-shirt with outlines of Nebraska and Kansas on it, plus an arrow and the words "Kansas is here."

Paul, who was visibly moved by the event but always ready with his wry sense of humor, made a little speech. "Today is pretty exciting for me. Most people have to die to get a building named after them, so I'm especially proud to be here."

It was the culmination of a dream that had taken root more than forty years earlier in Tipp City, Ohio. The Iams Food Company had certainly come a long way.

## CHAPTER 16

# People Are Your Best Investment

Decision-making is probably the most important skill we human beings have in our trusty box of tools that helps us to navigate successfully through life. You can't live properly, you can't realize your full potential, in short, you'll never be happy, if you make bad decisions. That seems so obvious it's hardly worth mentioning.

But decision-making is a highly intricate process that involves myriad complex emotions. The best decisions come when the head and heart, reason and emotion, are aligned—not an easy task by any standard and a particularly difficult one for entrepreneurs, who by nature rely heavily on gut feelings when making crucial decisions. The more success we entrepreneurs have, the more we tend to trust our own instincts and the more impressed we become with our amazing knack for betting on the right horse. As a result, we may make quick decisions that turn out to be on target or we may have to pay the price of failure for a misplaced hunch.

Ironically, a good decision maker must be comfortable with indecision. Entrepreneurs are famous for being overeager gunslingers, but as I studied and implemented new management strategies, I learned it's okay never to make a decision before you have to. "Haste makes waste" in most areas of life, but when the future of an entire company and the lives involved in it hinge on key decisions, haste can wreak not only waste but total devastation.

Along with learning how to make the right decisions comes learning how to delegate the decision-making process to others. This is perhaps the hardest thing for entrepreneurs to do, because it involves a phenomenal level of trust in others, and it requires a company's founder or leader to relinquish the overwhelming urge to control every aspect of the company's life.

One difficult decision I decided to delegate to someone else involved starting a new company that would manufacture the high-quality protein so essential to the Iams products. When I hired Tom Weinkauf in 1983, I presented him with the challenge of finding a better source and continuous supply of superior protein. I was deeply concerned that the explosive product demand growth I anticipated would soon outstrip our supply of high-quality protein.

More than once during our history, we'd been faced with a run-up in ingredient cost or the degradation or shortage of essential ingredients. I had never forgotten the disaster Paul experienced in the 1950s when Eli Lilly suddenly degraded the protein in the pig pancreases he was purchasing from the pharmaceutical giant for his dog and mink foods. Now, as the Delphos Avenue plant neared capacity, this issue weighed heavily on my mind.

I knew we had to provide our own source of high-quality protein. In fact, I already had a name picked out for what I envisioned as a division of The Iams Company: Protein Blending, Inc. Iowa stood out as the logical location for the new venture, not only because it produced more pork products than any other state, but also because it led the nation in corn production and would be central to our raw materials and convenient to both the Aurora and Lewisburg plants.

Tom immediately started working on a business plan for the new protein division. At the next planning meeting, he reported some interesting news. First, the name I had picked was already taken. Second, he wasn't convinced the best proteins were going to continue to come from the pork and beef by-products we'd been buying.

"I think we need to wait and see what happens in the market," Tom cautioned. "Meanwhile, let's continue testing other sources of protein."

Tom's plan sure put a pin in mine. I got nervous. What if he was making a mistake? And yet, wasn't that a core issue in delegating responsibility? If you purport to trust someone, you can't pull the plug on him just because his findings disagree with yours. Throwing my hat to the winds of employee-based decision-making was a monumental risk that has paid off many times over. I gave Tom the breathing room he needed to find a better and more reliable protein supply. Meanwhile, he designed a pre-screening process that made the fractionating machinery at Delphos much more efficient, freeing up quite a bit of additional capacity and easing the pressure to move on the protein division project immediately.

In the three years that had elapsed between the time I had initiated the idea and the time Delphos actually ran close to being out of capacity, the plans for the separate protein division evolved into something entirely different from what I had originally projected. In February 1987 Tom presented our board of directors with his business plan for An-Pro, Inc. The name stood for "animal protein," and the plan called for me to own the new company separate from The Iams Company, rather than having it fall under our corporate umbrella.

This was a brilliant idea, as it would allow Tom a great deal more freedom in reselling by-products to other pet food manufacturers, who in the past had eyed our by-products with suspicion. "If it's so good, why aren't you using it in your own products?" purchasing agents would invariably ask. "We don't want to buy your junk."

It wasn't junk, of course. The by-product under question was a great calcium and phosphorus supplement, perfect for the pet food industry. By setting up An-Pro as a separate entity and disassociating it from The Iams Company, we eliminated the perception that something was wrong if we were selling a by-product instead of using it ourselves.

Based on the proprietary technology that Paul Iams developed in the 1950s, Tom could identify the quality protein and separate it from the lesser quality materials. The residual was perfectly good for certain kinds of animal feed but not good enough for our pet food. An-Pro was positioned to offer a better protein that far exceeded the market's abilities, at a price that was favorable to the market. This arrangement allowed us to buy the protein wholesale, manufacture it into the form we needed for our products, sell the resulting protein to The Iams Company, and then sell our by-products to our competitors at a retail price. These benefits reduced the cost of making Iams and Eukanuba products.

Poultry sellers set five price levels. Human food manufacturers paid the highest prices; pet food companies, the second highest; animal feed manufacturers, the next highest; blenders followed next; and the lowest value was in feeding it back to the chickens. An-Pro was positioned in the marketplace as a blender, a kind of distributor that bought the protein at a deeply discounted price, just above chicken feed value. In the first year of operation, An-Pro contributed more than $3 million in cost savings to The Iams Company and still made a profit.

Tom estimated that An-Pro would eventually reduce our protein costs by 20 percent, a significant savings since we spent more than $15 million on that ingredient alone in 1986.

Extensive research and development had proven that chicken protein far surpassed other rendered proteins in terms of value and palatability. Chicken was also far more abundant than pork. Based on that fact, Tom had determined the new protein blending plant needed to be near the source of much of the nation's poultry supply.

Following the successful formula we'd employed in finding the Aurora location, Tom investigated every little town that met the requirements, finally choosing the small college town of Russelville, Arkansas, as the ideal site of the new plant. Forty percent of the nation's poultry was supplied regionally and all shipped via the interstate, a stone's throw from the new site. The largest poultry producer in the United States maintained several operations close by, and a shell of a 65,000-square-foot building from a failed manufacturing venture stood empty, ready for us to move in immediately. An-Pro was incorporated that month, and Tom ordered the equipment and signed everything by the end of May 1987. The townspeople, An-Pro's nine employees, and their families turned out for the grand opening that September, and An-Pro began shipping poultry meal in October.

With Tom Weinkauf doing his tour of duty at An-Pro, I needed a strong leader to step in and revamp Lewisburg. Years of running the operation flat out, coupled with the plant's original inefficient design and the authoritarian style of the plant manager and his supervisors, had left the Lewisburg troops dispirited. At that point, it was cheaper for us to make pet food in Aurora and ship it to Lewisburg than it was to produce product in Lewisburg. Aurora's labor costs were 35 percent lower than at Lewisburg, and the Nebraska plant beat the Ohio plant by $50 a ton on production costs. Shipping 200,000 tons per year meant a $10 million savings on products produced in Aurora. On top of that, we were in danger of running out of product again if Lewisburg wasn't drastically overhauled.

I could think of no better man for the job than John Polson, our vice president of manufacturing.

If you've ever had to remodel a home, you can begin to imagine giving a huge manufacturing plant a top-to-bottom makeover! Lewisburg was saddled with inefficient material flows, inadequate storage, and a lack of automation. We wanted to use what we'd learned building and operating the Aurora plant to revitalize the Lewisburg operation. Our plans called for adding a mill and a processing tower, both made of concrete to eliminate the noisiness of the metal construction, as well as a flavor enhancement room. We also planned to relocate packaging and greatly increase warehouse capacity. And we wanted to upgrade the extrusion process with the installation of two new Wenger 185 extruders, which could each produce eight tons an hour versus the five-ton capacity of the old Wenger 175s. Once again, we had an aggressive schedule, which called for the entire project to be completed before Christmas.

When he returned to Dayton right after Valentine's Day, John's first act was firing the plant manager, whose lack of people skills had steadily eaten away the reservoir of goodwill John and I had originally established with Lewisburg's workforce.

Andy Chance, an up-and-comer who had started in the plant laboratory as a technician, became the new plant manager. John soon replaced most of the senior management at Lewisburg. He promoted project engineer Kurt Petry to plant superintendent. Kurt educated the plant workers about the business, taught them how their decisions impacted our business, and assured them their ideas would be listened to and valued. Once the new leadership was in place at Lewisburg, it took about three years to reverse the situation. Shortly after naming the new team, John and his top operations managers attended one of W. Edwards Deming's seminars on quality. Dr. Deming's philosophy on management was credited with helping the Japanese rejuvenate their economy, and Japanese managers revered him. He preached:

- Quality leads to lower costs.

- Most defects are caused by the system.

- A company should buy from vendors committed to quality.

- Fear among employees leads to disaster.

- A company should work with suppliers.

Much of Dr. Deming's philosophy dovetailed perfectly with our beliefs at The Iams Company. A notable example was his recognition of the importance of small teams. Upon returning from the seminar, the plant managers launched "quality circles," which were small teams (usually five to eight people) assembled to work on improvements and address specific problems on an ad hoc basis. A team might be comprised, for example, of workers from quality control, packaging, customer service, R&D, and marketing. It was often made up of line workers with no managers involved.

These quality circles were informal, self-driven, and action-oriented. They didn't study an issue to death and file lengthy reports on their findings. Their focus was on getting the issue resolved rapidly, implementing the change, and moving on. Too many big companies strangle ideas by insisting on months of study and filtering every idea through layers of management. The teams gave employees a sense of ownership in solutions, and The Iams Company profited from listening to people on the front lines, those doing the work and dealing with customers every day.

The team format meshed well with our insistence that all departments work together for the common good of the company. In some companies dogfights break out among departments or divisions, and one part of the organization winds up dominating the others. At Iams everyone knew he or she was working for a greater cause: the well-being of dogs and cats. As a result, they cooperated with each other.

Building a strong, loyal, and enthusiastic employee base was always a top priority for me. I not only wanted to empower the Iams employee; I wanted him or her to be well compensated for excellence in performance.

So I hired Dave Smith, a human resources consultant from Mercer & Company, to help us develop a compensation plan that ensured everyone in the company got a bonus. To a union, this would have been the equivalent of waving a flaming cross in front of Dracula. After we put the bonus plan in place, morale was so high, unions couldn't get a foot in the door.

Good attendance was rewarded with a fifty-third paycheck. (Employees could take five personal days off during the year, but this program paid them if they didn't use those days.) After the year closed, a 10 percent bonus was paid on annual salary for hourly workers. Managers and salaried staff got up to 12 percent of their annual salary as bonus pay, based on the percentage of the plan that was met. At the other end of the stick, the CEO was the first to lose his bonus if targets weren't met. For instance, if 90 percent of the plan was achieved, salaried people got 50 percent of the targeted bonus. At 80 percent, salaried people got no bonus. Hourly people weren't penalized because managers developed a bad plan.

I also gave top priority to employee education. In December 1984 we launched a modest training and education program called Free Information for Learning Express (FILE). Because I've been such a voracious reader throughout my career and gleaned some of my best ideas from business books, I developed a special book collection for employees.

FILE also included written and video training programs that could be borrowed from our human resources group.

By 1986 we had invested in an in-house training center at Poe Avenue and hired a full-time training manager. Our own initial small effort started as a sales tool, but I wanted to help other employees, too. I knew the heavy demands we would be putting on them, as we rocketed forward toward my goal of being a $500 million company, called for a far more ambitious effort in training and education.

I've always believed in "invest $1 in a machine, get $2 back; invest $1 in a person, get $10 back." Many companies have set up corporate universities with varying degrees of success.

Dana Corporation, for example, based outside Detroit, Michigan, made truck parts. The company realized early that if it was going to control quality, it had to train the mechanics who installed the parts. So Dana University was established. I took a field trip with Iams board member Vernon Oechsle, senior vice president of Dana Corporation, to visit Dana University, where the energetic executive director impressed me with how in-tune he was with the company's corporate strategy. We also visited Steelcase University, the educational and training arm of the office furniture manufacturer based in Grand Rapids, Michigan.

Steelcase had a challenge similar to Dana, in that its customer satisfaction had more to do with installation and timeliness than the design and materials used in its office furniture.

Iams University started out as a department within the company. Four years later, in the fall of 1988, I announced that Iams University would operate officially as a stand-alone institution, with its own executive director and board of advisors.

My vision was to create a "university without walls" that provided courses and research, both about the company and about business practice in general.

I wanted everyone involved with The Iams Company to understand fully the nature of our products and of the consumers who purchased them. Studies showed that Iams appealed to the "family" dog owner, whereas

Eukanuba was the brand of choice for the "proud" dog owner. Both types of consumers were equally concerned about their animals' quality of life. Part of the mission of Iams University was helping everyone affiliated with The Iams Company understand the nature of that special bond and the role our products played in enhancing it.

By 1989 courses under the Iams University banner were being taught at all of our company locations, giving our people the tools to realize the vision of The Iams Company as the world leader in dog and cat nutrition.

Jack Tootson became Iams University's first director in November 1990. Soon after Jack joined the company, I asked him to research the average annual tuition cost of public college education in the state of Ohio. His answer was $4,000.

"Then we'll spend $2,000 on each employee, because I'm sure we can deliver more value and better education at half the cost," I said. That $2,000 per employee spent on training was more than double the amount the typical company spent on education for each employee in its workforce.

Relatively few companies treat training as a focused strategic initiative. Instead, they make training a departmental issue, where it invariably winds up on the lower end of priorities. In my opinion, this is an enormous strategic error. Training leads to quality improvement, which ultimately leads to productivity gains. When quality gets better, costs go down. Sounds simple, but I'm constantly amazed at how training's importance to an organization is overlooked in corporate America.

As early as 1984, I encouraged employees to take classes at Sinclair Community College in Dayton, Ohio, and if they maintained a C grade or better, 100 percent of the class cost and 50 percent of their book costs were reimbursed. That type of commitment is also unusual. Later, we expanded the program to include reimbursement for private tutors so employees could get their general equivalency degrees and high school diplomas. We also reimbursed them for tuition for associate and bachelor's degrees, MBA programs at local colleges and universities, and professional accreditation courses. For those who couldn't afford tuition up front, we made interest-free loans, eliminating another barrier that often stops employees from taking advantage of such opportunities. We were extremely flexible about the courses employees pursued; our only stipulation was that the employee's supervisor agreed the course would help boost skills or self-esteem.

Iams University was the deciding advantage that gave us the flexibility to stay abreast of the latest and best business practices to manage our company in a rapidly changing industry. The courses gave people confidence that they could do what they needed to do to help The Iams Company grow.

In his lectures, pre-eminent management expert Dr. W. Edwards Deming frequently cited an experiment with time and motion studies in a manufacturing facility. Researchers assessed productivity before any changes were made, then better lighting was installed in the plant. Productivity went up. Next, management painted the walls, and productivity

*Clay was the only CEO I'd met who really walked the talk. Iams University was a strategic partner in the Iams business, with a legitimate role in moving the company forward. It wasn't an afterthought or just a section of human resources. Iams University helped The Iams Company maintain control of its business process.*

*Clay was focused on building Iams University around the company's vision and mission, and he was determined that the courses should reflect commitment to CCPP (culture, customers, products, people).*

*Clay had always practiced Tom Peters' principle of management by wandering around. He was known for coming into an office, plopping down on the nearest chair, and asking, "What's your biggest problem?" Few CEOs are willing to allow people time to really orient themselves, but Clay encouraged me to spend my first year or so with Iams getting to know people and the particulars of the company. "You can't provide educational services if you don't understand your clients' business," he said.*

*(continued)*

went up again. Then the researchers had management do something surprising: Dim the lights. Productivity went up again. The study concluded that what management did had little to do with the increase in productivity. What was important to the workers was that management was paying attention to them. Likewise, we found what our employees were learning didn't make any difference. The simple fact that they were learning helped them feel better about themselves.

The better they felt about themselves, the better the job they did for the company. Although Iams University offered nuts-and-bolts courses, its most critical role emerged as the place where we formally transferred cultural knowledge.

"We've got to stay small while we get big," Tom MacLeod was fond of saying. Our culture, which encouraged risk-taking, entrepreneurial thinking, and individual initiative, thrived on our ability to stay flexible. We

*(continuation)*

*He was absolutely right. If I didn't understand sales, manufacturing, marketing, and R&D, I couldn't be prescriptive in providing training for all of those departments. What I ended up being was a performance consultant. I looked at processes and work streams and asked critical questions to find the root causes of problems. If it was a lack of knowledge or lack of skills, then an educational prescription was appropriate. My job was to provide the right training to the right people at the proper time and place. It was not just animal nutrition and well-being; it was also specialized subjects such as sales, business management, products, customer service, and leadership.*

*Clay told me, "It's been a vision of mine to have a university without walls, a system of education that provides outreach training for all our employees, our veterinarians, distributors, retailers, supportive influencers, and our customers." His dream came true, and I'm happy I was a part of it.*

JACK TOOTSON (DIRECTOR OF IAMS UNIVERSITY FROM 1990 TO 1997) viewed this culture as our heritage, our beliefs, and our organization's moral and ethical standards. It was the thread that held us together. As we hired more people to help us manage our rapid pace of growth, it became more difficult to pass along our values and culture.

Our solution was to create a course called "The Iams Way," a daylong, interactive course taught by senior management.

Each of our seven top executives taught the course four times a year, which represented a serious time commitment. All new hires attended the class together. There was no division by title or department. This meant that almost immediately after they joined the company, new employees were rubbing elbows with senior management and experiencing firsthand our casual, warm, family atmosphere. I cannot count the number of times employees who had worked at other companies told me they'd barely seen anyone from top management at their previous companies, much less spent any time with them.

Scott George, who joined Iams University in 1993, told me soon after he arrived that I startled him when I called him by name two days after he started with the company. "I spent six years at my former employer, and I never knew what the company's mission was," he said. "In all that time, my only contact with any senior executive was playing golf in a foursome with the CEO, but he never remembered my name."

As The Iams Company grew larger and larger, Tom Rowe, who by then was editor of *The Iams Times*, our monthly company newsletter, developed books that had photos and information on all our employees, field salespeople, and distributors. The books included everything from what sports their children played to the names of their pets. My rationale for these personal histories was simple: People need to know you care.

*The Iams Times* played an integral role in helping all of us feel connected and "in the know." Each issue included a "CEO's Corner" column, something on our history and our culture, and news from our locations around the world. Many companies undervalue such internal communications, but we saw our newsletter as a vital tool in keeping every member of the Iams family, from Dayton to Denmark, in the loop.

"The Iams Way" course was structured around my old CCPP philosophy: culture, customers, products, and people.

- *Culture.* The culture governed the way we did business with honesty and integrity. An integral part of the culture meant that we pledged to treat everyone with dignity and respect.

- *Customers.* The customers were the dogs and cats we fed. Our promise to them was that we would provide world-class products that enhanced their health and happiness. The other important customers were our distributors, retailers, and the people who purchased our products for their pets.

- *Products.* We were dedicated to making products that exceeded all expectations in terms of quality and were continually being improved. We sought to have every employee take responsibility for product quality.

- *People.* We put top priority on our people, whose enthusiasm, dedication, and excellence provided the distinction between the competition and us.

At Iams University new employees witnessed the friendly dynamics among our top executives at work. Too many companies are like dysfunctional families, whose members don't know how to communicate with each other. At The Iams Company, any such lack of communication simply wasn't tolerated. R&D's Vice President Diane Hirakawa and manufacturing's Senior Vice President John Polson might team up to teach "The Iams Way" together. Marty Walker, senior vice president of sales in North America, and Diane also would teach together.

They were both completely at ease as they shared personal experiences with the new employees, and their sessions were filled with laughter. Such courses helped dissolve any hierarchal barriers.

Other than "The Iams Way," the only required course was "Pet Nutrition." Every employee, from secretaries to machine operators, was required to know the basics of the science behind our products, because we viewed all of them as ambassadors for the company. We wanted them to understand what made our food better and to experience the difference with their own pets, so they could be knowledgeable about feeding dogs and cats when they talked to friends, family, and acquaintances about Iams and Eukanuba products.

Each year, we used the annual employee attitude survey conducted by the Center for Values Research in Dallas to help us chart our progress in human resources. In February 1986, the center's officials notified us that, based in large part on our commitment to education and the results of the most recent survey, Iams had won the group's top award. Since a number of large, well-known entities, including Hershey, Coleman Company, and Baldor Electric, numbered among the companies that had been surveyed, this was indeed a feather in our cap. We were invited to Dallas to attend a survey users conference with three dozen representatives from the more than one hundred companies surveyed. The companies ranged from Fortune 500 firms to small, privately held concerns in the service and manufacturing sectors.

Over the years, we've won many awards, but that one is particularly special to me, because it was a vote of confidence from our own employees. As an update, Hughes reports that today The Iams Company still ranks in the top 5 percent of the more than eight hundred companies surveyed in the years since by the Center for Values Research. Iams University branched out to all of our plants, each with its own training facility and full-time trainer.

In 1996, concurrent with our growing international expansion, we duplicated Iams University at our manufacturing facility in Eindhoven in the Netherlands to serve Europe. We also opened a smaller branch in Singapore. The beauty of both branches was that the core material all translated easily. Pet nutrition and The Iams Way were subjects all human beings could value and understand, no matter what language they spoke.

The influence of Iams University extended far beyond our own employees. Because of my belief in sharing knowledge with partners, we went operational with Distributor Education Development Institute (DEDI), a first in the industry, in August 1991. We held our first DEDI class with fifteen of our sixty U.S. distributors the week of September 29, 1991. Besides The Iams Way and the nutrition course, we offered the distributors training on sales and marketing, financial management, succession planning, technology, warehousing, and other areas relevant to their businesses. I believe that if we hadn't offered DEDI, as many as 70 percent of our distributors would not have been able to make the transitions we asked them to make over the next several years.

Eventually, training for folks outside The Iams Company accounted for 30 percent of Iams University's curriculum. Our suppliers from Bemis Bags to Wenger to our ad agencies became part of a vendor orientation program where their employees learned about the Iams vision, mission, culture, and beliefs. Iams U also designed training materials for our sales force to use with pet stores and veterinarians that carried our products. We didn't just teach them about pet nutrition, we offered them training on sales, business management, customer service, and personnel policy. Courses also were available to key influencers such as breeders and pet adoption centers.

In 1994 I established the Center for Entrepreneurial Education as a division of Iams University. I wanted to support the Dayton business community by providing a nurturing environment for entrepreneurs. We created a formal network of resources and forums to address the critical needs of aspiring entrepreneurs.

Earlier, in 1989, Mary and I had established the Mathile Family Foundation, with Mary serving as chairperson and CEO. We quickly saw the tremendous need to help nonprofits with their planning processes so that they could become more effective in serving the needs of their respective audiences. Starting in 1992, through Iams University, we offered courses on strategic planning to nonprofit organizations.

Being a good corporate citizen was enormously important to me. In the communities where we operated, our employees were expected to contribute their time and effort to causes. We didn't influence them; I didn't demand that people contribute to my pet charity or to a cause the company had chosen for them. Instead, we taught the heart behind the

213

philosophy and then let each individual decide where to focus his or her energies.

We also tried to lead by example. When Hurricane Andrew devastated southern Florida and Louisiana in August 1992, The Iams Company worked with the American Red Cross to bring swift humanitarian relief to the stricken region, and we donated 25 tons of pet food to the Humane Societies of Miami, Florida, and additional victims in Louisiana. This practice continues today as The Iams Company has contributed more than $30 million in support since 1992.

The Iams Way became not only a company mission statement but a force for good that reached out to people all over the world. I count that as one of my proudest accomplishments.

## CHAPTER 17

# If You Don't Listen, You'll Have to Feel

E ntrepreneurs are usually workaholics; with tremendous energy, they focus on their goals. With unwavering resolve and dedication, they forge paths where no one has dared go, and they don't stop marching until they've reached their destination. Then, because they feed off challenges and thrive on dares, they chart a new destination and begin marching all over again.

The tirelessness and visionary strength of entrepreneurs can inspire others. They become models of the work ethic on which this country was founded. They build business empires and accumulate wealth.

There is just one problem. As entrepreneurs, when we put all our energy into the vision that is dearest to us, we risk losing the people who are dearest to us. We may not be present for our wives, our children, or our friends. We may use others for support and sustenance but forget to give back part of ourselves in return. When we go into battle for our big dreams, there are always casualties of war. And among those casualties are the people we love the most, not to mention our own souls.

By 1988, with the money rolling in, I started acting like the big man on campus. I had single-mindedly devoted myself to The Iams Company for nearly two decades. I finally had plenty of money in the bank, and I became intoxicated with my increasing wealth and power, determined to enjoy both to the fullest.

It was understandable. I had worked so hard for so long, that I felt I was entitled to a good time. Unfortunately for me, a good time included alcohol. I had encouraged a hard-charging, hell-raising attitude at The Iams Company, particularly among the sales force, and it was about to catch up with all of us, especially me.

Dog shows were a great excuse to party. More than 3,500 of them took place every year across the country, with about 100,000 of the nation's 20 million purebred dogs competing. I'd attend the most prestigious events in big cities, including Atlanta, Charlotte, Dallas, Chicago, Denver, and New York.

These four-day events are spectacular. The prestigious Westminster Kennel Club Dog Show, held every year since 1877, attracts 2,500 of the nation's top dogs. The dogs compete during a black-tie affair at Madison Square Garden. Each entrant is an American Kennel Club champion, and breeders and owners often invest as much as $250,000 annually in a champion dog, much of it spent on salaries and travel expenses for professional dog handlers, on the road to Westminster. The dog shows were vital to Iams' sales, but they meant I was spending a lot of time on the road—and a lot of time in bars.

My dad used to say, "Nothing good ever happens in a bar after midnight." It took me a long time to understand the depth of that simple observation, because many an Iams employee joined me in shutting down the bars on the road, and that seemed like a good thing to me. I could relax with the guys, loosen up, have a little fun.

In the fall of 1987 one of my key sales managers had imbibed so much the night before his presentation at a regional sales meeting that he staggered to the podium in the throes of a hangover. I was livid. I'd also heard through the grapevine that he had taken to hanging out in bars when he was supposed to be working.

The national sales meeting was slated to start the next day in Dallas, and I decided to confront him about his drinking. Of course, we wound up having our little chat over drinks in the hotel lounge. Soon we were both drunk. Glaring at my errant sales manager, I wagged my finger at him.

"We've got to do something about this!" I declared, loudly enough for the whole hotel to hear. "Either you stop drinking and get some help, or I'll have no choice but to fire you!"

Unfortunately, I failed to see the irony in the situation. Hardly anyone was willing to challenge me on the alcohol problem that had gradually taken over my life, because there was subtle pressure to be part of the hellraising crowd in order to be "in" with me. This, of course, was directly at odds with the family-friendly culture I'd strived to cultivate at The Iams Company.

I had surrounded myself with an inner circle of people who wouldn't challenge my drinking. And the biggest problem was that I never perceived it as a problem. I was what you could call a functioning alcoholic: My drinking never really affected my ability to conduct day-to-day business, so it was easy to float along on the carefree cloud of denial.

My mother always said, "If you don't listen, you'll have to feel." In other words, those who don't learn the lessons of history will get their own private education in the school of hard knocks.

I was about to enroll.

On October 1, 1987, my oldest daughter, Cate, married Don Laden, the first employee Tom Rowe hired at the Chicago distribution center in 1978.

Before their wedding, Don had been promoted to marketing manager in charge of national sales promotion and transferred to the home office. I was excited about having this ambitious and creative young man in the family because I really liked him and admired the way he had worked his way up through the company.

The day of the wedding, I was in high spirits. The ceremony took place at 4:30 P.M. at a gorgeous former convent across from our parish, Precious Blood Church, and was followed by a sit-down dinner for three hundred guests at the Marriott in downtown Dayton. There was an open bar, and dancing went on until well after midnight. In the wee hours of the morning Mary approached me on the dance floor, where I was hanging out and drinking with some of the Iams guys.

"Clay, I'm tired," she pleaded. "Let's go to our room."

I wheeled around and drunkenly told her that I wasn't ready to leave the party. I don't recall my exact words, but I know they hurt Mary and deeply embarrassed Cate.

A few weeks later, Dave Tooker, our senior vice president of sales and marketing, and I flew to New England for a showdown with our east coast distributor. The meeting was tense, and on the flight home on the chartered jet, I was throwing down drinks, even though I was scheduled to attend a cocktail party with Dave, his wife Betty, and Mary later that evening. Mary and I went with the Tookers, but I barely remember what transpired because I was already half drunk before we went to the party.

On the ride home, Mary turned to me. "Clay," she said, quietly but firmly, "I can't live like this anymore. I don't believe in divorce, and I don't want to leave you. But I refuse to go on like this with you drinking, so what are we going to do?"

The next day I called John Rudisill, the psychologist who had helped me deal with my grief over the deaths of my mother and father.

Mary and I sat together on a low-slung, overstuffed leather couch in his office. Still smugly in denial, I wasn't convinced I had a problem. The old manipulator in me was looking for a way to finesse the situation so that Mary would stick by me, but I could still do what I pleased.

When Mary poured out the disappointments and hurts she'd experienced in our twenty-five years of marriage, however, I was chagrined. Most of them were directly linked to my drinking.

Dr. Rudisill sat in a chair across from us, listening intently. Finally, he leaned forward on the edge of his chair and looked me in the eye.

"I've known you for many years, Clay, and every time you've screwed up, you've been under the influence of alcohol."

It was one of those defining moments in my life. Images from the past flashed before me: the first time I ever took a drink and got blitzed with my fraternity buddies at college; hanging out after work with a group of guys from Campbell Soup who liked to raise Cain; the six-packs and pizzas I'd buy for the guys at the plant on Friday afternoon to celebrate the end of the week; the annual bus trips to the Cincinnati Reds games, where I always ended up getting drunk, no matter how much I told myself that I needed to be in control.

"Whoa. That's heavy," I mumbled.

I thought I loved Mary more than anyone in the world. But I loved my best pal Jack Daniels more. An alcoholic, I learned, will never quit drinking for somebody else, because he or she is completely self-centered. Dr. Rudisill made me come to grips with the damage I was doing to myself and made me face the devastating effect alcohol was having on my life. Three things stood out. When I was drinking, I made stupid decisions, people took advantage of me, and I made a fool of myself.

Dr. Rudisill also helped Mary see how she'd enabled my behavior. Being the spouse of a high-profile entrepreneur can be a lonely position, especially when there's a problem. Mary didn't really have anyone to confide in. On top of that, her loyalty and protectiveness toward me kept her from speaking up. Over the years she'd valiantly tried to make me look good in the kids' eyes and made excuses for me to others and to herself, excuses including "Clay's working hard," "Clay's under stress," and "Clay's business is tough."

After that memorable session with Dr. Rudisill, I vowed never to drink hard liquor again. I apologized to each of our children individually for my behavior, and we talked about the pain it had caused them. If I thought those truth sessions I endured at the AMA seminars were uncomfortable, they were nothing compared to the anguish I experienced as I was forced to admit the unhappiness I'd inflicted on those who were closest to my heart.

I attended a few Alcoholics Anonymous meetings. AA helped me to admit my alcoholism and, even more importantly, helped me to accept God as the higher power in my life.

In making business decisions, I always asked myself, "What's the right thing to do?" Now, for the first time in my life, I started asking, "What does God want from me?" Just as I had to learn to relinquish the need to control others in becoming a better manager, I now had to let go of the need to control my own life and give the reins over to a far greater, wiser manager.

I asked myself what I really wanted and realized that, like Dorothy in *The Wizard of Oz*, I was always looking somewhere over the rainbow for fulfillment, when what I needed most, my wife and kids, was right at the end of my nose. With the support and tough love of my family and close friends, I've stayed sober since October 19, 1988.

> *In making business decisions, I always asked myself, "What's the right thing to do?" Now, for the first time in my life, I started asking, "What does God want from me?"*

Rebuilding Mary's trust in me and repairing the damage I did to our relationship proved a much more arduous journey. Although I always gave lip service to her as my partner, I'm embarrassed to say that, in the tradition of my parents, we still kept separate checkbooks. And even though I had always presented The Iams Company as a family business, Mary did not technically own any of the business.

This was a fairly egregious oversight. For years Mary had always been by my side at any and every important function, the ribbon cuttings for new plants and new buildings, the sales and distributor meetings, the company picnics. She took a genuine interest in the well-being of our employees and their families. By nature a private person, she heroically showed up for as many of our employees' important life events as she could, from baby showers and weddings to funerals. It's no exaggeration to say that at The Iams Company, Mary was beloved by all. At company events, someone would often have to bring her food, because she was surrounded by so many people who wanted to talk to her that she couldn't get away to grab her own plate.

And I've already explained how much I depended on the Mary Test. Her deft, insightful interviews were integral to the hiring process of every candidate for every key position. Even my chief financial officer, Bob

Meyer, had to take the Mary Test. And I made it clear to him that I expected him to tell her anything she wanted to know about the business.

Now Mary started attending our board meetings and taking a more active role in the business. She set up an office adjacent to mine on the fourth floor of our Poe Avenue building and began running the Mathile Family Foundation, which she still manages. I set up a trust with both of us as equal trustees and put the stock of the company in the trust.

I came perilously close to losing the most important thing in the world to me: my family. Yet in the fire of the most painful inner work I have ever had to undertake, a new and deeper relationship was forged between all of us. Looking back, I see my alcoholism not as an affliction but a true blessing in disguise. After all, if it hadn't turned my life inside out, I might never have had the opportunity to turn it right side up.

## CHAPTER 18

# Inviting the Unknown

Over the years I got to know and respect Reuben Mark, CEO and chairman of Colgate-Palmolive Company, which acquired Hill's in 1976. We maintained a cordial relationship and started a dialogue in 1986 about the possibility of putting Hill's and The Iams Company together. At the time I rejected the idea of a merger, but when, at Reuben's suggestion, Rod Turner, executive vice president of Colgate-Palmolive, approached me once again about a Hill's-Iams partnership in June 1989, I seriously entertained the possibility. Fifteen years of nonstop working and the attendant stress had taken their toll. I was plumb tuckered out.

Although I was wealthy, the enormous capital needs of the company required taking on more and more debt to sustain the growth. Debt itself didn't bother me, as long as I knew I could get out of it fast. I was struggling with the question of whether to stay in the game. If we remained on our present course, we would soon be hitting $500 million in sales. Did I want to make the considerable monetary and emotional investments required to push The Iams Company to the $1 billion mark?

As we expanded in Europe, I faced shouldering far more debt than I'd ever imagined—and in an atmosphere of uncertainty. The important trade negotiations and treaties scheduled to take effect in 1992 were being hammered out in a political minefield. How the European Common Market (ECM) would behave with American agribusiness products, the category pet food products landed in, was a big question.

Some experts hailed these events as a great leap forward for U.S. products. My consultants, however, predicted the opposite. Dave Phillips, my auditor and trusted advisor, was the most skeptical of them all. He warned that the continent would likely become "Fortress Europe," meaning regulations would make the ECM practically impenetrable for U.S. companies.

In 1989 we were the largest exporter at the Norfolk, Virginia, port. We'd already completed site selection for a new $25 million plant in Henderson, North Carolina. Once again, we were almost out of capacity. The new plant was slated to manufacture most of the products for Europe to reduce our freight costs. Bringing the product in from the Midwest to ship overseas was adding $80 per ton to the cost. Long term, though, any hope of taking Europe by storm would require us to make an enormous capital commitment and negotiate the complexities of building a plant overseas, an astronomical capital expenditure, since we'd have to build an entire organization overseas, including distribution and logistics.

If I chose to move forward, it was going to be a long, hard ride. I called Dave Phillips.

"Dave," I said, "I want you to go to New York and work on this deal with Hill's. Talk to Reuben Mark, and see if you think we could consummate this marriage."

After three months of studying both companies' structures and how they would fit together, Dave and I met to go over his findings.

"I have mixed feelings, so I'll just lay the facts on the table," said Dave. "The opportunity for Iams management is substantial. From what I'm seeing, the caliber of people you have assembled outmatches the management at Hill's.

"On the other hand, I'm concerned about the culture clash. The large corporate mentality runs deep at Colgate-Palmolive, and it's deep at Hill's, too. I think that's a huge obstacle to making this merger work. Also, Hill's is a key operation for Colgate-Palmolive, but at the end of the day, it's a consumer goods company, not a pet food company.

"My other concern," Dave added, "is a possible major personality conflict between you and Rod Turner's replacement. You'd have to go to Reuben and get that guy pushed aside."

Rod, whom I liked very much, was retiring, and his replacement was exactly the corporate type who rubbed me the wrong way. Worse, he'd chalked up an even bigger demerit: an F on the critical Mary Test. If the deal were to go through, he would be an integral part of the negotiation and acquisition.

After listening to Dave, I said, "It's not the right time. I am willing to assume that next degree of risk in developing our business in Europe."

The merger was only part of the big decision I had to make. If I wasn't going to sell the company, I needed to bring in someone to operate the business. For some time my consultants and my board of directors had been after me to make myself chairman and hire a president and chief operating officer to run the company.

For more than two years I'd resisted their advice. After all, I reasoned, that's like asking a mother to hand her child to a stranger.

"I'm not ready yet," I'd say, whenever one of the board members brought up the topic. And it was true. I was wrestling with the most painful decision I had faced in my professional career.

By 1989 I had held the position of chief executive officer of The Iams Company for almost fifteen years. In the nearly twenty years since I had become the company's seventh employee in 1970, we had gone from $500,000 in sales to $172 million, with an extremely healthy bottom line. We now employed more than four hundred people. We had built two multimillion-dollar plants and a world-class research facility, and we had a third plant on the drawing board. We had formally established Iams University.

We'd gone from two independent distributors with limited regional distribution in five Midwestern states to more than seventy distributors handling our products nationwide. Less than five years after we shipped our first product to Germany, Iams products were being distributed in West Germany, France, the United Kingdom, Switzerland, Austria, Sweden, Norway, Denmark, Holland, Italy, Belgium, and Spain. In the Pacific Rim, you could find our products in Japan, Singapore, Hong Kong, Taiwan, Guam, and Australia. International sales, excluding Canada, only accounted for about $10 million in sales, but I was sure that number was poised for tremendous growth.

Our product line had expanded to include Iams Chunks, Eukanuba Dog Food, Iams Mini Chunks, Iams Puppy Food, Eukanuba Puppy Food, Iams Cat Food, Iams Biscuits, Iams Kitten Food, Iams Less Active for Dogs, and Iams Less Active for Cats. As operators, we had moved beyond constantly playing catch-up to meet product demand to becoming expert planners.

No wonder our competitors were constantly offering to buy us out. Could I entrust The Iams Company to someone else's guiding hand? Would an outsider change the tenor of the Iams culture that I'd worked so hard to establish?

Yet I knew that I needed help. If we were going to reach $1 billion in sales by the new millennium, we had to kick it up a notch in introducing new products and bolstering international sales, two areas where my skills were noticeably lacking.

At the December board meeting, Ed Wingate, a long-time board member who was at the time also senior vice president of Dayton-Hudson—now Target—once more broached the subject of bringing in an outside chief operating officer.

"Tell me again why you think I need to bring in someone from the outside to run this thing," I said.

Ed, Tupperware Worldwide President Al Nagle, and Senior Vice President of Dana Corporation Vernon Oechsle asserted that no one currently on my top management team was capable of taking The Iams Company to the next level. Bill Trubeck, chief financial officer of Northwest Airlines, brought up the lack of an obvious successor among my children.

"You need someone to bridge the gap," he said. "It would take a tremendous effort for one of your children to acquire the skills to run a business of this size, which has prospects of becoming a lot bigger. It's time to look to the outside."

I agreed that at that juncture none of my children appeared inclined to take the rigorous path that might one day lead them to that role. Mary and I had asked that they work for someone else for five years, and then they each had until the age of thirty to decide whether to join the family business.

Cate, who was working at LexisNexis in Dayton, and her husband Don were thinking about starting a family. Tim, who had graduated with a degree in mechanical engineering, had taken a job at Dayton Power & Light Company, the local utility. Mike, the star pitcher on his high school baseball team, had won a full athletic scholarship to Wright State University and was already getting interest from pro baseball scouts. Tina and Jen were still in high school.

*If I wasn't going to sell the company, I needed to bring in someone to operate the business. For some time my consultants and my board of directors had been after me to make myself chairman and hire a president and chief operating officer to run the company. For more than two years I'd resisted their advice. After all, I reasoned, that's like asking a mother to hand her child to a stranger.*

On more than one occasion I had shared with the board my dream of doing something meaningful to help the world at large.

"If that's an itch that you want to scratch, that's another reason to bring someone in now," said Al Nagle. "Realistically speaking, you cannot continue running The Iams Company day-to-day and hope to make a serious contribution to the world. There's only so much of you to go around."

"You are a visionary, Clay," added Ed Wingate. "Give yourself breathing room to do what you do best. Let somebody else take over the day-to-day operations."

Robert Johnston, president of Gerber, said, "Get somebody in here with a broader global perspective and a solid background in introducing new products."

s an example of why you need a chief operating officer," said ısle. "You're a starter, but not a detail guy."

ıs right. I'm a typical entrepreneur, after all; I get a new idea every fifteen minutes, and that can drive people nuts. Then, once I've got something up and running smoothly, I lose interest and move on to the next thing.

By the end of the meeting, I said, "Okay, I'm convinced."

"What kind of person would you want?" asked Ed Wingate. "Let's write a job description."

I gave my standard nonstandard requirements: "A Catholic Midwesterner with extensive consumer goods and international experience. A successful general manager who has been a competitive athlete, and, of course, a dog fanatic."

Vern Oechsle, who would have been qualified for the position himself, sputtered, "I don't know if that kind of job description is even legal, Clay!"

"I'm the one who is going to work side by side with this guy," I replied, "so he has to share my values and vision. Now, how do we find him?"

Ed suggested talking with Bob Lamalie, the headhunter who had sold his business a few years earlier and specialized in senior management searches. I called Bob the next day.

"At forty-nine years old, why are you doing this?" Bob bluntly inquired.

"Because I'm convinced it's the right thing to do for the company and for me," I replied.

"In all my years of doing searches, I've never encountered any entrepreneur as young as you who was willing to hand over the reins, especially when the company is successful," Bob said. "I usually get calls when a company is in trouble."

After Bob was satisfied that I was serious, he named his price. "The search will take approximately three months and will cost you $300,000. I'll take $100,000 now, $100,000 when I present the candidates, and $100,000 when the candidate starts work."

"I'll be in touch," I said.

My next call was to Ed Wingate. "Ed, the guy wants $300,000 to do the search!"

"That's a pretty steep fee," Ed agreed. "Let me think about it."

The next day Ed called me back.

"It is a lot of money, Clay, but think about it this way. If Lamalie finds us the right guy, it's the best bargain you'll ever get."

Because I've always believed in spending more to get the best, I decided to place my bets on Bob, who, true to his word, produced several candidates almost immediately. One stood out.

Tom MacLeod was such an uncanny match for my unorthodox criteria that he seemed to have been hand-delivered by Divine Express. Born in Butte, Montana, and one of six children in a Scottish-Irish Catholic family, Tom grew up in Kansas City, Missouri. His father was employed by a family-owned construction company, which promoted him and sent Tom's family to company headquarters in St. Louis. Moving was a rare thing in those days and especially painful for Tom as a sixteen-year-old sophomore and star athlete at his high school. At Cornell University he lettered on both the football and baseball teams and in 1969 won Cornell's Victor Grohmann Award for academic and athletic excellence.

In many ways Tom's life was a mirror image of mine. Soon after graduating from college, he married his high school sweetheart. Tom and his wife, Barbara, were Catholics and had four children a few years younger than ours. Like Mary and me, Tom and Barb rarely socialized. They preferred to devote time to their families and athletic activities.

Tom's first job was with Procter & Gamble, after which he embarked on a dazzling career at PepsiCo, rising through the ranks to become vice president and general manager of international operations for the company's Wilson Sporting Goods Division, all by age twenty-nine. When PepsiCo spun off Wilson, it asked Tom to move north and become president and CEO of Pepsi Canada, a position he accepted.

After eleven years with PepsiCo, Tom, still only thirty-four, accepted the challenge of turning around Sara Lee as the struggling company's new president and CEO. Under his leadership, Sara Lee soon saw $800 million in worldwide sales. A master salesman and great marketer, Tom brought the founder back in and made the founder's daughter, Sara Lee, the star of her namesake products' commercials. A big believer in quality, Tom led the charge to restore all of Sara Lee's core products to their original recipes, while introducing new products and building the company's international presence. It was exactly the formula for success I wanted to pursue at The Iams Company.

While I was doing my homework on Tom, he was doing his on us. He spent $10,000 of his own money on market research, using the mystery shopper approach. He made calls to various retail establishments and talked to our customers to find out what people were saying about Iams. He spent time with top pet nutritionists to get their take on our products. Prior to hearing about The Iams Company, Tom had always fed his dogs Purina Dog Chow. Now he started feeding his own two mixed-breed black Labrador retrievers Iams Chunks. When the dogs' black coats started to shine, Tom got excited about Iams, exactly as I had twenty years earlier when I saw Iams' effect on my dad's old dog Queenie.

Of all the candidates, Tom fired the most questions at me. "Why are your products positioned the way they are?" he asked. Many of his other questions revolved around the people at The Iams Company and their experience. And he grilled me on the science.

"If you have a better product, you can always win," Tom said, "and I like to win."

I liked the fact that he was doing the lion's share of the interviewing. Finally, I said, "We can't ask each other any more questions. I think we've both got to decide whether this relationship can work or not."

Next, Mary and I went out to dinner with each candidate and his wife. We shared many of the MacLeods' values and, as she had so accurately assessed John Polson ten years before, Mary sized up Tom as a strong, down-to-earth family man who could easily take me on.

Mary didn't hold back during our dinner with Tom and Barb at the Barnsider Restaurant in north Dayton. "How long do you think it will take before you and Clay learn to work together?" she asked Tom.

"We'll work together right away, but in terms of earning each other's trust, it will be two or three years before our relationship meshes," Tom answered without hesitation. "There will be some rough spots. It all depends on whether Clay really wants someone in this position. I know I'm qualified to do it."

The MacLeods passed the Mary Test with no problem.

There was one more hurdle for the three candidates before we made our final decision. Each was invited to our March board meeting and given a one-hour slot. I did not tell the board the conclusion Mary and I had come to, and I did not sit in on the meeting. Bob Lamalie introduced each man to the board with the instructions that he was free to ask anything he wanted to about the company and me.

Tom was last up. He immediately impressed the board with how much due diligence he had done on the company.

"Why would you want to leave a top position at a human food business to come to a pet food company?" Al Nagle asked.

"For the opportunity to use my skills to develop the brands into worldwide powerhouses," Tom replied. "In a private company you can use all your skills in building the business, whereas in a public company you have to use a significant portion of your time managing the impressions on Wall Street. By definition, you're more productive in a private business. This environment will be a better one in which to manage."

At the end of the day Tom was the unanimous choice. "He relates to you, Clay," said Al Nagle. "He'll relate to the employees, too. He's not an intellectual snob, but he's certainly got the intellectual and experiential horsepower to run Iams."

After the board meeting, we were in my car on the way to the airport when I realized we had not covered a key topic.

"Tom," I said, "we haven't talked about salary!"

"I'm not worried about that," Tom smiled. "You'll do the right thing."

That set the tone for our relationship. From the very beginning we had tremendous respect and trust for each other.

*I had never heard of The Iams Company when I read the job description the headhunter gave me. I was intrigued by what Clay had written, because it was so exclusionary that it appeared practically illegal. And it described me to a "T."*

*"Who has the hair on his chest to write this on paper?" I wondered. This guy was equally bold about how great his products were.*

*What was astonishing to me was that Clay, who was only eight years older than I was, wanted to bring somebody in. Ninety-nine percent of entrepreneurs would never think about doing that. I had to make absolutely certain during the interview process that Clay was serious about that. He was very humble about his own skills and his background in brand development, yet he'd built this incredible organization.*

*During the interview process, Clay told me his four dreams:*

*1. To have his own business*

*2. To make the Iams paw print recognized around the world as the symbol of excellence in dog and cat nutrition*

*3. To use the company's collective talents to help people*

*4. To give back to aspiring entrepreneurs*

*I looked Clay in the eye and said, "How committed are you to achieving this vision?"*

*"Completely," Clay said.*

*"Then I'll take responsibility for dream number 2," I told him. Clay grinned and said, "You've got a deal."*

TOM MACLEOD

232

I put a generous package together, because I didn't want money to be an issue. Bob Lamalie presented the package to Tom, who called me at our national sales distribution meeting in early 1990 at Marco Island, Florida, to give me his decision.

At the meeting I made the official announcement that Tom MacLeod would be coming on board as the new chief operating officer and president of The Iams Company.

## CHAPTER 19

# Letting Go and Letting Tom

om MacLeod officially joined The Iams Company as the new chief
operating officer and president on April 1, 1990. I retained the title
of chief executive officer and chairman.

Tom moved into my old office on the first floor of our Poe Avenue
building. He even took my desk. Mary and I moved our offices to the
fourth floor. Symbols are important in a company, and I wanted to send a
strong message to everyone from the outset that Tom was in charge. I never
looked at Tom as an employee; I considered him a partner.

Given my role in the company, neither Tom nor I expected employees to accept his leadership right away. I'd grown up professionally at Iams
and knew most of our employees by name. I knew their families, and they
knew mine. In many cases I even knew their pets' names. Our employees
felt like they each had an important part in the company, and they were
used to having direct access to me.

There was some trepidation and a good deal of skepticism because
Tom came from a big corporation. People were scared we would lose the
"one big happy family" aspect of our corporate culture and the open-door
policy would slam shut. I was particularly concerned about how the old-
timers, including Dick Buchy and Mike Major, would view Tom. Shortly
after he arrived, we embarked on what Tom dubbed the "legends tour." I
formally introduced Tom to the sales team, the plant workers, and our
distributors and suppliers. My gut told me it was vital for the troops to see

Tom and me united as a team. Enthralled with our rich company history, Tom was eager to get on the road and meet the characters who had made The Iams Company what it was. In his first hundred days with the company we spent a good deal of time together on a chartered jet.

Everywhere we went, I could tell Tom was making a positive impression, except perhaps with Paul Iams. We flew out to meet Paul in Sun City, Arizona. Our founder never minces words, and he had gruffly told me he thought I was crazy at age forty-nine to bring in a new leader from outside. Paul never had any use for the smart guys from corporate America, and he thought Tom would be gone in less than a year. Neither man was particularly impressed with the other.

Tom wanted to take his time learning the subtleties of the business when he came in. "Rug merchants call it the feel of the cloth," he told me. We agreed that he would steer clear of our international business for the first year.

It didn't take me long to realize that Tom completely embraced doing things The Iams Way. With his grocery store and mass-market experience, Tom was a big believer in walking the floors of retail stores to hear what was being said about our products. I hadn't visited as many stores during the entire fifteen years I ran the company as I did in the first few years after Tom came on board. In the process, I picked up valuable information about how our products were being positioned in the stores. We talked to clerks about how our products were moving, and we found out firsthand about service problems.

I believe you can learn something from anyone, and the wisdom of the decision has nothing to do with the power of the position. I could learn more about what was going on in the plant by talking to the third-shift extruder operator than I ever could sitting in my office looking at a status report. Gathering information from every available resource had become second nature to me.

During the first eighteen months after Tom MacLeod joined The Iams Company, he and I were still in the honeymoon stage of our relationship. But something was gnawing at me: I still hadn't found my place in the

new arrangement. Sure, Tom and I talked about me being t
company, the ambassador of the corporate culture. That so
theory, but exactly what that meant remained unclear to n

Every day, I struggled with deciding exactly what my n
be. I've always used mentors and modeled myself after people I admired,
but in this case I didn't know anyone who could fully relate to what I was
going through. Although there were many examples of entrepreneurs who
brought in presidents only to have the relationship end disastrously, success stories were hard to find. I forced myself to take a backseat position in
many situations, because I didn't want to interfere with Tom.

At times, though, that was just plain awkward. It didn't help to know
that bringing Tom on board had raised doubts about what was really going on at Iams. Many outsiders speculated that something must be terribly
wrong at the company and I'd brought in Tom to be the fall guy. Within
the company a faction believed my decision to hire Tom sprung from a
short-lived phase I was going through.

They predicted I'd snap out of my delusion that I needed anyone from
the outside and took bets on how long Tom would last.

For the first time in two decades I wasn't having fun at my job. Once
again Colgate-Palmolive floated a number by me. This time the figure
was large enough to get my attention. "That's a heckuva deal," said Bill
Trubeck, chief financial officer of Northwest Airlines and one of my board
members. "If you're ready to sell, this offer is about as good as it gets."

It was an awful lot of money to wave in front of a poor boy from
Portage, Ohio. If I sold the company, I'd have more money than I would
ever need, plus the freedom to work on my third and fourth dreams: helping other entrepreneurs achieve their dreams and supporting causes that
were important to Mary and me.

"You're right, Bill, that is good money," I said, "but how do I know
this number is real? We've never had a valuation of the company done, so
I don't know how much it's really worth."

I decided to find out. After interviewing several investment banking
firms, I hired the New York–based firm Goldman Sachs, which had been

business more than a century. Its experts evaluated The Iams Company's worth at $480 million.

But I wasn't ready to give up the business. We were about to expand our second brand, Eukanuba, and our veterinarian line; we had a number of new products in the pipeline; the retail phenomenon of pet superstores was just beginning; and the international opportunity loomed large. Every day we were one day closer to my dream of reaching $1 billion in sales. It would be like selling a champion show dog in his prime, while he still had a chance to win Westminster.

I decided a sale would be premature, and I knew Tom agreed. I went to his office late one Friday afternoon in the fall and gave him my vote of confidence.

"Tom, I'm putting the valuation books away," I said. "Let's pin our ears back and go sell some more pet food."

That June, our company got a call from a reporter at *Forbes*. "We understand The Iams Company is worth $450 million," said the voice at the other end of the line. "Is that number correct? If so, that puts Clayton L. Mathile on our list of the wealthiest people in America, with an estimated personal wealth of around $360 million. Are we in the ballpark?"

"I won't confirm that," Tom curtly replied. "Furthermore, since Mr. Mathile's company is private, I don't see where that's any of your business."

"That's okay," said the reporter. "We feel very confident of our source." With that, he hung up.

When Tom told me about the call, I was aghast. Obviously, one of the investment banking firms didn't maintain the confidentiality agreement. My temper flared. The trust issue is one of my hot buttons, and I felt like I'd just been sucker punched. To add insult to injury, the numbers *Forbes* printed were deceptive, because they didn't take into account that, like most family business owners, the bulk of our capital was tied up in the business. Indeed, the plans we had in the works—aggressively expanding internationally, launching new products, and building plants in the United

States and overseas—meant our family would shoulder a good deal more debt in the near future.

If the story went to print, it would have a huge impact on my estate planning and, worse, our competition would suddenly have a far better bead on our numbers. I immediately called our legal advisor, Dick Chernesky, to find out if there was anything we could do to stop *Forbes* from broadcasting our wealth. Unfortunately, there wasn't.

Mary and I are not ostentatious people. We have never flaunted our money. Don't get me wrong; we enjoyed life and the freedom from financial worry. But from the very beginning we were determined not to allow wealth to change our God- and family-centered values. We have always viewed money not as an end but as a tool that will allow us to live more productively and help others. Our shared goal was to use our resources to tackle problems such as hunger, poverty, and lack of education and to support other causes and institutions.

We didn't have a fancy house, lavish vacation homes, a garage full of sports cars, or any of the typical CEO trappings. Our biggest extravagances were building a pool in the mid-1980s for the kids to enjoy and taking yearly vacations with our siblings and their families.

As a result of our unpretentious lifestyle, our family had largely escaped the pressure that comes when outsiders know you have money. Not even my oldest and closest friends had any idea of the extent of our assets. Even our children were in the dark; my son Tim had been so blissfully unaware of our financial situation that when he was accepted to my *alma mater*, he dutifully went to apply for financial aid. Only when the bursar informed him that I gave more to the school each year than his entire four-year tuition would cost did Tim get an inkling of our wealth!

Apparently, a good number of folks make it a goal to be on the *Forbes* 400. When we didn't help the writer with the story, he decided to get even. I went through the roof when I saw the negative spin the magazine put on me as a newcomer to America's financial elite. The writer painted me as an opportunist who took advantage of the founder of Iams and bilked the public with "yuppie puppy" food.

As soon as the issue hit the stands, the switchboard at The Iams Company lit up with inquiries from job seekers and requests for donations for everything under the sun.

All through junior high and high school, Tim had been teased about his dad selling dog food. Now, I was virtually Father of the Year.

"Dad," Tim complained, "people who wouldn't even talk to me in high school are calling me and acting like my long, lost buddies."

My biggest worry was over my family's safety. I didn't know what to expect. We put a lock on our gate at home for the first time and started taking other security measures.

I was also concerned about how our employees and business partners might react. Although few within the company had a complete picture of our financial situation, we had routinely shared corporate results with our employees, especially when it pertained to their jobs and the bonuses they would receive. All employees clearly understood their bonuses depended on their contributions to:

- Improving the quality of our core products,

- Introducing new products,

- Aggressively growing our international business, and

- Becoming more efficient so we could invest more resources in the first three initiatives.

After I made the *Forbes* list, I got the feeling our employees had a sense of ownership in my success, because it was theirs as well. Everyone had contributed to the phenomenal growth of the company, and everyone stood to benefit.

In the end, integrity and fairness always wins. The employees of The Iams Company knew that I had their best interests at heart and had worked alongside them to achieve our goals. To the majority of them I was still just "Clay," and that's exactly how I wanted it.

On May 15, 1991, we opened a new chapter in Iams history when we made our first acquisition: Heartland Quality Foods in North Sioux City, South Dakota, the co-packer of our new Iams Canned Cat Food.

When our canned cat food's popularity took off, we felt we needed to control our own manufacturing, but we were in the middle of building our third plant at a cost of $30 million, in Henderson, North Carolina. Although we were reluctant to buy an existing company that might not fit into the Iams culture we had worked so hard to establish, this acquisition seemed to make more sense than suffering through the two-year lag time it would take to build another plant.

We bought Heartland and put a good deal of effort into quickly bringing the workers at Heartland on board. It took a while for them to get used to us, and we had to weed out a few employees who couldn't adapt to our culture and values. In the end it became a good plant with responsible workers.

As the new plant came to life, we bid farewell to our oldest plant. In December 1992, we locked the doors of the Delphos Avenue plant on Dayton's west side. For me it was almost like losing another parent. I had taken some of my first management steps in the rugged, unpretentious facility where Paul Iams had moved his fledgling business in 1950. Paul had been a father figure, as well as a teacher and mentor, to me. As I closed the Delphos doors for the last time, I thought of those wonderful coffee breaks when Paul would hold court on the state of the pet food industry and our long talks in his office about the latest book he'd read or a new theory on animal nutrition.

The Iams Company culture took root in that modest building where we froze in the winter, broiled in the summer, and devoted our hearts and souls to what seemed like the impossible dream. Eventually we razed the structure, donated the land to the community, and built a park on the property. To me it will always be hallowed ground, the place where I found my calling and began the toughest and most rewarding journey of my life.

CHAPTER 20

# Demanding the Unthinkable

By 1993, it was time to make a huge and risky move. If we wanted our new marketing programs, products, and other exciting plans to succeed, we needed 100 percent of our distributors' energy and attention. In other words, we were ready to push for our distributors to carry only Iams products.

That took raw nerve. Almost all our distributors were handling not only our products but several of our competitors' lines as well. Most of them carried Hill's, our biggest rival, and a number of our West Coast distributors also carried products by our most aggressive competitor, Nutro. I was determined to shift the focus to Iams, but I faced an uphill battle. Asking our distributors to handle just our products was like asking them to row out to sea and trust that if their boat capsized, Iams would be there with the life preservers.

Naturally, this didn't put them in the best of humor. Take, for instance, Marty Walker's experience with Bob Schober, owner of Super Dog Pet Food Company in Leola, Pennsylvania.

One of Marty's first missions in his new position as vice president of sales for North America was to convince Bob to become an Iams-only distributor. Bob, who'd been distributing Iams and Eukanuba since 1979, was one of our best distributors. By 1992 he had sold $3 million worth of our products. However, he was also selling about $2.5 million worth of other brands, including Triumph, Old Mother Hubbard, Wayne's, Quaker

Oats' Ken-L Biskit, and Purina. We offered Bob a new contract that gave him rights to sell our products to the pet specialty channel in the mid-Atlantic states, a substantial territory that included central New Jersey; eastern and central Pennsylvania; Delaware; Maryland; the panhandle of West Virginia; and Washington, D.C., along with the surrounding metropolitan area, in return for accepting Iams as his sole supplier.

"Why in hell would I sign a contract with a kick-out clause that says in seventy-two hours you can change the price and has a termination clause that would leave me without any customers?" he thundered. "My lawyers and accountant tell me I would be nuts to sign this contract! My wife Gloria is scared to death! I don't have any rights at all! It makes absolutely no business sense for me to sign!"

Bob's reservations were understandable; our lawyers had drawn up the contract in such a way that we had rock-solid protection of our brands and our interests, a reaction to the abuse the brands had suffered at the hands of renegade distributors. The distributors didn't feel the contract offered them much. But I was banking on them buying into my vision for the company and my reputation for operating by our beliefs, which required us to "treat everyone with dignity and respect."

Bob finally signed the contract. "The way I look at it, " he explained, "I can beat my chest as Mr. Independent or I can ride with the guy who knows where he's going. I'm going to ride with Clay. Now let's go eat."

Other distributors, however, weren't so convinced. Many of them flatly refused our proposition. By the end of 1992, only eight of our sixty-eight distributors had agreed to become Iams-only companies.

Over Valentine's Day weekend in 1993 we held our national sales meeting at the Westin Mission Hills, a luxurious golf resort in Palm Springs, California. We always put on the ritz for our distributors, and the meeting had become a highly anticipated event.

Every senior vice president, from manufacturing to research and development, gave a presentation. Distributors could talk to members of the veterinary support group, the manufacturing group, and representatives from all parts of the company and ask questions one on one.

Jim Butler, who had helped with the strategic planning process internally before leaving Iams to become a distributor, taught classes on financials and knowing costs. At the meeting we introduced new products and revealed our plans for the next year, because we treated our distributors as strategic partners in our business. The distributors loved it and came out of the meeting pumped to sell, sell, sell in the coming year.

I acted like a spectator. I wandered around the various department displays, set up as if they were representing The Iams Company at a trade show. I attended the seminars and took notes just like everybody else. I listened to conversations and asked my stock question: "What's your biggest problem, and what can we do to help?"

During our many strategic planning meetings over the past two years, we had spent a lot of time discussing different what-if distribution scenarios. What if Hill's asks for exclusivity from the distributors? What if it goes completely with company-owned distribution? What if it starts selling through grocery and mass markets? We looked at the distribution situation from every angle.

I was concerned that some of the distributors who figured prominently into our future plans would be left in a vulnerable position if Colgate-Palmolive's Hill's suddenly went strictly company-owned and pulled its business from them.

Hill's was accelerating the rate at which it was cutting distributors, some of whom found the bulk of their business wiped out overnight with the stroke of a pen. Fauna Foods Corporation, which distributed our products in New York City and the surrounding boroughs, was one of the casualties. On the day of the 1993 World Trade Center bombing Hill's informed Fauna's president Ira Slovin that his company was being cut as a Hill's distributor. We extended Ira a helping hand to stabilize his business, and he was one of the first distributors to become Iams-only.

We had the edge with our distributors in terms of trust. If they chose to go with us, we could help them weather the transition from a position of strength. I figured the odds were 70-30 the distributors would decide to go our way. I decided it was time to give the order at the speech I was scheduled to give on Saturday night. I strode to the podium and began with my favorite quotation: "'Dream no little dreams, for they have no magic to move men's souls.' Over the years I have shared my vision on a number of subjects: growth, retail channel changes, competition, and products. In 1990 I asked each of you to prepare to 'Come with me to Macedonia and fight!'

"Tonight I am officially announcing the beginning of the long march to the achievement of my vision that the Iams paw print will be recognized worldwide as the symbol of excellence in dog and cat nutrition.

> *Two years after Hill's cut us, we had made up all the volume we lost by selling more Iams and Eukanuba. A few years ago, we moved into a 65,000-square-foot warehouse. We thought we had died and gone to heaven. We had air conditioning, offices, even bathrooms that worked.*
> IRA SLOVIN, FAUNA FOODS CORPORATION

"I pledge to you that our distribution business is not a strategy; it's a laboratory where we test ideas to help make your businesses better."

Then I outlined our coming strategy as it related to CCPP.

I told the distributors what I expected from them in return. "I want you to accept my vision as your vision. Make a financial commitment to it by developing a long-range plan for Iams to be your only premium pet food. You can't pledge allegiance to more than one country."

The audience fell silent.

"Commit to establishing a partnership based on trust where together we can improve quality and eliminate waste," I continued. "Commit to professionally managing your business by having a long-range plan, a formal organization, a succession plan, and an outside board of directors. Continue to be a resource of information and knowledge. Thank your customers every day for their business, and let them know how much you appreciate them."

I don't think the distributors heard a single word I said after I asked them to make Iams and Eukanuba the only products that they carried.

For several of them, Iams products didn't even qualify yet as their top sellers. Yet here I was, asking them to hitch their wagon to the Iams star and dump their most lucrative accounts.

Although I got a standing ovation at the end of my speech, there was plenty of rumbling among disgruntled distributors afterward. The only ones who were truly jubilant were the eight who had already moved to become Iams-only.

After my speech, tight little groups formed. People were heatedly discussing what they should do. Some distributors were visibly angry; others looked downright shell-shocked. By the next day tensions were still running so high that our meeting planner, Janet Werner, caught Mary on her way to the pool and said, "I don't know if I'd go out there right now. A bunch of distributors are out there, and it isn't pretty. I left because I felt uncomfortable."

*I want you to accept my vision as your vision. Make a financial commitment to it by developing a long-range plan for Iams to be your only premium pet food. You can't pledge allegiance to more than one country.*

A week after I gave that speech, my turn to be shocked came when our southern California distributor filed suit against us for breach of contract and restraint of trade. As we mulled over the process of picking distributors and driving the future, Tom, Marty, and I had already tagged Steve as one of the distributors we wanted to keep. Smart and polished, Steve had been the leading candidate out of the half-dozen distributors in that part of the country. We had planned to make a move to just one independent distributor for the whole southern California territory, by far our largest market.

"It's a good thing we found out now," was all Tom MacLeod said.

A handful of other distributors also filed lawsuits. Not one of them won a case against us.

Although I purposely did not set a timetable in my speech, we verbally gave the distributors until the end of the year to make up their minds.

In moving toward distributor territories that did not overlap, we expected the distributors to upgrade their warehouses and technology, buy better trucks, and get to ongoing training for themselves and their employees with DEDI (Distributor Education Development Institute) through Iams University. We had committed a full one-third of Iams University's budget to educating distributors through DEDI. We were looking for distributors who had the vision to make significant investments in their own businesses.

We also asked that they devote resources to match our increased activity with influencers, attending dog shows, and calling on breeders. One of our biggest and most expensive initiatives was entering the veterinarian diet business, which we had long ceded to Hill's because the company was so entrenched in that segment.

However, the vets were too important as influencers to ignore any longer. We were hiring and training a whole new sales force to break into the veterinarian diet segment and pouring millions into developing the right products for the segment. Our distributors would need to make an equally serious commitment to what promised to be a protracted battle.

After the meeting, Buddy Baker, a distributor based in Cumberland, Rhode Island, was the first to decide to sell only our pet foods. In 1988, before he would agree to carry our line, Buddy, the third generation in the pet supply distribution business, asked me to meet with his semi-retired father George, who was wintering in Tampa. At the time, Buddy was doing $8 million worth of Hill's business and was understandably reluctant to put that relationship at risk without his father's blessing. By the end of our breakfast meeting, George and I shook hands, and the Bakers were our new distributors.

By 1993 Buddy's business was still stuck at about $8 million with Hill's. But his Iams business had grown to more than $10 million. One day, not long after the sales meeting, Martha Shaffer, our regional sales director in New England, visited Buddy in his office.

"If I dumped Hill's instead of waiting for them to cut me, would you give me all of New England?" Buddy asked her.

"You would drop Hill's?" Martha asked, incredulously.

Buddy replied, "I didn't say that. I said, 'What if?'"

Martha picked up the phone and left a message for Tom MacLeod, who was in Europe at the time. He immediately called back.

"Do the deal," he instructed.

It was an emotional time for us. As we started consolidating territories, we sometimes had to be ruthless with men we'd known for years. In a sense, I'd grown up with these distributors, entrepreneurs who had started out just like me. They had driven delivery trucks, stayed in the $6-a-night motels, worked the dog shows, loaded the bags, sweated getting paid, and struggled with integrating new technology into their businesses. I knew their wives and children. Some were introducing second and third generations into their businesses.

We stuck up for our distributors with the pet superstores, who, obsessed with getting our products at a cheaper cost, wanted us to deliver direct to their warehouses, cutting out the distributor. Our products had a much faster rate of turnover than many of the other products in the pet superstores warehouses. I was confident our distributors could keep those gargantuan stores fully stocked with our products much more cost-effectively than the superstores could using their own warehouses. Too many retail operations don't understand the real cost savings good distributors bring to their operations. Running more volume through our distributors continued to reduce their fixed costs. I took a strong stand with the pet superstores and argued that it was actually more cost-efficient for them to continue using our distributors. They finally capitulated, and our independent distribution system was preserved.

Craig Thoeny of RFG Distributing (formerly Robbinsdale Farm & Garden), based in Minneapolis, Minnesota, covered that state, western Wisconsin, North Dakota, and South Dakota. Craig, a second-genera-

*After the 1993 national sales meeting, we decided when we got back we were going to go exclusively with Iams. But it took us about six months to work it out, because it meant giving up half our business. We had $10 million in Iams and $10 million in Hill's. The folks from Hill's had made a pitch to us to be exclusive, and they actually offered a better program. However, they wouldn't give any guarantee that we'd still have the line after five years. The difference was Clay and his leadership. We understood where The Iams Company was going, and we decided to take our chances with the privately held company rather than the public one.*

*We got out of hard goods, dog leashes, collars, and other pet supplies, because margins were much better on dog and cat food, and then concentrated all of our efforts on Iams. It has been a fantastic ride ever since. I'd march anywhere with Clay.*

CRAIG THOENY, RFG DISTRIBUTING

tion distributor whose father purchased the feed-and-seed store in 1967 after twenty years as a salesman with Ralston Purina, grew up in a company town plastered with Purina's checkerboard logo. His father started as a sub-distributor in 1974, then signed on as an Iams distributor in 1978.

As a child, Craig revered Purina's founder, Donald Danforth, in much the same way I had worshipped my entrepreneurial hero, Harry Moran, the wildcatter who gave me my first paying job.

I considered it a real coup to sign the best distributor in Purina's backyard. After my famous, or infamous, speech, Craig, who co-owned the business with his brother Mark, came up to me and announced he wanted to get on board. About a week after the meeting, RFG contacted us to confirm that it planned on dropping Hill's and the other lines it was carrying.

Another distributor I especially wanted to focus only on our lines was Wolverton Pet Foods, Hill's top distributor. I wasn't sure if we could convince Wolverton to abandon Hill's, but I had been extremely impressed with the business acumen of Dave Rinckey, the second-generation co-owner who was running the company, and I wanted him on my team.

*We carried both Iams, which was gaining huge momentum, and Hill's. It was like having Pepsi and Coke. There wasn't a pet store in town that didn't want both. Then came the need for exclusivity. Both Hill's and The Iams Company were courting us. Hill's was following a similar strategy to Clay's, consolidating its distributors and giving the business to a select group.*

*Part of the reason Iams was so interested in Wolverton was that we had developed such a strong relationship with the veterinarians. The Iams Company, which was getting ready to launch Eukanuba Veterinary Diets, appealed to us, because it would allow us to utilize our existing relationships. The integrity of Clay and The Iams Company, as well as direct access to the decision makers and someone who would listen to me without having to go through a board of directors, were what convinced us to go with The Iams Company. Once I looked past the minutiae of the numbers and promises and started thinking about the culture and relationships, the fit was better with Iams. As an independent businessperson, you like dealing with other entrepreneurs where you can be eyeball to eyeball, shake hands, and do the deal.*

DAVE RINCKEY, WOLVERTON PET FOODS

We were exceptionally fair in terms of transition arrangements for distributors we were cutting or who didn't get extended contracts. We offered financial support during the transition on both ends. In some cases, we loaned money to distributors who were taking on additional territory to facilitate expansion.

The last thing we wanted to do was run someone out of business. For those who were being cut out of our organization, we considered each distributor's situation and any financial commitments the company was carrying. We didn't just cut them off, because that wouldn't have been the right thing to do. Although under no obligation to do so, we helped out and spent a substantial sum on the consolidation and reorganization of our distribution system.

I gladly served as a mentor to distributors who allowed me to take that role. I'd often give input, especially when it came to dealing with family issues in the business. During our golf outing at the distributors meeting the year after the "Iams-only" speech, Buddy Baker was my partner.

"Why don't you separate your Iams business from your supply business?" I asked him as we rode along in the golf cart.

"Why would I do that?" Buddy asked.

"Two reasons. First, estate planning. It takes it all out of your dad's estate and puts it into yours. Second, if you ever want to sell your hard goods business, you have two separate companies."

Buddy listened. He later decided to split the businesses and two years later sold off the pet supply business at a handsome profit.

Another thing we discussed that afternoon was the location of his stores. He had nine small retail stores in regional malls throughout New England. Each of his pet supply stores occupied a mere three thousand to five thousand square feet.

"The day of big-box stores is just around the corner, and it's going to change the whole complexion of the business," I warned. "Small stores aren't going to be that profitable going forward. You'll find it difficult to be a distributor and a retailer at the same time because the big-box retailers will be important customers for you, but they will see your stores as competition." As his leases came up for renewal over the next couple of years, Buddy got rid of his retail stores, too.

By the 18$^{th}$ hole, Buddy had asked my opinion on whether he should change the name of his distribution business, Rumford Aquarium, a holdover from the days of his grandfather.

"Don't be sentimental," I said. "It's confusing to your customers." I also advised Buddy not to bring his sons, Michael and Carlos, into the business right away. I explained what we were doing with our own children and my thinking behind it.

"They do so much better if they go out on their own for a while," I said.

At the end of our golf game Buddy said, "Clay, I've learned something important about playing golf."

I couldn't imagine what I'd taught Buddy about golf, because I'm not very good at the game.

"What's that, Buddy?" I asked.

"It's very important to share the cart with you," Buddy replied with a grin.

Why did I give Buddy business advice that had little if anything to do with the job he was doing for us? Because I cared. I love entrepreneurs. Family-owned, entrepreneurial businesses are the engine of our economy, and I think more entrepreneurs ought to help each other.

Bob Schober's son Fred and daughter Elizabeth Ann Garman have joined him in the business. Fred learned the business from the ground up. He developed his own routes and is now vice president of operations. Elizabeth Ann, who owned her own retail shop for six years before joining the family business, oversees human resources and information technology. Craig Thoeny's son Steve is being groomed to run RFG. Michael Baker, Fred Schober, and Steve Thoeny have all become good friends. Seeing those businesses thrive and being passed to the next generation and knowing we had a hand in it is deeply satisfying.

Our hand-picked group of distributors absolutely lived up to my expectation that they would become the A-team in the pet food industry.

## CHAPTER 21

# Winning Customers: Radical Relationship Marketing

With two premium brands, The Iams Company was in a unique position within the pet food industry. Both Iams and Eukanuba are top-of-the-line products, but from the outset they catered to different audiences. The Iams products were designed for the animal lover who thought of his or her pet as a companion whose health and diet were just as important as any other family member's. In contrast, consumers such as breeders, hunters, and show dog owners who were more concerned with their dogs' performance had traditionally selected Eukanuba.

In 1990, despite having been available for more than twenty years, Eukanuba was still a relatively unknown and undeveloped product line. Although it had a cult-like following among breeders and show dog and working dog owners, Eukanuba represented a scant 15 percent of our total sales and profits.

As early as the mid-1980s, I had begun thinking about making Eukanuba our second brand, but it was another one of those good ideas just kicking around the building at Poe Avenue. In the next decade, however, it became increasingly clear that Eukanuba had a definite place in the overall market. More and more dog and cat owners obviously considered their pets family members and wanted the absolute best for them. Giving them plenty of choices within the Eukanuba brand made perfect sense. We dubbed these consumers "proud pet owners." They were the ones who carefully studied the ingredients listed on the product label to find out exactly what their animals were eating.

Meanwhile, our customers kept telling us they wanted to be able to buy our products at their local grocery stores, rather than having to make a special trip to the pet store. This posed an interesting dilemma.

If we went mass market with Iams, we risked alienating the specialty retailers with whom we'd worked so hard to establish our brands in the first place.

Eukanuba used a richer, denser formula than our Iams brand, with higher protein and fat content. Fully developing it as our second brand and reserving it strictly for specialty pet food channels offered the ideal solution to our dilemma.

Having two premium brands, each with fully developed product lines, was a pioneering concept that was tricky to pull off. Toyota successfully accomplished a comparable strategic move in the auto industry by establishing its Lexus brand. Although consumers peripherally associated the Lexus brand with Toyota, the company was able to get consumers to accept Lexus as a luxury car, even though both lines shared the same parent company. But no one in the premium pet food segment could claim success with a two-brand premium strategy.

To establish Eukanuba successfully as a second brand, we needed to draw a much sharper distinction between our two lines of pet food.

I've often been asked why we didn't position our brands around a personality like Wendy's Dave Thomas or KFC's Colonel Sanders.

Identifying a product around its founder has become a popular strategy, especially in the last several years, because consumers are looking to connect products with the people who are responsible for them. But I wasn't convinced that was the right way to go. Relying on a personality to differentiate a brand struck me as risky on a couple of levels. For one thing, once the message gets stale, how do you change? Besides, neither Paul Iams nor I were particularly interested in seeing our names in lights.

If I had genuinely believed that putting my face out there would have helped us sell more pet food, I would have done it. In the end I rejected that idea, because in our field the proof is in the pudding—in this case, the vitality of the animals that consumed our products. The real story of The Iams Company lay in our science and superb research and development. So I made a conscious strategic decision to stake our brands on scientific differentiation.

Since Eukanuba was known for its nutritionally rich ingredients and high fat content, one of our biggest roadblocks was to create a Eukanuba product aimed at overweight and less active dogs. Normally, the trade-off for accomplishing pet weight loss was sacrificing a nice, lustrous coat. If a product contained less fat, the animal would shed weight but look nutritionally bankrupt. Obviously, that wasn't an option for us.

From his training in human nutrition and agricultural animals, Greg Reinhart, our vice president of strategic research, was aware of the many health benefits associated with balancing essential fatty acids in people and livestock. He guessed the same would hold true for dogs and cats.

Greg reasoned that a diet containing "good" fats, omega-3 fatty acids and omega-6 fatty acids, would allow animals to lose weight while retaining beautiful coats. Having the right balance of these vital fatty acids also reduces inflammation, which would benefit the skin and coat; kidneys, a commonly diseased organ as pets age; and joints. Greg's research showed the balanced approach was the right one. Dogs and cats thrived on a diet with a balanced platform of these two essential fatty acids.

Although the benefits of these essential fatty acids are well known today, this approach was considered radical at the time. Competitors slammed our new approach, deriding it as "voodoo science."

Greg developed a version of Eukanuba that contained less than 10 percent fat using fish oils and flax to achieve a perfect balance between omega-3 and omega-6 essential fatty acids. Thanks to the breakthrough formula, dogs lost weight but maintained or actually improved their appearance.

In May 1993 we debuted Eukanuba Light with OmegaCoat™. Diane Hirakawa realized she had formulated the same omega-3:omega-6 balance in our Iams Lamb & Rice, which explained why that product was quickly hailed as the "skin and coat" diet among breeders.

We decided to put this balance into our other products as well, but it wasn't easy. Retrofitting the plants to accommodate this plan was a big challenge for John Polson and his manufacturing team. By that point our plants were highly automated. The fish oils had to be metered into the kibble in precise amounts so that every bite contained exactly the right balance.

During the last half of 1993 we trotted out Eukanuba Natural Lamb & Rice Formula for Puppies and Eukanuba Natural Lamb & Rice Formula for Dogs.

We also formulated a specialty product called Eukanuba Ultra for show dogs and working breeds. By the end of 1994 all Eukanuba products included OmegaCoat. Today, achieving a balance between omega-3 and omega-6 fatty acids is viewed as the optimal way to feed dogs and cats.

From 1991 through 1996 we released more new products than we had in the company's previous four decades in business. With Tom MacLeod's extensive corporate experience and phenomenal drive, he was building the company faster and even more profitably than I had.

The bottom line for any product's success is knowing exactly who your customers are. To do this, you have to build your customer base.

For instance, since the mid-1980s, we had aggressively courted new puppy owners with our Breeder's Club program. Back then, we gave breeders free eight-pound bags of Iams Puppy or Eukanuba to give to new owners. For every new owner's name and address, along with the puppy's birth date and breed, we rewarded the breeder with a $5 bounty.

This didn't seem to me to be a stroke of genius. It was just plain common sense. It's the basic "free sample" strategy: If giving away one piece of candy makes a customer buy a whole box, you've made back your investment in spades.

Yet I remember that when I announced this scheme, some of my executives thought that $5 for a name was extravagant.

"Are you kidding?" I said. "Do you know what a new customer is worth to this company? I figure about $200 a year. If I can pay $5 and know I'll get a customer, I'm more than happy to shell out $5 bills all day long."

We continued courting the new puppy or kitten owners. We sent them a series of three follow-up letters, each containing high-value coupons for our products. We also made sure the toll-free number for our customer care center was prominently displayed.

We used an old-fashioned shoebox filing system to catalog these names and information. Not until the early 1990s did the files get keyed into a master database. In the course of researching our target customers, we asked typical demographic questions but also several psychographic questions, such as whether their dog or cat slept inside or outside, which gave us insight into our customers' attitudes about pet ownership.

In the past sixty years, attitudes about companion pets have changed tremendously. Originally, most dogs and cats slept outside. Dogs often were chained or tied to a tree or a doghouse, and cats were relegated to a barn or outside shelter. As owners became less likely to view their pets as "just animals" and more likely to see them as family members, our canine and feline friends made a steady progression into the home. They were allowed in the garage or on the porch, then into the house, then into the bedroom, and, finally, on the bed.

Our business grew along with that attitudinal shift. Our ideal customers wanted a nutritional diet that would help their pets live longer and healthier lives. If your dog slept next to a tree on a chain, you weren't likely to buy Iams or Eukanuba.

Tom's marketing strategy for Eukanuba was sheer genius. In our effort to increase Eukanuba's visibility and beef up the product line, we again focused heavily on capturing customer loyalty from the very beginning of the pet's life. Tom felt we needed to capture the new puppy or kitten owner at what he called "key transfer points": the breeder, the veterinarian, and the animal shelter.

We made a concerted effort to reach our target audience at each of those transfer points. Once you've established a puppy or kitten on a certain diet, it's difficult to switch. We worked hard to ensure breeders were feeding their puppies or kittens from our family of Eukanuba puppy and kitten products and offered them a price break for buying our products. We gave breeders, vets, and animal shelters Puppy Packs and Kitten Kits, along with brochures on pet nutrition for every puppy and kitten placed in a new home. We even sent out birthday cards to puppies and kittens.

Keeping close to customers was hard work but paid off handsomely. Our competitors had nothing that approached our devotion to relationship marketing.

A great product, combined with sampling and authoritative advice from an influencer, won customers early on. But our relationship marketing never stopped. Every new customer received an oversized, personalized welcome letter.

A lot of thought went into this letter because we were all too aware that much of what arrives in the mail gets tossed. For Iams users, the oversized envelope was decorated with images of dogs or cats playing with their owners, celebrating the close relationship between owner and pet. For Eukanuba customers, the image highlighted a dog or cat. We provided information on training a dog and answered frequently asked questions. In the process, we became a trusted ally in helping owners better understand their pets and helping the animals live long, healthy lives. All of this translated into customer loyalty.

Another wonderful tool we utilized in our effort to instill early loyalty was insertion of a 6-ounce sample of adult dog food inside each bag of puppy or kitten product. That way, when the animal reached adulthood, the owner already had a sample on hand, along with a high-value coupon.

This might sound like a simple strategy, but here's another detail about pet food manufacturing most people don't know: Putting coupons and samples into bags of puppy and kitten food was incredibly complicated. First, it had never occurred to us that the cellophane wrappers that kept the coupons from absorbing the oils in our products would cause static electricity. We wound up with coupons fluttering around our manufacturing plants! Second, dropping a coupon in a bag may look effortless, but when you work backward into a high-speed manufacturing operation, it becomes a delicate, precise process. In the automated line, there wasn't much time when the package was actually open. Getting the coupon in the top of the bag rather than at the bottom was a real trick. As usual, however, John Polson and his trusty team made it work.

Meanwhile, breeders continued to be a key part of our focus. Our sales force maintained a regular presence at dog and cat shows around the country, as well as at individual kennels. It's much easier to buy ten pages of advertising in a breeder magazine than to convert the influencers one by one, but we invested the time and effort, knowing that in business nothing can take the place of a personal relationship. We visited kennels, handing out samples, and ran raffles to collect names at dog shows weekend after weekend. We got down on our knees to admire a breeder's new litter of kittens or puppies. All the advertising in the world can't buy the kind of goodwill we got from going the extra mile to take a genuine interest in every breeder.

In the 1990s, just as people were according pets equal—and sometimes higher—status than other members of the family, attitudes toward animal shelters also underwent a transformation. As more awareness grew over the plight of animals in shelters, more and more pets were being adopted from these facilities. Keeping up with this trend, we extended the same program we had for breeders to the shelters. We began sponsoring Pet Adopt-a-thons across the country and helped the seven hundred shelters that participated with us.

Always one to walk the talk, Tom MacLeod and his wife Barb adopted an abandoned dog in 1994. Kramer, an endearing basset hound, subsequently became the animal most associated with The Iams Company in the hearts and minds of our employees.

One of our most successful relationship marketing efforts resulted from a cold call made by a salesman from Meredith Custom Publishing.

This fellow dropped by and asked the receptionist to speak to the person in charge of marketing. Rich Kocon, vice president of marketing, was out that day, so Joan Fedders, brand manager for Iams Dog Food, agreed to see him. The brand group was already evaluating the idea of creating a newsletter for our loyal customers, but he pitched her on the idea of creating full-blown, glossy magazines instead.

After extensive analysis, Rich, Joan, and Glenn Williams, category manager of cat products, decided custom magazines would be a great way to communicate with our customers. Within each issue there would be educational articles to deliver nutritional information, plus ideas to improve the owners' relationships with their pets. And each issue would include many different ways for pet owners to respond to what they were reading, giving us valuable customer feedback. They proposed the magazines to Tom MacLeod, suggesting one publication for cat owners and another for dog owners.

Tom listened carefully. "I'm concerned about the workload," he said. "I don't want to go into the publishing business. Are you sure you can produce enough articles to fill two 28-

*I started to bring my dogs to tapings of the quarterly meetings for our international employees. Shortly after that, I began to bring them to the quarterly meetings in Dayton for U.S. employees. There was no question Kramer was the crowd favorite, and he seemed to understand he was part of the presentation. He would come on stage, lie at my feet, and promptly fall asleep in front of four hundred people while I was delivering quarterly results. In fact, betting pools started among the audience to see who could predict when Kramer would become bored enough with my comments to fall asleep.*

*After I finished, I generally had to wake him up to get him off stage with me.*

(continued)

to-32-page magazines every quarter that will be up to our quality standards?"

"We have evaluated that, and we know it will be a lot of work," Joan agreed, "but we think this is a perfect way to cement the two-way relationship we want with our customers."

Tom shared my philosophy of allowing employees the right to try new ventures and the right to fail in the process. The brand team set to work, and in 1994 we launched two magazines, *You and Your Dog* and *Your Cat*. Each issue celebrated the relationship between owners and their pets.

We had strict standards for the publications; any dog or cat featured in a photograph was required to be on either Iams or Eukanuba products and to be the picture of health. Eventually, those publications became the largest circulation magazines aimed at dog and cat lovers. *You and Your Dog's* circulation reached 500,000, nearly twice the circulation of *Dog Fancy*, and *Your Cat* topped 250,000 readers. Once again, we broke new ground in the industry by producing custom publications.

*(continuation)*

*I persuaded R&D to "test" Kramer for fitness to participate in the Iditarod sled dog race and become a police dog, which led to some funny moments at quarterly meetings. He also became part of my presentations at our annual distributor meetings. I used to call him my private consultant and would share some of his thoughts about our plans. This sweet, abandoned dog that no one wanted earned his status as a real favorite in the Iams family.*

TOM MACLEOD

Although the magazines cost us more than $2 million a year to produce, they were actually more cost-effective than all the custom letters we had been writing. They also gave us a vehicle to test different ways to motivate our customers in a customized way. For example, if we knew a customer had a Chihuahua, we'd insert a coupon for a small breed product. We ran contests, published letters and photos from customers, and established a lively dialogue with users of our products. Every toll-free call and contact to our Customer Care Department, another pioneering concept in the industry when Joanne Weaver initiated it in 1980, went into our database. By 1994 we had more than four million names of customers with whom we had established an ongoing dialogue.

Our Customer Care Department had mushroomed to twenty-seven employees fielding more than 300,000 calls a year. Eighty percent of those calls generated a coupon or a Puppy Pack or Kitten Kit. Our highly trained specialists were available on the phone lines twelve hours a day, six days a week, answering questions ranging from how to feed puppies to how to relieve the pain of older dogs with arthritic joints. We also created special hotlines for breeders and veterinarians.

We even established a bereavement specialist. Many of our customers came to view our company as a friend, and when their pets died, they naturally turned to us for comfort. By 1995 we went live with a Web site that gave customers an additional link to us.

Meanwhile, our competitors, who relied almost solely on advertising to promote their products, stood by in shock as we zoomed by them. "Let's leave the $50 million advertising budgets to the competition and Harvard MBAs," Tom liked to say. "At the end of the day, we might have some crap on our shoes from visiting kennels, but we'll beat 'em, one customer at a time."

When we did eventually decide to embark on a print and television advertising campaign, we were fortunate to have Lori Antku. Before she came to us, Lori was secretary to William Anderson, then Chairman/CEO of the world-famous NCR Corporation, headquartered in Dayton. When she joined The Iams Company in 1981, Lori's interests had shifted to marketing and advertising. She devoted herself to learning about our company and products and became Iams' first official marketing person. Lori developed and placed our first print ad, which appeared in the pet food industry's top trade magazine, *Dog World*. She also worked closely with the W.B. Doner advertising agency in developing Iams' first TV commercial, "What Would Happen If Dogs Ran the World?" and its feline counterpart, "What Would Happen If Cats Ran the World?" This commercial series hit the airwaves in 1988 and was one of the eight winners of the "Ads That Broke Through" award sponsored by *Adweek Magazine*.

Lori also produced the very first "Tournament of Champions." This spectacular formal event recognizing champion dogs from around the country was the predecessor of what today is known as "The Eukanuba Tournament of Champions," an elite dog competition that leads up to the best of the "Best in Show," the AKC/Eukanuba National Championship, one of the most prestigious dog shows in the world.

By 1996 we were still relying primarily on our radical marketing ideas and in-store promotions to promote our rainbow array of products. We developed a 360-degree go-to-market strategy to reach customers:

- We emphasized new and better products that helped us grow exponentially throughout the 1990s. Diane Hirakawa made sure we had best-in-class products, so how could we lose?

- We targeted influencers, veterinarians, breeders, and retailers with best-in-class programs.

- We promoted our products with incredibly effective in-store activities.

- We concentrated on relationship marketing to build loyalty so our customers were not apt to switch brands if a competitor ran a price promotion or some other temptation came their way.

- We used modest levels of advertising to build brand awareness.

We got far more bang for our buck by putting our money in samples of puppy food rather than, for example, plunking down $60,000 or more for a one-time, one-page advertisement in *Time* magazine. We spent a modest 4 percent of our 22 percent marketing budget on advertising, compared to Ralston Purina's whopping $300 million advertising budget. But our straightforward messages were becoming more and more noticed:

Iams: Good for life.™

Eukanuba: The best you can do for your dog.™

The best you can do for your cat.™

My dream of the paw print replacing the checkerboard as the recognized symbol of nutritional excellence for dogs and cats worldwide was coming closer to reality, one customer at a time.

## CHAPTER 22

# Driven by Pride and Powered by Eukanuba

A t 1:34 A.M. on March 15, 1991, Rick Swenson and his sled-dog team sailed across the finish line in Nome, Alaska, to win an unprecedented fifth Iditarod sled-dog race. The Iams Company was the proud sponsor of Rick and his championship team.

"Driven by pride and powered by Eukanuba," Rick and his amazing huskies braved blinding whiteouts and a wind-chill factor of 70 degrees below zero along the Iditarod Trail, an arduous course that snaked over craggy mountains and desolate tundra, through dense forests and along windswept coasts.

Many other veteran mushers turned back when faced with a vicious snowstorm in the White Mountains, but Rick and his dogs refused to give up. With his lead dog, Goose, forging ahead, Swenson's team covered the 1,049 miles in 12 days and 16 hours to win the $50,000 purse. Rick became the only musher to have won the Iditarod in three different decades, an honor he still holds.

Throughout The Iams Company, excitement ran high. We posted big maps of Alaska on the walls and tracked the progress of Rick's team. Tom MacLeod; Bob Bardeau; Rich Kocon; Eukanuba Brand Manager Kevin Sharp; John Burr, a veterinarian from R&D; and Greg Reinhart all flew to Alaska to see Rick and his team off, and Kevin and John stayed to cheer him on as he crossed the finish line in Nome. Although I wasn't able to make that trip, I'd been on hand for many other Iditarod races.

Every summer since we began providing Rick with food for his dogs in 1976, Rick had made an annual trip to Lewisburg to discuss ideas for product improvements. Rick proved invaluable to us; he was completely tuned into his dogs and reported the slightest change in their performance on the trail, the texture of their coats, or the consistency of their stools. He kept meticulous records on every aspect of their health and the results he observed from feeding different formulas.

Rick's keen powers of observation, combined with the expertise of the Iams scientists, led to new nutritional approaches beneficial to the sled dog community. Small changes in the quality of a diet may not be obvious in a typical house pet, but they show up readily in a sled dog running the Iditarod. Based on our collaboration with Rick, we made a number of incremental improvements that ultimately helped all dogs.

The publicity surrounding the race and the fact that the champion musher fed his dogs Eukanuba brought in an avalanche of eighteen thousand phone calls the week after the race from consumers inquiring about Eukanuba. Rick's success carried more weight with them than a slick, expensive advertising campaign. Yet it certainly didn't hurt to capitalize on our newfound publicity with a daring promotional first.

The premium segment, which I estimated accounted for about $2 billion of the $10 billion pet food industry in the United States at that time, had never been very promotion-oriented. Retailers, especially pet superstores, relied almost exclusively on discount pricing tactics to generate sales. We didn't want to play that game. We'd established over and over again that our customers would happily pay $28 for a 40-pound bag of Iams, more than twice the cost of a bag of Purina Dog Chow, because they saw the value in our science. We decided developing value-added promotions would take the pressure off retailers to cut our prices to move product.

The following February we premiered a new marketing strategy. When a consumer purchased a 40-pound bag of Eukanuba, he or she would receive a canister emblazoned with a map of Alaska commemorating the

Iditarod Trail and giving a brief history of the race. The attractive canister featured convenient handles and could hold up to 22 pounds of dog food.

A lot of work went into designing the canister, delivering them to the distributors, and helping distributors get them to retailers. All kinds of problems popped up. We wrestled with how to ship the canisters most efficiently with minimal damage. They gobbled up significant space on the retail floor, and retailers were uncertain about where to put them. But they soon figured it out: right in front! Consumers are always on the lookout for an attractive container for their dog and cat food, and people loved those colorful canisters.

Before long, customers began clamoring for the next edition of the canister. Based on Rich Kocon's research on collectibles, we released a second Iams canister with an Americana feel. Each canister's rim sported a series number. On successive Iams and Eukanuba canisters, all numbered, we featured various breeds of dogs and cats.

We also ran a clever television commercial. The first twenty-two seconds of our spots focused on the nutritional efficacy of our products and the last eight seconds advertised the free Iams canister with a purchase of a 40-pound bag of Iams food. It marked the first time a manufacturer of a premium product advertised a promotional activity to generate foot traffic.

We encouraged competition among retailers by sponsoring a contest for the best canister displays. One store even went so far as to create an enormous sphinx out of our cat food canisters! During a canister promotion, it wasn't uncommon for a single PETsMART store to sell one hundred 40-pounds bags of Iams food in a weekend. Eventually, we were supplying the retail stores with 450,000 canisters on a promotion weekend.

Another successful value-added promotion for Eukanuba Cat was a Pampered Chef measuring cup giveaway with a purchase. The promotion did double duty by both providing consumers with a convenient food scoop and educating them about feline well-being. Many people buy into the myth that a fat cat is a happy cat. We wanted them to see how much a quarter-cup was to help them stop overfeeding their cats.

Eukanuba's visibility continued to soar. In April 1992 it hit the big screen in *Beethoven*. The Iams marketing staff worked closely with a Hollywood placement agency to get our product featured prominently in the movie. In a parody of the famous scene from *E.T.*, where E.T. followed a trail of Reese's Pieces, Beethoven, a lovable St. Bernard, followed a trail of Eukanuba. Other scenes featured Beethoven's family purchasing Eukanuba. We ran a national sales promotion awarding the winner a trip to Universal Studios and one hundred runners-up each won a 40-pound bag of Eukanuba food.

The following year, Iams food was featured prominently in Disney's runaway hit movie *Homeward Bound: The Incredible Journey*.

On the popular sitcom *Mad About You* the canine character, Murray, a border collie mix, also favored Iams food, which was frequently shown in his newlywed owners' Manhattan apartment. Our brands' premium image was in line with the upscale image the set designers were after, and the colorful packaging lent itself to a clean, crisp look onscreen.

At the beginning of the 1990s only four out of every ten dog or cat owners had heard of our brands. By the close of the decade eight out of ten recognized the names Iams and Eukanuba.

In 1991 we rolled out five different kinds of canned cat food. The following year we introduced four varieties of canned dog food. Until Tom joined the company, I had shrugged off the growing popularity of lamb and rice. Part of the reason was the poor quality of the lamb meal readily available in the marketplace. In fact, Diane Hirakawa was appalled at the low level of protein quality attainable from the lamb meal used by the rest of the industry. She complained that up to half of the lamb meal was filled with junk, wool filaments, and hide and hoof trimmings.

The other reason was that I had started to lose touch with customers, an enormous mistake for any leader. I was no longer spending much time in stores or at dog shows. Tom reinvigorated my thinking and inspired me to get out in the field again and listen to our customers.

When we visited pet stores in southern California, we were dismayed to see people carting out bag after bag of Nature's Recipe, a competitive dog food. Nutro, based in California, promoted its lamb and rice product as a good solution for dogs with allergic reactions and chronic skin problems. The company went after the "natural" market, emphasizing its products contained no artificial flavors, preservatives, or coloring.

One of Tom MacLeod's first acts upon his return was to urge Diane Hirakawa and her research and development team to make lamb and rice a priority.

We focused on procurement of the protein-rich ingredients we needed to produce quality lamb and rice products and sent John Polson to Australia and New Zealand to scout out the best source of lamb meat and meal. He found a trio of entrepreneurs in Auckland, New Zealand, who had previously operated a small lamb-processing business that produced meat for human consumption. John purchased some new machinery for them and contracted with them to take all their production. Their operation was not heavily mechanized and required a good deal of manual labor.

We decided against starting our own operation to produce lamb-based ingredients because we had no way of knowing how big the business was going to be. However, we didn't want to run the risk of pumping significant capital into their operation, only to have them become a lamb meat source for a competitor such as Ralston Purina or KalKan.

We employed a method similar to the process used with the de-boned chicken we used in Eukanuba foods. What resulted from the process was a purer, higher quality lamb meat worthy of the Eukanuba name.

One year and $10 million later, R&D had both an excellent quality lamb meat and lamb meal to work with. To achieve the protein level that would make our product far superior to any other lamb and rice pet food on the market, Diane supplemented the lamb with fish and eggs, both outrageously priced. That pushed the per-ton cost of the protein ingredients in the lamb and rice formula to almost double that of the protein in our Iams maintenance diet. But by eliminating a middleman, we were able to keep manufacturing costs to a reasonable level and maintain competitive pricing. We got to the point where we were producing so much volume that we had to offload containers of lamb meal in Houston and barge them upriver to An-Pro.

Our new Iams Lamb & Rice was an instant hit. The superior quality and novel protein sources that Diane installed in our lamb and rice diets were easier for animals to digest, and their owners quickly saw results. And our product got an unexpected boost with the discovery that some of our competition's lamb and rice products contained a measurable amount of wool. Our ad agency quickly developed a new campaign with the theme "Don't let them pull the wool over your eyes."

We've always insisted on the best ingredients possible. Now we could safely add the word "natural," which held great appeal for consumers, to our packaging. We added to the line and introduced Iams Natural Lamb Meal & Rice Formula for Puppies and Iams Lamb Meal & Rice Formula Biscuits.

We did not embrace natural diets and lamb and rice until we were thoroughly convinced we could do so and maintain quality. In the course of our long history, we had repeatedly refused to get caught up in the herd mentality and following trendy consumer whims.

Our mission was to serve the dog and cat, not the tastes of the owner who might think a pet should be eating a vegetarian diet or something that resembled pasta or miniature hot dogs. You might benefit from making food into visually enticing shapes for children, but—let's face it—a dog is best fed as a dog and a cat is best fed as a cat. When customers refuse to make that distinction and feed their pet as they would a child, the animal usually suffers. We never lost sight of the fact that our real consumer couldn't care less whether the food was shaped like a hamburger or a pepperoni pizza.

> *Our mission was to serve the dog and cat, not the tastes of the owner who might think a pet should be eating a vegetarian diet or something that resembled pasta or miniature hot dogs.*

In 1994 we finally introduced the first of what we called our veterinary diets. At that time Hill's Prescription Diet had cornered that segment of the market.

Like physicians, veterinarians are creatures of habit. They'd been taught in vet school to prescribe Hill's diets, so we knew we were in for a real battle. It would be hardball selling, and that's expensive. Starting up our veterinarian line represented an enormous commitment of resources for our R&D department. But Tom was certain we simply could not achieve our mission and vision without vet diets. "You can't be the world's recognized leader in nutrition if you don't have the vets' endorsement," he insisted.

Tom had a clear strategy. Any veterinarian diet we produced had to meet one of two criteria. Either it had to be completely innovative with great new science, or, if Hill's had a similar product, it had to raise the bar demonstrably.

Winning veterinarians' approval would strengthen our argument that what you feed your pet does matter in terms of the quality and length of the animal's life. We pioneered segmenting the different foods according to pet life stages and lifestyles. Of course, the critics and so-called experts attacked us, even though we had the science and research to back up our argument.

Hill's boasted a fifty-year head start in the therapeutic diet market. We needed to accelerate the understanding of our science and to build our reputation within the scientific community.

In mid-April 1996 we hosted the first Iams International Nutrition Symposium. We invited more than four hundred veterinarians, one-third of them from outside North America. All were top researchers, academics, or practitioners in the animal nutrition field. The symposium offered presentations of the best research, a chance for peer review of presentations, and the opportunity to present our science to the brightest minds in the field.

With a $1.6 million budget, we put on a top-notch event at The Boca Raton Resort & Club in southern Florida. We paid all the attendees' ex-

*When I joined The Iams Company, I looked at the formulas and saw we had beet pulp as the main fiber source. I planned on coming up with a better one, but what I did was validate what Paul Iams and Clay Mathile had already ascertained through their keen powers of observation. Beet pulp is a robust fiber source that promotes good stools. The animal's intestinal lining benefits from the fermentation of fiber, which creates an environment where healthy bacteria can thrive. A well-functioning intestinal lining allows more nutrients to be absorbed. You get smaller, firmer stools and less diarrhea and constipation.*

*Understanding how beet pulp works as a fiber source helped us tremendously when creating our new vet diets. We purposely promoted good bacteria in the intestinal tract and used fiber to help fight the symptoms of intestinal disease and kidney disease and manage diabetic dogs and cats. With kidney disease, nitrogen builds up in the blood, creating a toxic situation. Beet pulp fiber in the gut causes the beneficial bacteria to replicate rapidly.*

*When bacteria are growing, they remove nitrogen from the blood, essentially forming a nitrogen trap.*

*In some ways, we were ahead of the human medical nutritional area. When we introduced our canine renal products, they contained a nitrogen trapping fiber system that cleansed the blood of toxic nitrogen.*

GREG REINHART

penses. At Diane's suggestion, we asked all presenters to submit their papers to us in advance and published them in a hardcover book, *Recent Advances in Canine and Feline Nutritional Research: Proceedings of the 1996 Iams International Nutrition Symposium*, which we presented to all the attendees as they arrived.

The symposium opened many doors, especially in the international community, where veterinarians were less familiar with our company. We made contact with the leaders in the field and presented our science to them. We were no longer just another company peddling dog and cat food; we were partners in the quest to develop better nutrition for animals.

In February 1998, Tom got a call from a reporter at a Buffalo, New York, television station that *Consumer Reports* was giving our cat food front-runner exposure in a cover story about the "scandal" of the premium pet food rip-off. *Consumer Reports* was accusing us and other manufacturers of producing cat food that was deficient in potassium, which could be harmful to the cats. After receiving a videotape from *Consumer Reports* publicity people trumpeting that the story would soon appear, the Buffalo reporter called us for a comment.

"Would you be kind enough to send us a copy of that videotape?" Tom asked. "I haven't seen the article, but I can tell you right now our products are not deficient in anything."

The reporter sent us the video, and Diane and the lab went to work around the clock doing tests on potassium levels, not only in our products but those of our competitors as well. Our findings bore out the truth. *Consumer Reports'* scientific tests were fundamentally flawed. There are two tests for potassium levels and, being inexperienced with pet food research, the magazine's scientists had chosen the wrong test.

Tom called the magazine's editor. "You'd better not run that story," he said. "You need to ask your scientists how the tests were conducted, because our scientists have proof that they were done incorrectly. Besides that, potassium is a dirt-cheap ingredient that costs about six cents a pound. If we were going to cheat on something, that would be a poor ingredient to choose."

"We stand by our story," the editor snapped and hung up.

We were furious. Here was the world's most respected consumer products magazine, with a circulation of five million, accusing us of being cheaters. Although the story slammed the premium cat food industry as a whole, the cover story and the illustrations all featured our products.

"That's the price of being recognized as the best," Tom said dryly.

While the rest of the industry shrank up and crawled into their holes, we repeatedly demanded a meeting with the scientific research team that had conducted the flawed experiments. When *Consumer Reports* had finally agreed to a meeting, we dispatched our ace scientists to their offices in Yonkers, New York, to present our case.

*Consumer Reports'* scientific team rarely granted meetings and appeared supremely confident of their position. In the conference room Diane neatly laid out her research and explained how easy it is to perform the wrong test for potassium, which would explain the incorrect results. "I'm afraid you used the wrong methodology," she concluded quietly.

The magazine's chief scientist had been sinking lower and lower in his chair. The editor-in-chief and technical team cleared the room and returned, ultimately admitting the initial testing was done incorrectly. The meeting was over, but the problem wasn't.

That issue of *Consumer Reports* had already hit the newsstands and had been mailed to subscribers. And those publicity videotapes had been sent to hundreds of TV stations around the country, blasting us. We were extremely concerned about the damage that had been inflicted on our good name and on the trust we had worked years to establish with our customers.

Eventually, Iams was vindicated. We won a retraction, only the second *Consumer Reports* had issued since its inception in 1936. It was buried on page seven and printed in tiny type, but it was a retraction nonetheless. The magazine also scrambled to retrieve the erroneous videotapes.

Then we ran a counter-offensive and wound up getting some wonderful press out of the incident. My favorite headline ran on one of the nightly news programs: "Dog Bites *Consumer Reports.*" Our toll-free number rang off the hooks. We packed off a copy of the retraction statement to every single person who inquired about the story. It was a scandal, all right, but in the end we emerged stronger than ever. As 1998 drew to a close, The Iams Company had more than $800 million in sales, with one hundred different products sold in seventy-five countries around the world. Most of the industry pegged our sales at around $400 million to $500 million. That was fine by me.

## CHAPTER 23

# A Family Forever United

L osing both of my parents and Mary's father while we were only in our mid-forties caused me to contemplate my own mortality. In 1986, with our oldest daughter Cate working at the company and our son Tim likely to step in as well after college graduation, I mulled over what the future might hold in terms of my successor. I started wrestling with the question of whether to bring the kids into the business.

In his seminal book *Beyond Survival* family business expert Léon Danco addressed many of my concerns as an owner-manager of a thriving family business.

Dr. Danco outlined the cycle family-owned businesses typically experience.

- *Wonder:* The owner-manager, usually in his or her early thirties, starts the business to pursue a dream. The owner works all day, seven days a week. For the family this period is a nightmare.

- *Blunder:* Despite all the blunders of the startup period, money starts coming in, and the business grows rapidly. The owner doesn't trust anyone and is still harassed, overworked, and scattered in his or her efforts. He/she seeks advisors, especially when there's trouble with accounting, unions, the IRS, or the bank.

- *Thunder:* The owner has attained relative security and comfort. The knockwurst and beans days are over. He's loud, obnoxious, and opinionated; he knows it all. In this corporation, he is the major, if not the sole, stockholder. Secrecy and lack of review are the hallmarks of the family-owned business at this stage. As the business expands, the company is still too often dependent upon second-rate legal and accounting talent and banking connections made when the operation was the size of a fruit stand.

- *Plunder, Sunder, or Renaissance of Wonder:* By the time the owner reaches age fifty to sixty, he has usually become disenchanted with this flamboyant thundering stage. The wear and tear begins to show. The owner is fearful the dream will not live after him. He tries to sell out, merge, close up, or go public. The alternative is the possibility of vesting his successors with his own sense of wonder in the joy of risking and building the business so they can provide the leadership the business needs to continue to grow, without repeating all the mistakes and hardships of a first generation.

I had experienced all the emotions Dr. Danco described. I felt lonely, scared, tired, and misunderstood. I also felt like I was running out of time and didn't know where to go for help. I've always made it a habit to hire the best consultants I can afford, and Dr. Danco immediately had my vote because he had developed a reputation for firing clients whom he decided weren't trying to live up to their end of the bargain.

After Mary and I attended a family business seminar in Kentucky where Dr. Danco and his wife Katy were speaking, I wrote a letter telling him how much I'd gotten from his speech and his book and enclosed brochures about my company.

As soon as he received my letter, Dr. Danco invited me to come see him at his office in Cleveland.

"I'm forty-four years old," I told him, "and I don't want to crash and burn like the entrepreneurs in your book."

Dr. Danco, a formal man with ramrod-straight posture and an incisive intellect, studied me a moment, then said, "You're the first business owner who has called me while you're still in the Thunder stage. Most founders wait until they're well into their fifties, when it's basically too late for me to help them. I think I can help you a great deal."

Dr. Danco observed that the average person lives only one thousand months, a sobering thought. Thinking of your life in terms of months instead of years is a real wake-up call. As Dr. Danco saw it, the first third of your life (up to thirty) is spent acquiring knowledge, the second third (ages thirty to sixty) is spent accumulating and climbing the ladder to success; and the final third (ages sixty to eighty and older) is spent accepting the fact you're not going to be around forever, so you should be giving it all away. I met Dr. Danco at the end of my startup years and became his first client under age fifty or, as he liked to say, under six hundred months.

Dr. Danco asked to tour one of the Iams plants right away. After the tour, he told me the plant revealed that I was hardworking, honest, and loved the business. "I can see you're honestly asking for help, and you are a man worthy of respect on a business level," he congratulated me. "The clients I have the most success with believe in God, and they want to do the right thing for their families and their companies."

We met once or twice a month after that for six years. Dr. Danco also spent a good deal of time with Mary, and we all explored the issue most critical to us: where, when, and how our children would fit into the business.

Dr. Danco believed that having children join the family business straight out of school is a dire mistake. It puts terrible pressure on kids and puts them at a disadvantage with employees. By working somewhere else first, the children get a chance to make mistakes and learn from them. In the process they gain confidence and experience and genuinely have something to offer the company if they choose to return to it.

Mary and I completely resonated with this approach. With Dr. Danco's guidance, we established the process by which one of our children could assume the helm of the company. We had two main rules: First, after graduating from college, any child with this goal had to work outside the company for at least five years. Second, the deadline for the kids to express an interest in joining the company was age thirty.

The children had grown up spending their summers and school breaks working for the company, and we never coddled them with cushy jobs.

At fourteen, Tim started working five to six days a week during the summer. By the time he was sixteen, he was working in maintenance in the plants, and one summer he joined the team we sent out to build the plant in Aurora. All through college, Tim spent his breaks at The Iams Company. He never shied away from the hard jobs. Every Saturday morning during the summer months he cleaned the air scrubber at the Lewisburg plant, a dirty job that no one else wanted.

After Cate graduated college in 1985 and began working full-time at Iams, she noticed that none of the names of the people who carried our products were entered on a computer system. She volunteered to create the first database for that information. Thanks to Cate, by using the zip code of the specialty pet retailers and dealers who sold our products, the Customer Service Department could quickly let consumers know the closest source for purchasing our products.

As a high schooler, Mike often spent eight hours a day hoisting 100-pound bags of ingredients to the bins where they needed to be dumped. One day he came to me and asked to get off early, because he was pitching in a game that evening. "Check with your boss," I replied. Don Fox, man-

*Growing up, I often saw Mom and Dad picking up trash. Everyone was respected, no matter what his or her job happened to be. The Iams Company was a fun environment, but when it came to the work, the employees didn't mess around.*

*I started working at The Iams Company when I was in college. My best friend and I were groundskeepers. We pulled weeds and painted bins. Over two years, I got to know the shift workers and what kind of people worked for the company. It was certainly an unusual situation; the employees got to see the boss's kid picking up cigarette butts.*

JEN MATHILE PRIKKEL

ager of maintenance at the Lewisburg plant, refused to let him end the day early. Mike never asked for special treatment again.

Jen and her best friend Shelley spent the summer making sure the campus-like grounds of the Lewisburg plant and research centers were litter-free and neatly manicured. Jen took great pride in making sure not even a blade of grass was unkempt.

The kids had had a firsthand glimpse of what it took to run our organization. They were also well aware that part of Tom MacLeod's job was to groom a successor, should one of them choose that path.

My children would find themselves in an unusual and difficult position. My ownership of The Iams Company in some ways compromised their ability to pursue their chosen careers. The fact that I didn't hire them upon college graduation made them suspect to potential employers, who reasoned that either my kids would merely be cutting their teeth at their companies on the way to joining the family business or, worse, that they didn't have the necessary talent to work at The Iams Company.

On the other hand, if they had worked at Iams, they would have lived in the shadow of being the owner's kids. Either way it was a no-win situation.

In 1989 we had formed the Mathile Family Foundation with $300,000 of The Iams Company profits. Mary had always been profoundly interested in the welfare of others and was an ideal person to be at the helm. She assumed the titles of chairperson and CEO, and I became its president.

Learning to work together within the foundation was a new experience. In more than thirty years of marriage, our roles had been clearly defined. I was CEO of the company, and she was CEO of the household.

Almost immediately, we discovered we had different management styles. Mary would often become frustrated with me, because my old shoot-from-the-hip style had the annoying habit of resurfacing.

For example, I'd go to lunch with someone and listen to a pitch for a contribution to a charity. Off the cuff, I would indicate we would be interested. My circle of advisors had repeatedly warned me that I was a soft touch. I used to make all kinds of personal loans to employees in tight spots. However, in the mid-1980s my advisors had helped me see I could get myself into a world of trouble by continuing that practice. Now I was essentially doing the same thing with the family foundation, responding emotionally to anyone with a seemingly worthy cause.

Understandably, this irritated Mary, who methodically selected appropriate recipients for our charitable contributions, wielding the same sharp instincts for people that had served us so well in choosing Iams employees. As CEO of the foundation, Mary went on site visits to not-for-profit organizations and quickly figured out which organizations weren't what they appeared to be or weren't making good use of the donations they had received.

Over the years, I have gotten too much credit, and Mary hasn't gotten enough. I'm convinced The Iams Company would not have happened without her. Mary has been my best friend and most loyal supporter. When push comes to shove, she is in my corner. We've hung in there during the tough times because

*I didn't want the kids thinking money was the be-all and end-all. Health, love, and family are what nurture your soul. It's hard when people judge you because you're wealthy, and automatically put a label on you without knowing you.*

*I used to worry about my kids being judged and labeled, and I actually used to feel bad because we had money and everywhere I looked, there was so much suffering. I feel much differently about our wealth now. I believe God had a plan. He knew that we would use the money to make a difference. The important thing to me is whether our children and grandchildren are good human beings and good citizens who consider the needs of those less fortunate than they are.*

MARY ANN MAAS MATHILE

our marriage was built on mutual respect and trust. That commitment to maintain a solid relationship speaks volumes to your kids. When you have someone you respect and love by your side, that is a tremendous help. Mary's the best person I've ever known.

After we established the foundation, Mary and I pondered how the wealth we were rapidly accumulating was going to affect successive generations. That was a big question for both of us. I wanted to be assured the company would outlive me and thrive for generations.

*Mom and Dad lived so simply relative to their wealth that few people outside the family, not even close friends, had any idea until that* Forbes *article came out.*

*I was on my fifth interview for a job with a machine tool company. The regional sales manager had flown in from Cleveland to interview me. He looked at my name, opened up his briefcase, and pulled out the day's newspaper. "Is your dad Clay Mathile?" he asked.*

*When I answered affirmatively, he said, "This article says that your dad is one of the five richest guys in Ohio. We're not interested in having you stay around two or three years and then go work for your daddy." That's how I found out about the* Forbes *article.*

*Dad called and apologized to me. I told him, "When you grow a prize rose, you have to put up with the scent of fertilizer around it. I enjoy the fruits of being a Mathile, so I'll put up with the fertilizer."*

TIM MATHILE

With the establishment of our family foundation, the extent of our wealth had become obvious to our children. We had never tried to hide it from them; however, like many family business owners, we had failed to discuss the topic thoroughly. With the bombshell of being named to the *Forbes* 400 wealthiest list in 1992, the cat was out of the bag. Watching our grandchild Abby grow further underscored the need to include the next generation in my thinking about succession and the company's future.

By the mid-'90s, the chances that any one of our offspring would succeed me in the business were rapidly diminishing.

Mike, a junior at Wright State University who lived and breathed baseball, was drafted as a pitcher by the Montreal Expos. After completing his MBA, Tim took a position at Dayton Power & Light. Jen graduated St. Mary's College with a BA in religious studies. Tina majored in psychology at Wright State.

The only offspring who became directly involved in the company was Cate, along with her husband Don Laden, who had taken a sabbatical from The Iams Company to finish his bachelor's degree in marketing at Wright State.

Before leaving The Iams Company to get his degree, Don had climbed the ranks from a truck driver delivering dog food for our Chicago distribution center to director of new product marketing. On January 2, 1992, he assumed the position of president of Complete Petmart, the small chain of pet supply stores Mary and I had launched in the mid-1980s to test retail theories and which had lost $500,000 the previous year.

Although I didn't expect it to be a huge moneymaker, I believed the operation had a good deal of untapped potential. With Don's background in sales and marketing, his skill as an operator, and his strong work ethic, I thought he'd do a good job. Cate was distressed that by all appearances we were making few contributions on the charitable front, although that was far from the truth. At the time the Mathile Family Foundation was operating anonymously.

Mary and I took to heart God's admonition about doing good deeds in private and didn't want to draw attention to our charitable efforts. Although it was becoming more and more difficult, we were determined to keep a low profile.

In fact, at that time, 75 percent of the local population didn't even know The Iams Company was headquartered in Dayton. Our corporate contributions were virtually nonexistent. Requests for donations came from all over the place, and there was no rhyme or reason to the few we chose to honor. We sponsored baseball and softball teams here and there, but our efforts were completely haphazard. My rationale was that we were already giving large sums through our foundation, so why should I give more through the company?

But Cate argued that The Iams Company should be more of a presence in the community. Tom MacLeod shared my view, although for slightly different reasons.

"The best thing I can do with our profits in the communities where we operate is create more jobs," he said, whenever someone brought up the subject of charitable contributions. His other argument was that if we were to do something charitable under The Iams Company banner, it should be on a national basis and aligned with our mission of serving the world's dogs and cats.

"Let me be in charge of corporate contributions," Cate asked Tom and me. "I'll do the job until I can prove it's a job worth doing."

Cate installed professional management and established a philanthropic strategy that related to our philosophy as a company. After doing a lot of benchmarking to find out how other companies were handling philanthropy, she launched an employee committee comprised of twelve people from all parts of the organization. This committee, which turns over on an annual basis, decided that all requests should flow through the human resources department and that our charitable efforts should be concentrated on the welfare of children, companion animals, and dogs that help people. For example, we often stepped in to fund the purchase and training of police dogs for communities that could not afford them and of service dogs for people with disabilities.

The employees on the committee were given a great deal of autonomy regarding how best to put our charitable dollars to work. Cate met with each location's plant manager once a year to discuss plans. Each facility maintained its own budget for philanthropy, and each location had a point person who determined how to use the budget to serve his or her particular community best. In Aurora, for example, the employees decided it was important to sponsor a baseball team.

During the holidays our employees traditionally made donations to an effort that eventually became known as Paws for a Cause. Years earlier, Jan Dinges had suggested that instead of exchanging gifts at the company, we should host a holiday luncheon and donate the money that would have gone to gifts to a worthy cause. We also raffled off gifts that came into our executive offices and matched the funds raised by the employees from the raffle.

Again, the employees in each location decided where the contributions went. I'm immensely proud of the major impact Cate had on the shaping of our corporate charitable contributions. I admire her creativity. She developed some breakthrough ideas. That whole idea of nonprofit education, increasing their ability to do more with the donations they receive, is still a big part of our philanthropy today.

Regardless of what happened with the succession issue, I was acutely aware that a large percentage of prominently owned family businesses in this country are destined to self-destruct over the same emotionally charged issues—money, power, and relationships—our family was facing.

To avoid this dismal scenario and to help our family negotiate the treacherous waters ahead, I hired John L. Ward, PhD, a world-renowned expert in family business and author of *Keeping the Family Business Healthy*, and Mary Whiteside, PhD, a family business consultant and psychologist.

John and Mary were skilled at running family meetings and dealing with family issues. Mary and I were designated "G1s," shorthand for the first generation. Our children and their spouses became known as the "G2s," and the grandchildren were dubbed the "G3s."

One of the first steps the consultants insisted on was regularly scheduled family council meetings.

So Mary and I met once every quarter with the children and their spouses. John and Mary kept us on track.

In the beginning they served as referees more than facilitators. The meetings sometimes digressed into blowups, complete with yelling and tears. Most of our conflicts were typical of first-generation family business owners and second-generation misunderstandings.

"We busted our tails to build this business," I would think. "Why these kids are having problems is beyond me. What on earth do they have to complain about?" I genuinely thought I'd set the kids up to win by spending so much time laying the groundwork for succession and building an enormously successful company. I felt unappreciated and hurt.

Meanwhile, the second generation was saying, "You don't understand." I optimistically expected to be able to handle generational issues just as I would any other thorny business issue. It was quite a surprise to realize that, unlike problems in business, family issues are matters of the heart. There are no clear-cut or fast solutions.

Although softening my autocratic style a decade earlier had transformed me as a leader within The Iams Company, I had yet to tame my authoritative tendencies when it came to the family. As much as I wanted to listen, I found it hard to relate to what our now adult children were dealing with. But with the wise guidance of John Ward and Mary Whiteside, and a deep-down belief in the process and everyone's ultimate desire to do what was best for the family, the Mathile Foundation, and The Iams Company, we all made it through. The family council meetings became a great place to discuss feelings and to bond as parents, children, siblings, and spouses. They eventually became a place of support and an active part of the family. Soon after we formed the family council, we commenced work on estate planning. Instead of having our children wait until after we were gone to get their inheritance, we decided we wanted them to learn how to live with wealth while we were still alive. Limiting our taxes was not our first concern. If that had been our top priority, we would have passed our assets to the grand-children. We determined the best option for our family was to establish living trusts for each of the children.

At the end of 1995 we put a portion of the company stock into a Grantor Retained Annuity Trust (GRAT). Shares were divided equally among each of our children. As the business grew, the children's equity would grow along with it.

Meanwhile, the G2s formed a special committee to hash out the answer to who, if any of them, would succeed me.

By early 1995 I was catching more and more flack both from outside forces and from within my own company regarding our ownership of Complete Petmart.

No matter how many times I argued that I kept it largely as a learning resource to test out retail theories and promotions, questions arose. We even pointed out that we carried a full line of our competitors' products, and Complete Petmart bought Iams and Eukanuba products

*I know my parents have struggled a lot with this decision. Money was a hard thing, especially for Mom, coming from nothing and then having so much. I know they worried about whether we would be responsible stewards. But in the end they trusted that they had taught us basic values and to work hard. Dad said, "I don't want you thinking about when you are going to get the money. I'd rather you get it at age twenty-eight than fifty-eight. This way you can do what you love. You don't have to do anything for money." They have done a good job of refraining from criticizing us.*

JEN MATHILE PRIKKEL

from a distributor just like any other retailer. Still, our ownership of the small chain was a bone of contention with national pet retailers, especially PETCO and PETsMART.

During the four years Don had presided over Complete Petmart, he had done an admirable job, expanding it to twelve units with a profit of $250,000 in 1994. I finally conceded we'd reached a point where we either needed to expand the chain or sell it. Don expressed interest in buying it, but we would have faced the same conflicts I had, since he was my son-in-law. After many discussions, we agreed selling the chain outright made the best sense.

From his many years with The Iams Company and Complete Petmart, Don knew all the channels, the players in the industry, and the distributors. Following our sale of Complete Petmart, he started his own business, PetOvations, to design and market new dog and cat products.

In early 1997 the G2 committee officially informed Mary and me that none of the children or their spouses wished to pursue the top spot at The Iams Company. I completely understood and respected their decision. Dr. Danco used to say I had the happy misfortune of creating an incredibly successful company while my children were still young. By the time they reached the age when they might have considered joining the family business, it had grown so multifaceted that getting one of them up to speed to run it would have been a Herculean task.

Deep down, I think I'd known all along that none of them was going to want the job. After Tom took on the role of COO, they saw up close what it took to run a company of the size

> *The children have passed the test. They are down-to-earth, caring human beings with Christian values. As long as they stay close to God and focus on answering the question, "How can I make a difference?" they'll be fine. After we distributed money, they were free to handle it however they saw fit. We don't ask what our children have, and they don't ask what we have. We want to be a family that's concerned with more important things than money.*
> MARY ANN MAAS MATHILE

and complexity The Iams Company had become. None of them wanted to live that life. I felt a little regret, but in another sense, having a final answer came as a relief. The kids' decision simplified our estate planning tremendously. Now we could set up a system for the succession of the business.

Meanwhile, family business consultant John Ward thought having the Mathile Family Foundation in the Iams home office on Poe Avenue was a big mistake.

"You are confusing your employees by having the foundation in the building," he said. "On one floor you are trying to figure out how to make money, and on the next floor you are figuring out how to give it away." On the advice of my board, we moved the family office and foundation away from The Iams Company and formed CYMI, Ltd., Greek for Clay and Mary Inc., to manage our family's personal business issues and investments.

*I was relieved to move the foundation away from the corporation's home office. In this city, everybody goes to Clay, and being in the Iams office was confusing to people. The move clarified that the Mathile Family Foundation was different from Iams charitable works. Once we had our own space, I felt I had much more say in and control of the foundation.*

MARY ANN MAAS MATHILE

We then had to hire a president for the family office. The first choice, a man who had worked with Mary when she had served a brief stint as president of Complete Petmart, didn't work out. The next time around, we hired the right guy: Les Banwart, who had taken over the Arthur Andersen relationship for The Iams Company account when my long-time advisor Dave Phillips transferred to California in 1988.

Les started on October 1, 1997, the first day of Mary's and my annual month-long vacation. I teased him that we sure must have had a lot of confidence in him if we already were letting him run the show his first day on the job.

Les's duties include overseeing our investments, handling security issues, and taking care of other family business concerns. He also oversees the Center for Entrepreneurial Education, which I formed in 1994 with Bill Matthews and Dave Sullivan as an expansion of Iams University. The center focuses on helping business owners take their organization to the next level and is transitioning to become known as Aileron as it reaches its next milestone of growth. The family office, which now employs eleven people, also handles backroom operations for the Mathile Family Foundation and our corporate jet charter operation called Corporate Flight Alternatives, which we acquired in 2001.

With Mary officially in the driver's seat of the foundation, she and I were grappling with how to work together as a team. John Ward and Mary Whiteside suggested we hold weekly partner meetings.

*We've learned to work very well together. We support and teach each other, and Clay compliments me frequently. We are working more as a family group to make an impact on children's lives. Part of that is through helping their parents, the community, and education. The spiritual aspect is woven through all of it. We believe spirituality should be part of everything we do. Our job is to be good stewards of the gifts God bestowed on us and to be servant leaders for Him. That's the culture. That's why we don't put our name on many things. It's not about the family; it's about the people we help. We've learned so much about running a foundation. Helping other people is the reward in life. Families who have money have to find their own way. The path we have chosen brings the family together for a common purpose.*

MARY ANN MAAS MATHILE

"You've got to present a united front to the employees of the family office and the foundation," Mary Whiteside explained in no-nonsense terms.

These partner meetings opened my eyes. Running the foundation requires a different mentality than running the family office. It was much more about spirituality. I didn't understand this subtle distinction at first, but Mary did. If I'd been running the foundation, we would have been very efficient at writing checks. Mary's vision, compassion, and values made the foundation an efficient spiritual engine. Together, we worked on a mission and vision for the foundation. With the combination of her input and mine, we ended up with much better answers than if either of us had operated independently.

Mary and I met with John Ward and Mary Whiteside to begin crafting a mission and vision statement for our family, too. The G2s also had a big part in this effort. It took two years, but we were determined to get every word right.

## Our Family Mission

To be responsible stewards of God's many gifts by growing together through mutual love and commitment to our family values.

## Our Family Vision

A family forever united.

## Our Family Values

Mutual respect, honesty, and integrity are basic elements of our family and business relationships. Without these, we cannot achieve our vision and mission.

When we started the foundation, we wanted to focus on basic human needs, education, and our community. Gradually, we decided our approach to helping the entire world was too broad. We became more focused on our own community and specific audiences within it. A town like Dayton doesn't have many folks who can give in a big way. We believe the old maxim that charity should begin at home. We've refined the foundation's focus with all our children actively participating.

## The Foundation Mission

To create opportunities for children in need by focusing support to children and their families who have already exhibited the motivation to succeed.

## The Foundation Vision

Sharing God's blessings by perpetuating a multi-generational foundation committed to philanthropic excellence.

*It's about one word: unity. Without a family council, a family will never accomplish its vision and mission. If our kids grow up with something similar to the values our family has worked so hard to embrace, then we will have done a good job.*

MIKE MATHILE

## CHAPTER 24

# The Iams Company Turns Fifty

A t our 1995 national sales meeting at the Grand Floridian in Orlando, I celebrated my twenty-fifth anniversary with the company. The staff surprised me with videotaped congratulatory messages from many people whom I greatly admire, the highlight of which was best wishes from former President George Bush, Sr. As the meeting concluded, several distributors asked us, "How in the world are you going to top this one?"

We had a whale of a surprise in store for the distributors and Iams employees. The fiftieth anniversary of The Iams Company was coming up, and we were planning a celebration that just might go down in history as the mother of all blowouts. Relatively few companies make it to the half-century mark. I used to worry about The Iams Company's life span. I felt enormous pressure, knowing all those employees were betting their livelihoods on us. "Are we going to survive?" I would wonder.

Then in 1996, as we approached our fiftieth anniversary, I was confident at last that we would deliver on the promises we'd made to all those who had hitched their wagons to our star.

How do you celebrate the Big 5-0 of a company like Iams? With a worldwide yearlong party, of course. We saw this milestone as a marvelous opportunity to say "thank you" to all our employees, suppliers, distributors, and many others who had a hand in our success over the years.

The occasion would give us a chance to reflect and rejoice in our achievements and to revel in the simple fact that we'd made it.

Naturally, such an undertaking required some serious planning. In 1994 Tom MacLeod was already putting the process in motion. He designated a fiftieth anniversary planning committee. It was a massive undertaking, because our goal was to touch every Iams employee around the world.

We had agreed that if Janet Werner, our meeting planner, could keep the 1995 sales meeting under budget, we'd kick off our fiftieth anniversary celebration in the fiftieth state. She met the goal, and we gave her a budget of $4 million for yearlong festivities celebrating our success around the world.

The yearlong anniversary bash began during our annual national sales meeting held in February 1996 at the breathtaking Grand Wailea Resort on Maui in Hawaii. The theme for the meeting was, appropriately, "Dream no little dreams, for they have no magic to move men's souls."

We brought in our national and international distributors, our international and national sales and marketing teams, the board of directors, five hundred employees, and, of course, our family.

I sat with Paul and Jane Iams during the opening laser light show. It was an unforgettable experience, watching Paul's emotion as he witnessed this dramatic display of the incredible growth of the little backyard company he'd started fifty years before.

There was an enormous map showing the world distribution of The Iams Company with paw prints landing on various parts of the world. The Iamses were overwhelmed. "I could never have even imagined bringing this company to this level," said Paul. Our keynote speaker was none other than General H. Norman Schwarzkopf, commander of Operation Desert Storm. He delivered a rousing message on responsible leadership and excellence.

"The secret to modern leadership is simple," he told the audience. "When placed in command, take charge. The leader is the person who is willing to take responsibility." He then ticked off the characteristics of a good leader: character, competence, selfless service, and caring about people.

The general, who completed two tours of duty in Vietnam, continued, "There's no question about the fact that you have to have competence to be a leader, but you also have to have character. Good leaders are men of competence and character. Many times character is more important."

Finally, he stressed the importance of caring about people. "I've known a lot of leaders who said, 'I really care about my troops.' But when you got right down to it, they didn't give a damn." He related a story of one U.S. helicopter pilot who initially refused to transport wounded South Vietnamese troops in his helicopter because he didn't want it to get bloody. The general recalled how he had climbed inside, pointed his cocked .45 at the pilot, and said, "Don't you ever put machinery over men again."

Schwarzkopf asked every person who served our country in Vietnam to identify himself or herself, and he made a point of shaking hands with each one and thanking each individually. Many of the Vietnam veterans broke down and wept openly. General Schwarzkopf also graciously spent a good deal of time signing autographs for our employees who were veterans and couldn't make the trip.

Mike Major, a decorated Vietnam veteran who joined the company in 1983, had just started an assignment in London to sort out our distribution in the United Kingdom. He was puzzled by my insistence that he fly to Hawaii from his new post, as he would only be able to stay one day for the main gala. I surprised Mike by arranging to have his photograph taken with General Schwarzkopf. I hope he'll talk about that moment forever!

As usual, we offered a full array of classes for our distributors and used the occasion to unveil our latest new product: Eukanuba for Cats in a vacuum-sealed bag. The celebration culminated with a big luau on the beach with Chubby Checker performing. During our courtship, Mary and I had loved to dance to his rollicking hit "The Twist." Could we ever have dreamed way back then that someday we'd be dancing on a beach in Maui to the live music of our musical idol from our teen years?

Right after the sales meeting, we took the show on the road. Mary, Tom MacLeod, and I went to Australia. The archives were set up in each location, so that employees could walk through them. At every location we held a catered sit-down dinner to which all employees and their families were invited. Many employees met Mary for the first time at these warm, open gatherings.

We continued during the summer months to our plants in Aurora, Heartland, and Henderson. In September we wound up our U.S. celebrations at Lewisburg, which we combined with the home office at Poe Avenue. Our German distributor, Helmut Grönemeyer, who had been with us for thirteen years, brought his wife Christa, his daughter Maike, and his entire staff to Dayton for the celebration. The highlight of the event, especially for the employees' kids, was a traveling dog show that brought the house down.

The last leg of the festivities was held in Europe for 350 people, including our European distributors and our sales and marketing team, whom we took on a Mediterranean cruise. Our children and their spouses accompanied us on part of these trips, and they got the opportunity to experience firsthand the global impact of The Iams Company. It was an unforgettable experience for all of us.

As our 50th year drew to a close and I looked back on that remarkable journey that was The Iams Company, I thought of something General Schwarzkopf had said in his keynote address, which seemed to sum up in a handful of words a lifetime of work and passion.

"You have to understand what leadership is all about," he said. "Leadership is not managing an organization. Organizations are made up of people. Leadership is about people."

In the end it was the people who made The Iams Company what it was. When praised for his courage and devotion to England and the Allied effort during World War II, Sir Winston Churchill replied, "The British people were the lions. I was only the roar." The members of the Iams family were the lions, the ones whose courage, faith, and commitment ensured our success. I was only the roar. A pretty loud roar, to be sure, but had I not had such a marvelous team of employees, managers, distributors, and other advocates, not to mention my remarkable wife and children, that roar might have ended up being merely an echo in that empty part of the universe reserved for failed dreams.

Instead, it was heard around the world and paved the way for animals to be given the same chance at optimum health that we give ourselves and those we cherish. I am so proud of this legacy and of everyone who helped to bring our mission of enhancing the well-being of every dog and cat that much closer to reality.

# INDEX

If you would like to order additional copies
of this book, please contact Aileron at
8860 Wildcat Road,
Bethel Township, Ohio 45371
or email director@aileron.net
or visit our website at www.aileron.net.